Yale Publications in Religion, 3
David Horne, editor

Published under the direction of
the Divinity School

Jefferson on Religion

in Public Education

by ROBERT M. HEALEY

New Haven and London, Yale University Press, 1962

to Edith, of course

Preface

This book had its beginning in a question raised in a Yale Divinity School seminar on religion in public education. Subsequently the research necessary to answer that question became a dissertation presented for the degree of Doctor of Philosophy at Yale University. The present version has been somewhat revised but is substantially the same. From start to finish I enjoyed this project, partly because Jefferson's thoughts, deeds, and historical era are continually fascinating, partly because the question here pursued shows no signs of becoming a dead issue, and not least because at every stage of the work numerous people have invariably given me generous and competent cooperation. That most of them will not here be named is no sign that I have forgotten the debt I owe them for illumination and assistance. In particular I must mention Seymour A. Smith, who served as friend and advisor to me in my studies at both the Divinity School and the Graduate School of Yale University; and Professor Sydney E. Ahlstrom, who joined him in guiding the development of the dissertation. My thanks also go to the American Association of Theological Schools for a Faculty Fellowship Grant, and to the Theological Seminary of the University of Dubuque for all its help but especially for furnishing me with a year free from academic responsibilities, without which this study would probably still be only a plan.

ROBERT M. HEALEY

University of Dubuque
February 1962

Contents

CHAPTER 1

The Current Controversy

Thomas Jefferson and the McCollum Case

In 1948 the Supreme Court of the United States of America handed down its decision in the McCollum case. This case reflected the growing interest on the part of many Americans concerning the proper role of religion in public education in light of the United States Constitution's First Amendment clause: "Congress shall make no law respecting an establishment of religion, or prohibiting the free exercise thereof." At issue was a "released time" program in which, at the request of their parents, children were being released from regular classes during the school day to receive religious instruction elsewhere in the public school building from teachers employed by religious organizations.

The Court ruled, eight to one, that this specific form of released time violated the religion clause in the First

2 THE CURRENT CONTROVERSY

Amendment. The majority opinion reaffirmed a statement
made in a previous decision and intended to spell out the
meaning of that clause:

> The establishment of religion clause means at least
> this: Neither a state nor the Federal Government can
> set up a church. Neither can pass laws which aid one
> religion, all religions, or prefer one religion over an-
> other. Neither can force nor influence a person to go
> to or to remain away from church against his will or
> force him to profess a belief or disbelief in any reli-
> gion. No person can be punished for entertaining reli-
> gious beliefs or disbeliefs, for church attendance or
> non-attendance. No tax in any amount, large or small,
> can be levied to support any religious activities or
> institutions, whatever they may be called, or whatever
> form they may adopt to teach or practice religion.
> Neither a state nor the Federal Government can, open-
> ly or secretly, participate in the affairs of any religious
> organizations or groups and *vice versa*. In the words of
> Jefferson, the clause against establishment of religion
> by law was intended to erect "a wall of separation be-
> tween church and state."[1]

This statement is basically an attempt to determine how
the American founding fathers intended the First Amendment to govern public education. In the Supreme Court decision the statement is preceded by a discussion attempting
to fathom the history leading up to the writing of the First
Amendment or the circumstances out of which it came. The
opinion focuses on one father in particular, Thomas Jefferson, and cites his ringing phrase: "a wall of separation between church and state." Jefferson deliberately intended
those words to bear fruit in American thought on religious

1. McCollum vs. Board of Education of School District No. 71 Champaign County, Illinois, 333 U.S. 203, 1948. The passage appeared originally
in Everson vs. Board of Education, 330 U.S. 1, 1947.

freedom; they are part of his well-known Reply to the Danbury Baptist Association,[2] in essence a brief expression of his understanding of the meaning of the First Amendment. Yet this reply, it should be noted, was not concerned directly—if at all—with public education.

Jefferson's Effect on American Institutions

There is good reason why Thomas Jefferson should be consulted and quoted by those who are trying to determine the fathers' view of the proper relationship of religion to public education and how the First Amendment was intended to govern that relationship. Jefferson was a leader in the battle for civil rights, and the rights he listed as essential always included freedom of belief. He wrote the Virginia Statute for Religious Freedom and worked tirelessly to have it passed. Although he was in France at the time the Constitution was framed, he campaigned so vigorously by mail to have a bill of rights added to it that he has received credit for delaying constitutional ratification in several states and for spurring on Madison to the fight for amendments concerning human rights in the opening session of Congress.[3]

Equally important, this statesman and patriot was also a pioneer in the field of education. Throughout his life Jefferson insisted that public education was essential to the survival of democracy. In 1776, as a member of the committee appointed to revise the laws of the state of Virginia, he prepared three bills providing for elementary and secondary education, for higher education, and for a public library.

2. Jan. 1, 1802, in Andrew A. Lipscomb and Albert Ellery Bergh, eds., *The Writings of Thomas Jefferson* (hereafter referred to as LB), *16* (Washington, D.C., 1903), 281–82. See also letter to the Attorney General, Jan. 1, 1802, in Paul Leicester Ford, ed., *The Writings of Thomas Jefferson, 8* (New York, 1892–99), 129.

3. See Adrienne Koch, *Jefferson and Madison, the Great Collaboration* (New York, 1950), pp. 40 ff.

In 1779 he reorganized the College of William and Mary, anticipating that it might shortly become a state college. Subsequently he discussed his plans for public education thoroughly in *Notes on Virginia*. In 1806, as President of the United States, he suggested that Congress apply surplus revenues to the founding of a national university. Finally, during retirement he devoted a major portion of his time and energy in an effort to have his state develop a system of public education like the one he had proposed in 1776, and saw his endeavors bear fruit in the founding, building, and first year of classes of the University of Virginia.

Jefferson's ideas about religious freedom and education proved to be vigorous and enduring. In the United States the acceptance of the right to freedom of belief as an essential concept in a democracy has become an American tradition. It has become customary to use his words "separation of church and state" to designate the principle by which religious freedom is to be safeguarded. The effects of his ideas and accomplishments in the field of public education are not as well known, but equally far-reaching. The University of Virginia became the model for American state institutions of higher learning presenting curriculum offerings heavily influenced by utilitarian considerations. Jefferson's organization of the curriculum was a precursor of the system of free elective offerings. His concept of a system of public elementary education for all citizens was taken over by the American people, who made it compulsory and expanded it to include secondary education for all as well. The exact form of the system he envisaged, on the other hand, affected the development of European education, particularly in France.[4]

In education, as well as in government and politics, the thought of Jefferson has continued to have its effect, often in ways of which most Americans are unconscious. Similar-

4. See Gilbert Chinard, *Thomas Jefferson, Apostle of Americanism*, 2d rev. ed. (Ann Arbor, 1957), p. 98.

ly, his records have been consulted by many citizens seeking
to interpret the Constitution or hoping to find there understanding or insight concerning contemporary problems of
the republic he helped to found. Two of his major concerns
were religious freedom and democratic public education.
Many people have therefore tried to plumb his thought to
discover what he felt to be the proper role of religion in public education in a democracy. The result of such an attempt
was the citing of the words "a wall of separation between
church and state" in the McCollum majority opinion concerning the constitutionality of one form of released-time
religious instruction. When the results of a number of different attempts are compared with each other, the most
striking thing about them is the lack of unanimity of opinion or consensus concerning Jefferson's view of the matter.
In order to get a clear view of how fundamental the divergence of opinion is concerning Jefferson's thought on this
question, let us consider in some detail the discussion that
occurred after the McCollum decision.

O'Neill's Rebuttal to the McCollum Decision

The McCollum decision was received in a variety of
ways. It was expected by many Constitutional lawyers. It
caused consternation among advocates of released time. It
disappointed most Roman Catholics and many Protestant
Evangelicals. It was praised by most Jewish agencies, *The
Christian Century,* Unitarians, other liberal Christian
groups, and many Baptists.[5] The first extended rebuttal was
a book, *Religion and Education under the Constitution,* by
J. M. O'Neill, a Roman Catholic layman and professor of
speech and debating.[6]

O'Neill's line of reasoning was as follows. Both the Mc-

5. See Anson Phelps Stokes, *Church and State in the United States,* 2
(New York, Harper, 1950), 522.
6. New York, Harper, 1949.

Collum decision and its reasoning were unconstitutional and historically fallacious (the dissent of Justice Reed excepted). The First Amendment was intended to allow the federal government to support all religions equally. Even if this were not true, the First Amendment does not apply to the several states, to which the Tenth Amendment reserved all powers concerning religion and education. Therefore, the reasoning behind the McCollum decision and the decision itself are actually attacks by the Supreme Court on civil rights.

Focusing on Jefferson, O'Neill strongly protested the Court's defining the First Amendment by means of the phrase, "a wall of separation between church and state," which is not in the Constitution. He felt also that the Court had seriously misinterpreted Jefferson. Throughout Jefferson's life, said O'Neill, he constantly sought to protect and promote three basic principles: (1) democratic political decisions; (2) freedom and equality in religion; and (3) the reservation of authority in such matters as religion and education to the several states rather than to the federal government. The idea of complete separation of church and state, O'Neill maintained, was subversive to all three. Tax support of religion or religious education certainly did not mean "establishment" to Jefferson. Indeed, no evidence whatever exists that the idea of prohibiting equal, impartial, public support of religion or religious education ever entered Jefferson's mind. To show that Jefferson favored cooperation between church and state, and also as examples of how this affected his activities in public education, O'Neill states repeatedly that Jefferson advocated the use of public funds for a school of theology for the training of clergymen (a department of "Theology and Ecclesiastical History"), and that he advocated partial support for sectarian schools for religious instruction to be set up around the University of Virginia, and desired provisions for sectarian use of university facilities for instruction and worship. O'Neill insists that no record exists of Jefferson ever having protested Virginia's continuing use of tax money in various ways to promote religion and religious education in the forty years he remained a leading citizen of his state after the passage of his Bill for Establishing Religious Freedom in 1786.[7] O'Neill's position concerning Jefferson's intentions can be summed up by his own words: "Jefferson's total record is consistent proof. In fact he never did or said anything at any time to indicate that he thought the states could not do whatever they thought wise in regard to government provision for religion or religious education so long as they treated all religions alike and preserved religious freedom."[8]

Strict Separationist Replies to O'Neill

This strong comment provoked equally strong rejoinders. Among those who wrote books opposing O'Neill and supporting the Supreme Court's interpretation of the First Amendment and its application in the McCollum case were R. Freeman Butts,[9] an authority on the history of education, Leo Pfeffer,[10] a lawyer, and Conrad Moehlman, a professor of church history.[11] The position of all three on the First Amendment can be summed up in the words of Butts: "The clause 'establishment of religion' included all the desires to prohibit a single established church, but it also applied to plural support of many or all religions . . . it prohibited any financial support, directly through tax funds, or indirectly through land for any one or more churches, or for religion in general."[12]

7. See ibid., pp. 63, 75–77, 205–06, 215.
8. Ibid., p. 248.
9. R. Freeman Butts, *The American Tradition in Religion and Education*, Boston, Beacon Press, 1950.
10. Leo Pfeffer, *Church, State and Freedom*, Boston, Beacon Press, 1953.
11. Conrad H. Moehlman, *The Wall of Separation between Church and State*, Boston, Beacon Press, 1951.
12. Butts, p. 91.

With respect to Jefferson, all three maintained that he had been a thoroughgoing separatist concerning the relationships of church and state, and therefore concerning the proper role of religion in public education as well. Butts cited the fact that Jefferson's proposed draft for a constitution for Virginia in 1776 said that no one could be compelled to maintain any religious institution, and that his Statute for Religious Freedom stated that the legislature could not compel a man to contribute to the support of any religious belief. Butts therefore rejected O'Neill's contention that Jefferson never entertained the idea of prohibiting the use of public funds for equal, impartial support of religion and religious education. If Jefferson was a strict separatist, his practice in public education should have been very different from that described by O'Neill, and Butts tried to show that it was. He conceded that Jefferson proposed the establishment of a theological seminary in 1814, but observed that this was at Albemarle Academy, a private school, and that no mention was made of the use of public funds, whereas in the 1817 proposals for a state university, which resembled the Albemarle Academy proposals in every other respect, theology and religion were conspicuous by their absence. Butts felt that the suggestion that sectarian schools should be established on the confines of the university was an expedient compromise, unenthusiastically received by Jefferson to gain support of religious groups that might otherwise prevent the institution from getting under way. He points out that Jefferson later declared that previous regulations permitting religious exercises on campus were superseded by the suggestion that sectarian schools be built on the confines of the university. This, to Butts, would be consistent with Jefferson's earlier acts in collegiate education. When he had still hoped that his own College of William and Mary would become Virginia's state university, he submitted a bill to the legislature to amend the college's constitution by removing the two professorships of theology and divinity, and not replacing them with any in religion. The bill was not passed, but nevertheless Jefferson helped to eliminate the schools for divinity and for Greek and Latin when he was a member of the college's board of visitors.[13]

Butts puts his own conclusion in very strong terms:

> A careful study of Jefferson's entire career and his views on education from 1779 to 1825 will show that Jefferson was one of the earliest advocates of a public education divorced from all sectarian religious influences. He saw clearly that the principle of separation of church and state for which he worked so long must mean a secular educational system. . . .
>
> The education bill recognizes that if no person were to be compelled to support "any religious place whatsoever," then education must be available freely to all and should contain no religious instruction.[14]

In other words, Jefferson's efforts on behalf of public education had their roots in his efforts on behalf of religious freedom.

Among others who agreed with Butts' interpretation of Jefferson as a strong separatist were Moehlman and Pfeffer. Moehlman had previously observed that Jefferson's bill for elementary schooling in the state of Virginia carried a clause forbidding any religious reading, instruction, or exercise not common to all religious sects.[15] Now he also suggested that Jefferson's total plan for education in Virginia failed because of his absolutism concerning separation of church and state.[16] Leo Pfeffer challenged O'Neill's statement that Jefferson wished education to be reserved to the authority

---

13. See ibid., pp. 47–57, 119–29.

14. Ibid., p. 119.

15. See Conrad H. Moehlman, *School and Church, the American Way* (New York, 1944), p. 84.

16. See Moehlman, *Wall of Separation*, pp. 108–09.

of the several states. He observed that in 1806 Jefferson had urged an amendment to the Constitution specifically giving the federal government control over education.[17] Pfeffer also noted an example of Jefferson's absolutism concerning separation of church and state in the draft of a constitution for Virginia which included a clause barring ministers of the Gospel from holding public office.[18]

A Third Interpretation of Jefferson

Jefferson's position on any question of importance to the American people is subject to varying interpretations. His political and private statements, actions, and maneuvers contained many ambiguities and paradoxes. Jefferson was a partisan figure to whom reference is often made for partisan reasons.[19] So far we have seen two mutually exclusive roles assigned to Jefferson with respect to religion in public education. On the one hand he is claimed as an advocate of impartial government support for religion and religious education. On the other, he is set forth as a rigid separatist utterly opposed to government support of religion, including any form of religion in public education.

These are not the only possibilities, however. Somewhere in between lies the interpretation of Anson Phelps Stokes. In his massive work, *Church and State in the United States,* he imputes to Jefferson the double interest common to most of the fathers: to support religion, because Jefferson was himself religious and felt that without religion democracy could not succeed, and to support religious freedom by doing away with any form of interference by the govern-

17. See Pfeffer, p. 479.
18. See ibid., p. 194.
19. For an analysis of the significance of the many aspects of Jefferson's posthumous reputation up to the present, see Merrill D. Peterson, *The Jefferson Image in the American Mind,* New York, 1960. Clinton Rossiter recently counted seven Jeffersons still being "batted around the political arena"; see "Which Jefferson Do You Quote?" *The Reporter, 13* (1955), 33–36.

ment in religious matters. To uphold this interpretation, Stokes, in addition to citing many documents referred to by O'Neill, says that Jefferson secured works on the evidences of Christianity for the library at the University of Virginia, and concludes: "even in establishing a quasi-state university on broad lines, the greatest liberal who took part in founding our government felt that instruction in the fundamentals of Christian theism and Christian worship were both important and proper."[20]

The Problem Caused by the Usual Approach

We have now seen three different and conflicting interpretations of what Jefferson intended concerning religion in tax-supported education in a democracy. Let us first examine the process by which such different answers to one question can be attributed to one man. The insights we gain from this step will help us when we move on to the next problem, that of determining just what Jefferson *did* intend concerning religion in public education.

Despite their different conclusions, all the parties to the discussion we have been examining have taken the same approach to Jefferson's thought. They have invariably first raised the question, "What position did Thomas Jefferson take regarding the relationship of church and state in the United States?" Each participant answers this to his own satisfaction. The answer he arrives at then becomes the basis for the next question, "How does this position concerning church and state demonstrate itself in Jefferson's thought and practice concerning public education?" Or perhaps, "How did it determine his philosophy and practice in public education?" Or even, "How can it be proved and illustrated from his practice in public education?"

Each of the men we have considered thus far presents a good example of this process of reasoning about Jefferson.

20. Stokes, *1*, 338–39, 515–16.

For instance, O'Neill upholds his belief that Jefferson was in favor of equal, impartial governmental support for all religions and religious education by citing the plan for a school of theology in 1814 and the plan for divinity schools on the confines of the University of Virginia in 1822. Butts bolsters his position that Jefferson believed in absolute separation between church and state by stating that the school of theology was proposed only for a private academy to be privately supported, and that the plan for divinity schools on the confines of the University of Virginia was only an expedient compromise to overcome the opposition of religious sectarians to a state university where religion was not to be taught. Stokes backs his belief in Jefferson's dual interest—to support religion as the basis of democracy and to support religious freedom—by saying that Jefferson provided works on the evidences for Christianity for the library of the university and felt that instruction in Christian theism and Christian worship were both important and proper.

It is not enough to say that this approach is inadequate. It actually does violence to the thought of Thomas Jefferson. A flagrant example of the extremes to which it can be carried is Butts' statement that Jefferson's Bill for the More General Diffusion of Knowledge recognized that if no person were to be compelled to support any religious place whatsoever, then education must be made freely available to all and should contain no religious instruction. The bill recognizes no such thing. Its preamble states that the best way to prevent tyranny is to educate the people so that they can recognize it and be prompt to defeat its purposes, and that the best way to promote public happiness is to educate all men of genius and virtue so that they may be called to offices of leadership and government without regard to wealth, birth, or other accidental condition or circumstance.[21] No other reason for sponsoring public education

21. See Julian P. Boyd, et al., eds., *The Papers of Thomas Jefferson*, 2 (Princeton, Princeton University Press, 1950), 526–27.

is given. No mention is made in this bill of any relationship it may have to the Bill for Establishing Religious Freedom, nor to religious freedom in general, nor to the doctrine of separation of church and state, nor to how that doctrine might affect education in Virginia whenever the Bill for Establishing Religious Freedom should be passed. An examination of Jefferson's correspondence at the time provides no more evidence for the kind of linkage which Butts maintains exists between the two bills than do the bills themselves.

Butts' own desire to answer a question of great current importance causes him to bridge the gap here between two strands of Jefferson's thought for which Jefferson himself did not supply the connection. Except as Butts' interpretation manufactures it, no evidence exists here of any such cause-and-effect relationship between religious freedom and public education. Nor is it to be seen elsewhere in the records of Thomas Jefferson. During the fifty years he was active as patriot, politician, diplomat, and educator, he wrote many times on the problem of religious freedom and the need to guarantee it by means of the separation of church and state, and also on the impossibility of guaranteeing the continuation of freedom and democracy without public education for all citizens. But at no point did he develop religious freedom or the doctrine of separation of church and state as an educational philosophy, nor does he use the First Amendment as an educational directive. Rather, he repeatedly discussed both his concern for religious freedom and his plans for religion in public education without bringing these two areas together at times when it would have been easy for him to do so if he had desired.

A typical example of this can be seen in his *Notes on Virginia*. The answer to Query 14, concerning justice and Virginia's laws, contains an extended statement on the role of education in a democracy and dwells for some time on Jefferson's Bill for the More General Diffusion of Knowledge. Query 14 mentions the fact that the Bible is to be omitted from the curriculum of public elementary schools (which, incidentally, is not stated in the bill itself). A reason is given: the age of the children. "Their judgements are not sufficiently matured for religious inquiries." This is certainly not the principle of separation of church and state, and no mention is made of that principle anywhere in the discussion.[22]

Similarly, the answer to Query 17, concerning the different religions in the state of Virginia, develops a lengthy statement on the desirability of religious freedom and separation of church and state. After pointing out the unfortunate consequences of constraint of opinion, he makes the following statement: "Reason and free inquiry are the only effectual agents against error. Give a loose to them, they will support the true religion by bringing every false one to their tribunal, to the test of their investigation. They are the natural enemies of error, and of error only."[23]

If there are implications here for public education and for the role of religion in public education, they are not developed by Jefferson. Nor do we find in this whole discussion of religious freedom any recognition by Jefferson that the separation of church and state meant that "education must be available freely to all and should contain no religious instruction."[24] These two examples from the *Notes on Virginia* are typical of Jefferson's discussions of these topics. Neither area of his thought stands in a cause-and-effect relationship to the other. Nor can his understanding of the proper role of religion in public education be seen rightly as a development of his concept of the doctrine of separation of church and state.

This is not to say that he was unaware of implications in the First Amendment for public education. Twice while

22. See Ford, *Writings of Jefferson, 3,* 251–55.
23. Ford, *3,* 264.
24. Butts, p. 119.

helping to establish the University of Virginia Jefferson showed his awareness of them. These statements have been cited by every person who has attempted to prove that Jefferson's understanding of the First Amendment governed his thought and practice concerning the role of religion in public education, and to show how it did. In the Rockfish Gap Report of 1818 Jefferson claimed that his plans for religion in the curriculum—the teaching of those aspects of religion on which all sects agree and the leaving of those aspects on which they do not agree for the sects to handle themselves—were in conformity with the Constitution.[25] He reiterated this statement in the 1822 Annual Report of the Board of Visitors as a preamble for the proposal that schools of divinity be established on the confines of the university.[26]

To dwell on this point, however, is to miss the thrust of the discussion of religion in both documents. The question being answered by Jefferson is not, "How does the First Amendment govern what we can do in the field of religion at the University of Virginia?" but, "Given the First Amendment as a condition under which we work—and which we take seriously—what can we do to make certain that the University of Virginia will provide the fullest instruction possible in all useful sciences, of which (in Jefferson's estimate) religion is most important?"

This is a specific question concerning practice, and answers to it which are actual plans seriously put forward by Jefferson himself are available to us. But these only show us practices he approved at particular times. They do not of themselves tell us what his thought was concerning the role of religion in public education. By themselves they are blind alleys, not highways through his thought. We have

25. See Nathaniel Francis Cabell, ed., *Early History of the University of Virginia as Contained in the Letters of Thomas Jefferson and Joseph C. Cabell* (Richmond, 1856), p. 441.

26. See ibid., pp. 473–74.

already seen what violence can be done to the thought of Jefferson when one of its implications is raised to the role of a major philosophical emphasis.

The Approach in This Discussion

Did Thomas Jefferson believe the principle of separation of church and state to be the reason why public education was necessary in a democracy? Certainly not! Did he believe that the First Amendment determined whether or not religion was to be included in public education? Again, no! In Thomas Jefferson's literary remains there is no evidence to prove either contention. He never considered public education in any way to be merely a logical derivative of religious freedom. Both were essential to democracy. They were parallel developments rooted equally in his total philosophy of man, religion, education, and government. Only by exploring that philosophy as a whole can we come to an understanding of Jefferson's concepts of the relationship of religious freedom and public education, and of the proper role of religion in public education.

In the following chapters I shall explore that philosophy and try to reach that understanding. I shall try to fathom his religion, his view of the world and man, his understanding of society and the purpose of government, and his complete philosophy of education. At times I may seem to be straying from my course, but there is good reason to cover all the ground. Only when we see the interrelationships that Jefferson saw between all these areas will we also understand his concept of the proper relationship of religion to public education.

CHAPTER 2

The Creator and His Handiwork

At first glance Thomas Jefferson's own faith may seem to have very little to do with his position on the proper relationship of religion to public education. As we proceed, however, we shall discover first that Jefferson's belief that a particular kind of God had created a particular kind of universe and a particular kind of man is the logical basis of the rest of his thought; from this belief his ideals for society, government, and education are derived. Second, we shall see that the kind of religion which Jefferson believed had a place in public education corresponded exactly with his own beliefs. To understand what he believed is therefore of prime importance.

The Evolution of Jefferson's Beliefs

JEFFERSON'S COMMONPLACE BOOKS

Very little is known about Thomas Jefferson's youthful religious beliefs. He had yet to develop the voluminous correspondence in which he discussed so much of what he was thinking from day to day. He did keep notebooks, however, into which he copied or summarized passages from his reading. These give us some insight into his growth.[1]

In all probability Jefferson experienced a religious crisis just after turning twenty. The religious training he received as a child and adolescent from his family and tutors was probably in orthodox Trinitarian Christianity. He was no doubt familiar from early boyhood with the liturgy of the Church of England and with the language of the King James Version of the Holy Bible. The effect of all this can be seen in Jefferson's letter to John Page, July 15, 1763, in which "Christian Stoicism" resulting from his early religious training is evident in such phrases as "perfect resignation to Divine will."[2]

Subsequently in his notebooks, the "Commonplace Book" and the "Literary Bible," Jefferson copied selections reflecting a great and developing interest in skepticism, materialism, and misogynism. The last may have just been due to unrequited love.[3] The others, however, showed a growing acquaintance with English thought of the eighteenth century and especially with the works of Bolingbroke. From these he learned historical criticism of the Bible. He copied Bolingbroke's statement:

> It is not true that Christ revealed an entire body of ethics, proved to be the law of nature from principles of reason and reaching all duties of life. . . . A system thus collected from the writings of the ancient heathen moralists, of Tully, of Seneca, of Epictetus, and others,

---

1. See Gilbert Chinard, ed., *The Literary Bible of Thomas Jefferson* (Baltimore, Johns Hopkins Press, 1928), *The Commonplace Book of Thomas Jefferson* (Baltimore, Johns Hopkins Press, 1926), and especially Chinard, *Jefferson*, Bk. I, chaps. 1, 2.

2. Boyd, *Papers of Jefferson, 1*, 9–11; Chinard, *Jefferson*, pp. 5, 20.

3. Chinard's comment in *Literary Bible*, pp. 22–23.

would be more full, more entire, more coherent and more clearly deduced from unquestionable principles of knowledge.[4]

From Bolingbroke Jefferson also learned the principles of scientific doubt, and copied the sentence, "No hypothesis ought to be maintained if a single phenomenon stands in direct opposition to it."[5]

During this period Jefferson was questioning the Bible and his own religious beliefs. The critical attitude he developed was in all probability augmented by his contact with William Small at William and Mary College.[6] It was perhaps inevitable that a young man of his intellectual capacity should share in the eighteenth-century movement to put religion on a rational basis.

BACKGROUND TO CRITICISM

I shall recall this movement briefly.[7] It was essentially a quest for valid authority in religion. From the Reforma-

---

4. Chinard, *Literary Bible*, p. 50. See also Chinard, *Jefferson*, p. 526. The effect of the ancient Stoics and Epicureans upon the American founding fathers was profound. E.g. see Morison, *The Young Man Washington* (Cambridge, Mass., 1932), pp. 18–21, 41–43, and passim. Madison, Franklin, and John Adams all reflect the same climate of thought.

5. Chinard, *Literary Bible*, p. 41. See also Dumas Malone, *Jefferson, the Virginian*, Vol. I of *Jefferson and His Time* (Boston, 1928), p. 106.

6. See Marie G. Kimball, *Jefferson: The Road to Glory* (New York, 1943), p. 124.

7. There are a number of excellent detailed discussions of various aspects of this movement already available. For its development in America, see Herbert W. Schneider, *A History of American Philosophy* (New York, 1946), chap. 2. For England, see Mark Pattison, "Tendencies in Religious Thought in England, 1686–1750," *Essays and Reviews*, 12th ed. London, 1865; and Leslie Stephen, *History of English Thought in the Eighteenth Century*, 2 vols. New York, 1876. For Europe, see Ernst Cassirer, *The Philosophy of the Enlightenment*, trans. F. C. A. Koelln and J. P. Pettegrove (Boston, 1955), chap. 14. See also J. H. Randall, *The Making of the Modern Mind* (Cambridge, Mass., 1926), Bk. III, chaps. 11, 12, 15; and Paul Hazard, *European Thought in the Eighteenth Century*, trans. J. Lewis May (New Haven, 1954), Pt. I, chaps. 3–7. Other references will appear below.

tion on, the foundations upon which Christians had tried to base their theology had successively failed. In England, for instance, the authority of the universal church had given way to the national church, that to the authority of scripture, and that to the inner light or witness of the Spirit in the soul of the individual believer. The reaction to the extravagances of the last led to the attempt to base revealed truth on reason.[8]

Reason had a peculiarly powerful appeal during this era. In the late seventeenth century Isaac Newton had used it to perform the unprecedented task of explaining the material world. By means of relatively few fundamental laws of immense scope and power, he had made it possible to determine, at least in principle, the properties and behavior of every particle of every material body in the universe. After searching into things themselves, man could formulate the general laws by which they were formed and come to an understanding of nature by means of reason. Laws based on the observed order and conjunctions of things and events were sufficient, without introducing impalpable entities and forces, to describe all that could be described and predict all that could be predicted.[9]

This was an immense and widely acclaimed victory for reason. The typical reaction is expressed in Alexander Pope's couplet:

> Nature and Nature's laws lay hid in night:
> God said, *Let Newton be!* and all was light![10]

At first glance nature was obviously a balanced whole of order and law, and man (hitherto in darkness but now beginning to be enlightened) wanted to place himself spiritu-

---

8. Pattison, pp. 350–52.

9. See Isaiah Berlin, ed., *The Age of the Enlightenment* (New York, 1956), pp. 15–17; J. H. Randall, chap. 11.

10. "Epitaph Intended for Sir Isaac Newton."

ally and physically in harmony with it. Locke provided the rationale for doing this when he said that man had no innate ideas but received all of his ideas by means of his sense experiences and intuition.[11] Locke's authority on all questions of psychology and the theory of knowledge remained unchallenged throughout the first half of the eighteenth century, except for the tendency of philosophers such as Berkeley, Hume, and Condillac to minimize the difference between sensation and intuition, and finally to wipe it out altogether. Condillac expanded Locke's attack upon innate ideas to include the prejudice concerning innate operations of the mind.

Once it could be seen that mental operations were merely transformed sensations, it could also be seen that no upper limits must be set for the process of the constant growth of the mind.[12] Reason could show men how nature worked when men no longer impeded that work by unnatural institutions and habits. Reason could make them aware of natural laws they had been violating in their ignorance. It would be possible for men "barely by the use of their natural faculties" (a phrase Locke had used only with respect to man's ability to come to certain knowledge) to bring ideas, conduct, and institutions into harmony with the universal natural order.[13]

In eighteenth-century thought science, religion, morality, and the social sciences became inextricably interwoven.[14] For example, the inevitable conclusion toward which Locke's *Essay on Human Understanding* moves is the cer-

11. See John Locke, *Essay Concerning Human Understanding*, Bk. II, chap. 1, secs. 1–5, quoted in Berlin, pp. 40–42; J. H. Randall, pp. 269–70; Stephen, *1*, 34–36.

12. See Cassirer, pp. 99–104.

13. See Crane Brinton, *The Shaping of the Modern Mind* (New York, 1956), p. 122; Carl Becker, *The Heavenly City of the Eighteenth Century Philosophers* (New Haven, Yale University Press, 1932), pp. 64–65.

14. See Gladys Bryson, *Man and Society: The Scottish Inquiry of the Eighteenth Century* (Princeton, 1945), chap. 1.

tain knowledge of God's existence.[15] In other words, reason becomes the means of testing and supporting the truth in Christian revelation. For Locke's time the *Essay* also had the significance, however, of demolishing the doctrine of total depravity in man.[16] Now by using reason, man could hope to develop and perfect true morality and the natural society here on earth. He could become good and achieve happiness.[17]

But reason and observation went on to prove too much. They made the conclusion inescapable that nature did contain evil. Since it was unthinkable that nature did not accurately reflect the God who had created it, three unpalatable but thoroughly reasonable alternative conclusions could be drawn about Him: (1) if benevolent, He was also incompetent; (2) He was malevolent; (3) He did not exist. (There was a fourth choice available: a return to Christian revelation based on the authority of church, scripture, or inner light, which was not only unreasonable but reactionary.) To accept any one of these conclusions meant that reason could provide no motivation for morals or virtue.

The problem then was to set up a standard by which to judge results of reason. Not only did they have to be limited to the conclusions reason can draw from observations or sense data, but conflicts between different individuals were to be settled by an appeal to the multitude.[18] It was generally assumed that each person is equipped to attain truth for himself and that all the truths he needs are universally accessible and verifiable. Whatever is beyond the grasp of the majority is certainly unreasonable (however "rational" it may be), unnecessary, and probably untrue.[19]

15. See G. R. Cragg, *From Puritanism to the Age of Reason* (Cambridge, 1950), p. 115; Stephen, *1*, 36.
16. See Becker, pp. 54–65.
17. See Hazard, pp. 14–25.
18. See ibid., pp. 26–30.
19. See Arthur O. Lovejoy, "The Parallel of Deism and Classicism," *Modern Philology*, 24 (1932), 281. Summarized in Bryson, pp. 13–15.

As a result Christian revelation was subjected to relentless criticism. No body of doctrine given by divine inspiration to particular individuals could be accepted as true except for those tenets which were universally reaffirmed on some other basis by the human race. Metaphysics similarly fell into disrepute because it dealt with matters which were exclusively rational and beyond the range of sense data and empirical testing. The concern for moral behavior, on the other hand, was enhanced because it seemed obvious that all men at all times had been concerned with the problem of morality and that its basic principles were the common possession of humanity. Morality seemed somehow to be inherent in men irrespective of their particular religious beliefs. For example, there was the atheist Diderot, "his mind unable to find any sufficient reason for virtuous conduct, his heart unable to renounce the conviction that nothing is better in this world than to be a good man."[20]

JEFFERSON'S PHILOSOPHY OF LIFE

All of this formed the climate of thought in which Jefferson approached religious maturity.[21] The themes we have seen to be typical of the century appear in his own advice to others concerning religion. In 1787 he wrote a letter to Peter Carr containing advice on how to study religion and morality. This letter may have reflected his own previous religious crisis and his way of attacking it.[22] The similarity between some of the advice given in this letter and Diderot's dilemma is striking:

> Religion. Your reason is now mature enough to examine this object. . . . Shake off all the fears and servile prejudices, under which weak minds are servilely couched. Fix reason firmly in her seat, and call to her

20. Becker, p. 80.
21. See Schneider, pp. 56–59, 67–72.
22. See Kimball, *The Road to Glory*, p. 125; Chinard, *Jefferson*, pp. 19–21.

tribunal every fact, every opinion. Question with boldness even the existence of God; because, if there be one
he must more approve of the homage of reason, than
that of blindfolded fear.

Do not be frightened from this enquiry by any fear
of its consequences. If it ends in the belief that there is
no God you will find incitements to virtue in the comfort and pleasantness you feel in its exercise, and the
love of others which it will procure for you.[23]

Thus it seems that if the religious superstructure Jefferson received as a child collapsed, his foundation of morality
remained unshaken. He was conscious of being of good
stock. The self-discipline of the Stoics appealed to him as
it had to Washington. After a brief period of skepticism and
cynicism, Jefferson took Bolingbroke's advice and built
himself a philosophy of life involving personal discipline
and scrupulously moral behavior. He also responded in
Stoic tradition to the call of duty to the life of public service,
and soon enlisted in the movement to bring about the amel-
ioration of society and mankind. From ancient moralists
such as Cicero, Seneca, and Marcus Aurelius, Jefferson derived a conception of patriotism and public duty which
molded his life.[24]

Adrienne Koch has taken issue with Chinard's appraisal
of Jefferson's philosophy as "pessimistic yet courageous,"
and maintained that Jefferson's enduring philosophy of life
was marked by cheerfulness, not gloom. Happiness, she
says, was the end of life to Jefferson. He was engaged by
"the peculiar conjunction of duty with happiness," and
blended Epicureanism and Stoicism, with the result that
happiness was to be attained by self-discipline.[25] Actually

23. To Peter Carr, Aug. 10, 1787 (LB, 6, 258–61).

24. See Chinard, *Jefferson*, pp. 19–26; Morison, pp. 18–21, 41–43, and
passim.

25. See Adrienne Koch, *The Philosophy of Thomas Jefferson* (New York,
1943), p. 6, and chap. 1.

the philosophy that Jefferson evolved by 1770 was neither "pessimism" nor "cheerfulness." He never seems to have doubted the goodness of the Creator, the essential goodness of nature and men, or the final victory of the rights of men in all societies. Over against this, however, he was always aware that many difficult, painful problems lay between his hopes and their achievement. Basically he was "optimistic," cautious, conscious of barriers to be hurdled, but confident of the ultimate victory. However, more important than assigning a name to this attitude is recognizing that from 1770 on, Jefferson had an enduring philosophy of life. He had emerged upon a plateau of religious belief which, although subject to some modification of detail in the light of later personal experience (and sometimes because of personal inconsistency), nevertheless remained relatively stable until his death.

Jefferson's "Reticence" about Religion

Some biographers of Jefferson have expressed reluctance to deal with the religion of Thomas Jefferson because he himself insisted so often that it was a private matter.[26] "Say nothing of my Religion: it is known to myself and God alone," he wrote the "fan-coloring biographer" Delaplaine and repeated to others. Many have decided since then that Jefferson's religion was intended to be Jefferson's secret.[27] Actually, he was far from secretive about his faith. He would not answer questions about it whenever he felt that they were violations of his freedom of conscience. But if he seemed defensive or touchy with inquisitive strangers and people he did not trust, he explained his beliefs fully and without reticence to close friends and confidants, such as Charles Thomson, Benjamin Rush, John Adams, William Short, Joseph Priestley, and Thomas Cooper. In his letters

26. E.g. Chinard, *Jefferson*, p. 519.
27. To Charles Thomson, Jan. 29, 1817 (Ford, *Writings of Jefferson*, *10*, 75–76); To John Adams, Jan. 11, 1817 (LB, *15*, 99–100).

to them he called himself "Deist," "Theist," "Unitarian," and "rational Christian." In one letter he declared, "I am a *real Christian,* that is to say, a disciple of the doctrines of Jesus."[28] In another he said, "I, too, am an Epicurian [*sic*]," explaining that he meant he followed "the genuine (not the imputed) doctrines of Epicurus."[29] Jefferson also said, "I am of a sect by myself as far as I know,"[30] as well as, "I never submitted the whole system of my opinions to the creed of any party of men whatever, in religion, in philosophy, in politics, or in anything else, where I was capable of thinking for myself. Such an addiction would be the last degradation of a free and moral agent. If I could not go to heaven but with a party, I would not go there at all."[31] It might be well, then, not to take the labels Jefferson applies to himself at face value without first investigating his writings to discover what they reveal about his beliefs.

Jefferson's Theism

Jefferson believed in God. He rejected the accusation that he was an atheist, calling it a calumny and a lie.[32] He founded his belief in the existence of God on two well-known arguments, the order of the universe (or the argument from design) and the general consensus of opinion. Both these arguments are found in his letter to John Adams

28. To Charles Thomson, Jan. 9, 1816 (Ford, *10,* 5–6, and LB, *14,* 385).

29. To William Short, Oct. 31, 1819 (Ford, *10,* 143). Jefferson's orthography was far from conventional even for his own time. In matters of spelling, grammar, capitalization, and punctuation his writings are by now thoroughly unorthodox. (See Boyd, *1,* xxviii–xxx.) A consistent use of *sic,* to indicate that vagaries in particular passages should be attributed to Jefferson, would be excessive. Further, each editor of Jefferson's writings has used a different editorial policy with respect to this matter. For this reason, the reader may assume that any particular quotation from Jefferson in this discussion represents the author's efforts to reproduce the version given in the source stated in the footnote.

30. To Ezra Stiles, June 25, 1819 (LB, *15,* 203).

31. To Francis Hopkinson, March 13, 1789 (Ford, *5,* 76).

32. To James Monroe, May 26, 1800 (Ford, 7, 447–48).

of April 11, 1823.[33] Here he says that the evidences for the existence of God are "irresistible." This belief actually can be detected underneath Jefferson's words even when he is trying to be neutral and encourage a reasonable investigation of the problem of whether God exists. For example, after saying to Peter Carr, "Question with boldness even the existence of God," he writes a few lines further on, "Your reason is the only oracle given you by heaven"![34]

Jefferson liked to believe himself free from unwarranted theological speculation. He once wrote to Ezra Stiles that Jesus "has told us only that God is good and perfect, but has not defined him. I am therefore of his theology, believing that we have neither words nor ideas adequate to that definition."[35] It is true that he never engaged consciously in systematic theological speculation. Nevertheless, he had definite ideas concerning what God was like and refused to accept certain ideas concerning God put forth by others. Consistent with his ideas concerning God, he developed a system of thought comprehending the nature of creation and the nature and destiny of man.

Some insight into what Jefferson believed concerning God can be obtained, first, from examining the names by which he referred to Him. They are numerous, and include "God" (as well as "my God," "God of the universe," and "God of justice"), "Deity," "Almighty," "Supreme Being," "Creator" (as well as "our Creator," "benevolent Creator," "Creator of the Universe," "common Father and Creator of men"), "intelligent and powerful Agent," "ultimate cause," "He who made us," "Giver of Life," "Author of nature," "Holy Author of our religion," "Author of morality," "Providence" (and also "overruling Providence"), "Being who presides over this world," "benevolent Governor of the World," "Infinite Power which rules the desti-

33. LB, *15*, 426–28.
34. To Peter Carr, Aug. 10, 1787 (LB, *6*, 256).
35. June 25, 1819 (LB, *15*, 203).

nies of the universe," "Fabricator, Preserver, and Regulator," and "Creator, Preserver, and Supreme Ruler of the universe." Two other names may be serving as synonyms for God when they are referred to as the sources of man's endowments: "heaven" and "nature" or "the hand of nature" ("nature" usually draws a feminine pronoun). The word "Lord" is rare; apparently he used it only in an excerpt from the Litany to provide an ironic ending to his list of the appalling characteristics of Kings, such as, "And so endeth the book of Kings, from all of whom the Lord deliver us."[36] Most of these names were in common use during the Enlightenment, and a good deal of what they indicate about Jefferson's concept of God was common belief.

God as Creator

THIS WORLD

Like most of the intellectual leaders of the period, Jefferson believed in God as the Creator of the universe and man. He uses the word "Creator" more often, it seems, than any other, except possibly "God." He accepted the argument from design and the argument from consensus as rational proof of "the hypothesis of an eternal pre-existence of a Creator, rather than in that of a self-existing universe."[37] The means by which he refers to the source of the universe are "Creator," "Agent," "Ultimate Cause," "He who made us," and even "Fabricator!"

That source had created a universe of matter. In this belief Jefferson was an eighteenth-century materialist who held that anything in existence had to be of matter. "To talk of *immaterial* existences is to talk of *nothings*. To say that the human soul, angels, God are immaterial is to say, that they are *nothings,* or that there is no God, no angels, no

36. To John Langdon, March 5, 1810 (LB, *12*, 379). See also letter to David Humphreys, Aug. 14, 1787 (LB, *6*, 280).
37. To John Adams, April 11, 1823 (LB, *15*, 247).

soul. I cannot reason otherwise."[38] Things immaterial could only be said to be things nonexistent; the doctrine of a nonmaterial God was simply disguised atheism.[39]

In the universe created by God one could perceive:

> design, consummate skill, and indefinite power in every atom of its composition . . . movements of the heavenly bodies, so exactly held in their course by the balance of centrifugal and centripetal forces; the structure of our earth itself, with its distribution of lands, waters, and atmosphere; the animal and vegetable bodies, examined in all their minutest particles; insects, mere atoms of life, yet as perfectly organized as man or mammoth; the mineral substances.[40]

The skill manifest in the construction of the universe caused such wonder in Jefferson, as it did in many another *philosophe,* and so strongly supported his belief that God was to be seen in His works in nature, that he could not understand those who reverted to medieval Christian practices: "And Madame Cosway in a convent! I knew that to much goodness of heart she joined enthusiasm and religion; but I had thought that very enthusiasm would have prevented her shutting up her adoration of the God of the universe in the walls of a cloister; that she would rather have sought the *mountain top.*"[41]

38. To John Adams, Aug. 15, 1820 (LB, *15*, 274). Italics Jefferson's. The emphasis on matter and void alone making up the universe was undoubtedly one of the reasons Jefferson appreciated the doctrines of Epicurus so greatly. See his letter to William Short, Oct. 31, 1819 (Ford, *10*, 145).

39. Jefferson was exceeding Priestley in this respect; see Stephen, *1*, 432. For the variety of religious alliances materialism could make, see Hazard, pp. 122–29, and J. H. Randall, pp. 294–306. Jefferson consistently shied away from atheism, whether it was materialistic or immaterialistic; see Koch, *Philosophy of Jefferson,* pp. 92–99.

40. To John Adams, April 11, 1823 (LB, *15*, 427–28).

41. To Mrs. Church, Nov. 27, 1793 (Ford, *6*, 445).

Within the world of nature God had created man. This belief has outcroppings in documents such as the Declaration of Independence ("that all men are created equal; that they are endowed by their Creator . . .") and the Reply to the Danbury Baptists ("the common father and Creator of Man").[42] From this Creator, man has received the gifts and endowments which make him human: his life, his rights, his capacities, his instincts. One of the most important of these was conscience or the moral instinct, a human faculty of whose existence Jefferson was as sure as he was of the existence of organs of sight and hearing:[43] having intended man for a social animal, God had put social dispositions into him. Further, even the relationships between men found their source in the Creator, "the author of all the relations of morality, and of the laws and obligations these infer."[44] Thus the natural law of the universe included not only physical but moral law.

THE AFTERLIFE

Part of creation, in the thought of Jefferson, was the afterlife. Jefferson was, of course, a true reformer; during most of his active career his attention and energies were directed to the improvement of this world rather than the anticipation of the next. Chinard writes: "In his later years Thomas Jefferson's thoughts turned to the hereafter. In his youth he had declared that 'the business of life is with matter' and that it serves no purpose to break our heads against a blank wall. But he was human and returned to the riddle as his term grew nearer every day."[45] Yet it is not wise to conclude on the basis of these words of Jefferson that he denied either the existence of an afterlife or the value of

42. LB, *1*, 29; *16*, 282.
43. To Thomas Law, June 13, 1814 (LB, *14*, 138–44).
44. Rockfish Gap Report, Aug. 1, 1818 (Cabell, *Early History*, p. 441).
45. Chinard, *Jefferson*, p. 519.

contemplating it at any time in his life. Two comments must be made. First, the statement, "the business of life is with matter," may mean that the existence of heaven cannot be proved, but may also mean that any heaven that does exist must be material. Second, by the time Jefferson began discussing the afterlife, he did not consider its existence a riddle but believed in it with a firm assurance. His statements concerning the future life show no real doubt but only those qualifications any intelligent man will include when he discusses a subject which cannot be proved one way or the other.

Chinard's statement that Jefferson never denied the existence of a future life actually gives us a false picture; he affirmed it, especially in his old age. Much earlier than that, however, his records reveal his willingness to believe in life after death for a good utilitarian reason: its value as an incentive to virtue and moral living. "[If you find reason to believe] that there be a future state, the hope of a happy existence in that increases the appetite to deserve it."[46] The education by which society could hope to make up the defect of the lack of a moral sense in the individual included "ultimately the prospects of a future state of retribution for the evil as well as the good done while here."[47]

Remarks reflecting his belief in life after death came with ever increasing frequency from 1787 until his death. They appeared not only in his private correspondence but in public utterances such as the statement that the American people acknowledge and adore "an overruling Providence, which by all its dispensations proves that it delights in the happiness of man here and in his greater happiness hereafter."[48] His concept of the afterlife included customary attributes such as immortality and rewards or punishments for each individual, appropriate to his behavior during life

46. To Peter Carr, Aug. 10, 1787 (LB, 6, 260).
47. To Thomas Law, June 13, 1814 (LB, 14, 142).
48. First Inaugural Address, March 4, 1801 (LB, 3, 320).

on earth. Jefferson, incidentally, seemed to have had no doubt about his own future lot. He wrote in 1820 to Mrs. Cosway that "the religion you so sincerely profess tells us we shall meet again; and we have all so lived as to be assured it will be in happiness."[49]

Perhaps the most striking emphasis in Jefferson's concept of heaven is its prospect of reunion. He used that prospect to comfort himself and friends whenever he considered actual or possible bereavement. His need for such comfort may have had its roots in the shock he received in 1782 at the death of his wife.[50] The death of his daughter Mary in 1804 undoubtedly reinforced the need to reassure himself that his separation from his loved ones was not eternal. Such a reassurance appears in his letters and certainly reaches the peak of its expression in his extraordinarily sensitive letter of condolence and hope to John Adams after the death of his wife Abigail: "The term is not very far distant, at which we are to deposit in the same cerement our sorrows and suffering bodies and to ascend in essence to an ecstatic meeting with the friends we have loved and lost and whom we shall still love and never lose again. God bless you and support you under your heavy affliction."[51] Essentially he tried by the same means to comfort both himself and his daughter Martha in the "Death-Bed Adieu" he wrote to her:

Life's visions are vanished, its dreams are no more;
    Dear friends of my bosom, why bathed in tears?
I go to my fathers; I welcome the shore
    Which crowns all my hopes or which buries my cares.

49. Dec. 27, 1820 (LB, *18*, 310).

50. See Chinard, *Jefferson*, pp. 137–39; Marie G. Kimball, *Jefferson, War and Peace* (New York, 1947), pp. 306–07; and Malone, *Jefferson*, *1*, 394–98.

51. To John Adams, Nov. 13, 1818 (Ford, *10*, 114). Other letters touching this anticipation of heavenly reunion are to the Marquis de Lafayette, Feb. 14, 1815 (Ford, *9*, 510); and to Mrs. John Adams, Jan. 11, 1811 (Ford, *10*, 70–71).

Then farewell my dear, my loved daughter, adieu!
The last pang of life is in parting from you!
Two seraphs await me long shrouded in death;
I will bear them your love on my last parting breath![52]

In the light of all this, perhaps too much is made of Jefferson's words to Isaac Story when he was acknowledging receipt of the latter's book on transmigration of souls:

> When I was young I was fond of speculations which seemed to promise some insight into that hidden country, but observing at length that they left me in the same ignorance in which they had found me, I have for very many years ceased to read or think concerning them, and have reposed my head on that pillow of ignorance which a benevolent Creator has made so soft for us, knowing how much we should be forced to use it.[53]

Although disclaiming speculation, the letter also contains a plain statement of Jefferson's belief that the Creator has prepared an afterlife in which to reward the deserving. In other letters he does speculate about its nature. More than once he entertains the possibility that "perhaps . . . one of the elements of future felicity is to be a constant and unimpassioned view of what is passing here."[54]

Immaterialist spiritualism had no place in Jefferson's view of the hereafter. He rejected out of hand Plato's arguments for the immortality of the soul.[55] Even in his remark to John Adams that "we are to deposit in the same cerement our sorrows and suffering bodies and to ascend in es-

52. Quoted in Saul K. Padover, *Jefferson* (New York, New American Library of World Literature, 1955), p. 185. The "seraphs" were Jefferson's deceased wife and younger daughter.

53. To Isaac Story, Dec. 5, 1801 (Ford, *8*, 107).

54. To Mrs. John Adams, Jan. 11, 1817 (Ford, *10*, 70–71).

55. To John Adams, July 5, 1814 (Ford, *9*, 464).

sence," the word essence refers to something material—
thin, nonearthly, but material, nevertheless. This stubborn
materialism caused Jefferson some trouble in reconciling
his views with those of his favorite moralist, Jesus of Nazareth. In April 1820 Jefferson reluctantly admitted that they
differed. "It is not to be understood that I am with him in
all his doctrines. I am a Materialist; he takes the side of
Spiritualism."[56] As Jefferson continued to mull over the
question, he began to wonder whether the spiritualism of
Jesus was the same as that of Platonists and other metaphysicians. In August of the same year he put the problem in
this way: "At what age of the Christian Church this heresy
of *immaterialism,* or masked atheism, crept in, I do not
know. But a heresy it certainly is. Jesus taught nothing of it.
He told us, indeed, that 'God is a Spirit,' but He has not
defined what a spirit is, nor said that it is not *matter.*"[57] As
time went on, Jefferson became acquainted with evidence
enabling him to proclaim, "Jesus himself, the Founder of
our religion, was unquestionably a Materialist as to man.
In all his doctrines of the resurrection, he teaches expressly
that the body is to rise in substances."[58] The reconciliation
had been effected. On this question Jefferson now believed
he and Jesus were in almost complete fundamental agreement.

Preserver and Regulator

Unlike many of his contemporaries, Jefferson did not
believe that once the Creator had set the great world-ma-
chine going, He had left it to spin on to its end governed
solely by natural law:

56. To William Short, April 13, 1820 (LB, *15,* 244).

57. To John Adams, Aug. 15, 1820 (LB, *15,* 274–75). Italics Jefferson's.

58. To Augustus S. Woodward, March 24, 1824 (LB, *16,* 18). Thomas
Cooper claimed credit for giving Jefferson this evidence. See Koch, *Philosophy of Jefferson,* p. 36, n. 54.

[The] Fabricator of all things from matter and motion [is also] their Preserver and Regulator while permitted to exist in their present forms and their regeneration into new and other forms. We see, too, evident proofs of the necessity of a superintending power, to maintain the universe in its course and order. Stars, well known, have disappeared, new ones have come into view; comets, in their incalculable courses may run foul of suns and planets, and require renovation under other laws; certain races of animals are become extinct; and were there no restoring power, all existences might extinguish successively, one by one, until all should be reduced to a shapeless chaos.[59]

This was the Being Jefferson called "Preserver," "Being who presides over this world," "benevolent Governor," "Infinite Power who rules the destinies of the Universe," "Regulator," "Supreme Ruler of the universe," and "Providence." God was an assiduous, divine mechanic or repairman, keeping the universe from stopping or lapsing into chaos. He also proved by His works to be benevolent, the "overruling Providence which by all its dispensations proves that it delights in the happiness of man here, and in his greater happiness hereafter."[60] The benevolence of this Governor, working through all natural events, may be seen in the termination of an epidemic[61] or in the preparation of the aged for death.[62]

God is also evident as benevolent guide and ruler in the relations of morality between men. Jefferson periodically expresses a prayer that God will safeguard the thought and efforts of public officials in words such as, "And may that Infinite Power which rules the universe, lead our councils

59. To John Adams, April 11, 1823 (LB, *15*, 427–28).
60. First Inaugural Address, March 14, 1801 (LB, *3*, 320).
61. Fifth Annual Message to Congress, Dec. 3, 1805 (Ford, *8*, 384–85).
62. To Mrs. John Adams, Jan. 11, 1817 (Ford, *10*, 70–71).

to what is best,"[63] or, "God bless you, and all our rulers, and give them the wisdom, as I am sure they have the will, to fortify us against the degeneracy of our government."[64]

Supreme Judge

Since this God was good, perfect, not withdrawn from His creation but attending upon it every moment to prevent its lapsing into chaos, He could be expected to see also that justice would prevail. Jefferson's optimism was based on this belief. That justice would certainly triumph in the afterlife provides the threat to Jefferson's statement: "If ever the morals of a people could be made the basis of their government, it is our case; & who could propose to govern such a people by the corruption of a legislature, before he could have one night of quiet sleep must convince himself that the human soul as well as the body is mortal."[65]

Throughout most of his career, however, Jefferson kept his attention and energies focused on this life, and his optimism was based on the belief that here, too, God's justice would prevail. If, as he believed, the Almighty had not decreed that men should never be free (the contrary, to Jefferson, was blasphemy),[66] this meant also that the day would come when God would liberate men on earth. There is an Old Testament ring to some of the passages in which he proclaims this belief. "If there be a God & he is just his day will come. He will never abandon the whole race of man to be eaten up by the leviathans and mammoths of a day."[67] Here is the Old Testament concept of the "Day of the Lord." It is comparatively mild, however, and not in-

63. First Inaugural Address (LB, *3*, 323).

64. To Joseph C. Cabell, Feb. 2, 1816 (Cabell, p. 55).

65. To John Adams, Feb. 28, 1796 (Ford, 7, 57).

66. To Joseph C. Cabell, Feb. 2, 1816 (Cabell, p. 55).

67. To the Marquis de Lafayette, Jan. 20, 1811 (Ford, *9*, 302). The "leviathans and mammoths" are countries like England and France, the naval and military oppressors of man.

consistent with the general impression of the God of the philosophe.

The expected Jeffersonian solutions to the problem of human evil are the benevolence of God and the natural progress of man. The Supreme Ruler of the Universe worked through the normal course of natural events to correct injustice. He spread enlightenment and education to bring about human improvement and perfection. After sufficient progress, man of his own desire would abandon the abuses in which he had previously indulged, or rise and smite the minority of kings, nobles, and priests too blind to learn. All this is in keeping with the suspicion Jefferson showed of biblical accounts which described events requiring a divine suspension of natural law.[68]

During one period of his life, however, Jefferson added to all of this a note distinctly out of key. In his discussion of Virginia's slavery problem, he wrote in 1782:

> And can the liberties of a nation be thought secure when we have removed their only firm basis, a conviction in the minds of the people that these liberties are of the gift of God? That they are not to be violated but with his wrath? Indeed, I tremble for my country when I reflect that God is just; that his justice cannot sleep forever; that considering numbers, nature and natural means only, a revolution of the wheel of fortune, an exchange of situation is among possible events; that it may become probably by supernatural interference! The Almighty has no attribute which can take side with us in such a contest. But it is impossible to be temperate and pursue such a subject. . . . We must be contented to hope they will force their way into every one's mind.[69]

---

68. E.g. letter to Peter Carr, Aug. 10, 1787 (Boyd, *12*, 15–17).
69. *Notes on Virginia*, Query 18 (Ford, *3*, 267).

Several years later he discussed the same subject and said:

> But we must await with patience the workings of an overruling Providence, & hope that that is preparing the deliverance of these, our suffering brethren. When the measure of their tears shall be full, when their groans shall have involved heaven itself in darkness, doubtless a god of justice will awaken to their distress, and by diffusing light and liberality among their oppressors, or at length, by his exterminating thunder, manifest his attention to the things of this world, and that they are not left to the guidance of a blind fatality.[70]

The aspect of Jefferson's thought revealed by words such as "wrath," "supernatural interference," "tremble," and "exterminating thunder," may have been temporary, since it is not evident elsewhere in his writings. If temporary, however, it was not momentary, since it appears in passages he wrote several years apart. The rarity of this theme makes it difficult to account for. One clue to an understanding of it may come from the fact that neither of these writings was intended to be confidential (as were all of the letters in which Jefferson discussed religion in his later years), but each was intended in its own way for publication. Jefferson published *Notes on Virginia* (from which the first passage is taken) himself, and hoped at one time to place a copy in the hand of every student at the College of William and Mary. The second selection was part of a critique in which Jefferson placed a great deal of material to be used to amplify and correct someone else's article submitted to him for review in advance of publication.[71]

70. "Observations on the Article 'États-Unis' Prepared for the *Encyclopédie Politique*," June 22, 1786 (Ford, *4*, 185).

71. Jefferson discusses his own attitude toward these corrections and comments in a letter to John Adams, Aug. 27, 1786 (Ford, *4*, 296).

Another clue may come from the fact that both passages concern slavery. There is a possibility that Jefferson, purely for political effect, put his case in theological terms reflecting concepts in which he personally did not believe. If this was simply a political expedient, it is the sole example of that type in his career. Why did he not use the same tactics to fight other human injustices? It is probable, rather, that the institution of slavery itself was the cause of the overwhelming emotion in Jefferson. He took it so seriously that its presence in the world put his belief in a God of justice to the test. He had learned from experience in the Virginia legislature and in the Continental Congress that slavery might not be removed from the American scene for a long time, if ever. It must also be kept in mind that Jefferson wrote *Notes on Virginia* during a period when he was personally distressed by criticisms of his administration as Governor of Virginia, and that he had it published after the death of his wife. All of these factors probably combined to make him psychologically ready to affirm the possibility that his good and perfect God would show wrath, even to the point of upsetting the natural order, when men had gone too far.

CHAPTER 3

*M*an

The Jeffersonian science of man was more than an anthropology. It was at once an aspect of cosmology and theology, and an avenue to ethics and political theory.[1] Its base was reason applied to external observation. God had created man as a unique and single species of animal whose humanity lay in his physical needs and his physical attributes. Any eye could see that the bodies of all men were basically similar. Their fundamental physical needs were everywhere the same. Needs must be satisfied. It followed that the Creator intended all men to achieve satisfaction of their needs in the world in which He had placed them. In this they

1. See Daniel J. Boorstin, *The Lost World of Thomas Jefferson* (New York, 1948), p. 59. Boorstin's discussion of the beliefs held in common by the members of the American Philosophical Society provides insight into Jefferson's own thought. See esp. chap. 2. See also Bryson, *Man and Society*, chap. 1, for a discussion which shows to what extent this aspect of Jefferson's thought was typical of his age.

were all the same. From these propositions Jefferson derived
his doctrine of man.

Man's Rights

The first of the truths held to be self-evident in the
Declaration of Independence is that all men are created
equal. Jefferson never tired of proclaiming this. It was self-
evident to him that God had made men equal. All humans
were descendants of the original parents created at the beginning of time. They derived equal rights from their common physical and biological humanity.[2] Fifty years after
the signing of the Declaration of Independence he declared
that "the mass of mankind has not been born with saddles
on their backs, nor a favored few booted and spurred, ready
to ride them legitimately by the grace of God."[3]

The equality of men consisted in the "rights" (or "liberties" or "freedoms") with which their benevolent Creator
had endowed them,[4] and in certain "natural" duties which
they assumed upon entering into the compact of society
with their fellows. Rights were actually based upon needs.
Since all men had the same needs organically, the claim to
equal rights for every individual was universal: "Under
the law of nature all men are born free, everyone comes
into the world with a right to his own person, which includes the liberty of moving and using it at his will. This
is what is called personal liberty, and is given him by
the author of nature, because necessary for his own sus-

2. The first draft of the Declaration read: "that all men are created
equal & independent; that from that equal creation they derive rights inherent and unalienable." See LB, *1*, 29, illustration facsimile of Jefferson's
Rough Draft; Boyd *1*, 423; Boorstin, p. 61.

3. To Roger C. Weightman, June 24, 1826 (Ford, *Writings of Jefferson*,
10, 391–92).

4. See Carl Becker, *The Declaration of Independence* (New York, 1922),
chap. 2, for the effect of the philosophy of natural rights upon the thought
of the American revolutionaries.

tenance."[5] The Creator had given certain abilities in common to all men to enable them to satisfy common needs. Jefferson traced one right after another back to this belief. For example:

> I believe . . . that right to property is founded in our natural wants, in the means with which we are endowed to satisfy these wants, and the right to what we acquire by those means without violating the similar rights of other sensible beings; that no one has a right to obstruct another, exercising his faculties innocently for the relief of sensibilities made a part of his nature.[6]

If men had not been created equal, the matter might have been quite different. This aspect of Jefferson's thought can be seen excellently in his anecdote concerning the Revisal:

> I proposed to abolish the law of primogeniture, and to make real estate descendible in parcenary to the next of kind, as personal property is, by the statute of distribution. Mr. Pendleton . . . proposed we should adopt the Hebrew principle, and give a double portion to the older son. I observed, that if the oldest son could eat twice as much, or do double work, it might be a natural evidence of his right to a double portion; but being on a par in his powers and wants, with his brothers and sisters, he should be on a par also in the patrimony.[7]

All humans were physically equal. They had the same needs, the same abilities, the same capacities.[8] Therefore,

5. Howell vs. Netherland, April 1770, in Thomas Jefferson, *Reports of Cases Determined in the General Court of Virginia* (1829), pp. 90–96. Quoted in Kimball, *Road to Glory*, p. 94.

6. To Dupont de Nemours, April 24, 1816 (LB, *14*, 490).

7. *Autobiography* (LB, *1*, 64). For further discussion of Jefferson on rights see Koch, *Philosophy of Jefferson*, chap. 15, and esp. pp. 143–44.

8. The effect of this tenet of faith upon scientific discussion in the A.P.S. was to take in all evidence, however contradictory, as proof. See Boorstin, pp. 61–68.

the Creator had given each man the same rights, so that he might achieve happiness through the satisfaction of his natural needs.[9]

Since man's particular needs varied with his situation, his specific rights were numerous. The list of those mentioned by Jefferson seems endless. There were "life, liberty, and the pursuit of happiness." There were the individual's personal liberties of conscience, thinking, speaking, writing, movement, commerce, and correspondence. There were the rights to the use of one's faculties, to property, to acquisitions from one's industry, to honor and confidence from one's fellow citizens, stemming from their sense of his worthy actions. Man had the right to regulate and control society jointly with all who have concurred in the procuring of it; this involved the rights to information concerning government, to rebellion when misinformed or unsatisfied, to expatriation (emigration), to freedom from oppression by the majority and from perpetual service to the state, and the right to alter or abolish any form of government that becomes destructive of these other rights. If any single right mentioned by Jefferson sums up the rest, it is that of self government: "Every man and every body of men on earth, possess the right of self-government. They receive it with their being from the hand of nature. Individuals exercise it by their single will; collections of men by that of their majority; for the law of the *majority* is the natural law for every society of men."[10]

Man's Capacities

In their rights men were absolutely equal. But God had also given men important capacities. Concerning these, Jefferson was no equalitarian, since he recognized fully

9. To James Monroe, May 20, 1782 (LB, *4*, 196).
10. "Opinion . . . whether the seat of the government shall be transferred to the Potomac," July 15, 1790 (Ford, *5*, 205–06). Italics Jefferson's.

that they had been given to individuals in greater or lesser degree. He believed that these capacities entered properly into the definition of humanity, nevertheless. He also felt that the want of certain human capacities in certain individuals might be made up by education, and he was definite in his belief that want of talents was no measure of the individual's natural rights.

REASON

Reason was one capacity given to men by God. As he wrote to Peter Carr, "Your own reason is the only oracle given you by heaven."[11] Jefferson's belief in the essential rationality of man lies behind his optimistic statement in the Bill for Establishing Religious Freedom, "that truth is great and will prevail if left to herself; that she is a proper and sufficient antagonist to error, and has nothing to fear from the conflict unless by human interposition disarmed of her natural weapons, free argument and debate; errors ceasing to be dangerous when it is permitted freely to contradict them."[12]

Jefferson, however, did not consider reason an infallible guide in all things. Reasonable men did not show uniformity of thought; but the differences in opinion to which reason could lead individuals in no way excused them from using it to the best of their ability. That the responsibility was God-given can be seen in the words from a letter to William Carver. Speaking about those whose conclusions differ from his, Jefferson assures his correspondent:

> I respect their conclusions, however different from my own. It is their own reason, not mine, nor that of any other, which has been given them by their creator for the investigation of truth. . . . For the use of this rea-

11. Aug. 10, 1787 (LB, 6, 261).
12. Boyd, *Papers of Jefferson*, 2, 546.

son, every one is responsible to the God who has plant-
ed it in his breast, as a light for his guidance, and that
by which alone he will be judged.[13]

MORALITY

Man had other important capacities besides reason. In
1816 Jefferson wrote to Dupont de Nemours, "We consider
society as one of the natural wants with which man has been
created; that he has been endowed with the faculties and
qualities to effect its satisfaction by concurrence of others
having the same want."[14] He goes on to say later, "I believe
with you that morality, compassion, generosity are innate
elements of the human constitution." In other words, Jefferson felt that man is not natively depraved. As a being intended by his Creator for society, man's most important endowment was "a love of others, a sense of duty to them, a
moral instinct in short, which prompts us irresistibly to
feel and succor their distress."[15] Jefferson found his real
authority in the conscience within the individual's own
breast, the special moral sense which was as truly a part of
man's nature as his sight, hearing, arm, or leg.[16]

In the realm of morality Jefferson felt reason was a broken reed. He went on record, very explicitly putting reason's limitations and defects in strong terms, in the "Dia-
logue" between the Head and the Heart in his letter to

13. To William Carver, Dec. 4, 1823 (Ford, *10*, 284–85).
14. April 24, 1816 (LB, *14*, 487).
15. To Thomas Law, June 13, 1814 (LB, *14*, 142).
16. Malone, *Jefferson, 1*, 108. The Hutcheson-Hume theory of conscience
was commonly held in the eighteenth century. See, e.g., Richard Price, *A
Review of the Principal Questions in Morals*, ed. D. Daiches Raphael (Oxford, 1948), pp. 13–15, 215–17, 235–36, and passim. But cf. Schneider *(History
of American Philosophy*, p. 48) who maintained there was "no enthusiasm
as yet" in America for the theory. Jefferson's position is made clear by the
quotations that follow below.

Maria Cosway in 1786. Among the remarks with which the
Heart finally put the Head in its place are these:

> When nature assigned us the same habitation, she gave
> us over it a divided empire. To you she allotted the
> field of science; to me, that of morals. . . . [In] denying
> to you the feelings of sympathy, of benevolence, of
> gratitude, of justice, of love, of friendship, she has
> excluded you from their control. To these, she has
> adapted the mechanism of the heart. Morals were too
> essential to the happiness of man to be risked on the
> uncertain combinations of the head. She laid their
> foundations, therefore, in sentiment, not in science. . . .
> A few facts . . . will suffice to prove to you that nature
> has not organized you for our direction.

The Heart then tells of two actions performed by Jefferson
and which had shown him to be ungenerous. (Since he
wrote this letter in France, and both incidents had taken
place in America, they must have weighed on his conscience
for several years.) The Heart delivers the *coup de grâce* to
Reason with the statement, "In short, my friend, as far as
my recollection serves me, I do not know that I ever did a
good thing on your suggestion, or a dirty one without it."[17]
   A year later, in answer to Peter Carr's request for advice
on what to study in the realm of moral philosophy, Jefferson had this to say:

> I think it lost time to attend lectures on this branch.
> He who made us would have been a pitiful bungler, if
> he had made the rules of our moral conduct a matter of
> science. . . . Man was destined for society. His morality,
> therefore, was to be formed to this object. He was en-
> dowed with a sense of right and wrong merely relative
> to this. This sense is as much a part of his nature as the

17. To Maria Cosway, Oct. 12, 1786 (LB, 5, 442–44).

sense of hearing, seeing, feeling; it is the true foundation of morality. . . . The moral sense, or conscience is
as much a part of man as his leg or arm. It is given to
all human beings in a stronger or weaker degree, as
force of members is given them in greater or less degree. It may be strengthened by exercise as may any
particular limb of the body. This sense is submitted,
indeed, in some degree, to the guidance of reason; but
it is a small stock which is required for this.[18]

He was essentially of the same opinion in 1814 when discussing the subject in a letter to Thomas Law. Admitting
that individuals without social dispositions exist, he continues, "There is no rule without exceptions; but it is false
reasoning which converts exceptions into the general rule.
Some men are born without the organs of sight, or of hearing, or without hands. Yet it would be wrong to say that
man is born without these faculties, and sight, hearing,
and hands may with truth enter into the general definition
of man." He goes on to say that the lack of a moral sense in
an individual is "more degrading than the most hideous of
the bodily deformities," and that when it is lacking, "we
endeavour to supply the defect by education."[19]

EDUCATION

The capacity for education was another endowment the
Creator had given to man. It was part of man's native ability
to copy others, "for man is an imitative animal. This quality is the germ of all education in him. From his cradle to
his grave, he is learning to do what he sees others do."[20]
This capacity, like the others, was given to individuals in
greater or lesser degree. Not only that, but Jefferson also

18. To Peter Carr, Aug. 10, 1787 (LB, *6*, 257–58).
19. June 13, 1814 (LB, *14*, 138–44).
20. *Notes on Virginia*, Query 18 (Ford, *3*, 266–67).

entertained the lasting suspicion that it was given to the different races in greater or lesser degree as well, and that the Negro race in particular was comparatively deficient in educational capacity. He was impelled to face this conclusion because he honestly believed that many Negroes had been given ample opportunity to become educated. He discussed the problem at length in *Notes on Virginia,* Query 14. Although admitting his observation was incomplete, adding all sorts of qualifications and setting it forth as a doubt rather than something beyond dispute, Jefferson's position is that "the improvement of the blacks in body and mind, in the first instance of their mixture with the whites, has been observed by every one, and proves that their inferiority is not the effect merely of their condition in life. . . . It is not their condition, then, but nature which has produced the distinction."[21] Hesitatingly expressed, it was nevertheless a doubt to which Jefferson adhered. He had neither hesitation nor doubt, however, about insisting that "whatever their degree of talent, it is no measure of their rights."[22]

Jefferson showed no doubts about the native talents of the American Indians. He attributed their lack of cultural development to the fact that they had not yet devised an alphabet and that they were not sufficiently numerous to enable one improvement to beget another in sufficient numbers over a long enough period of time.[23] Yet even without the advantage of the Negro in his association with civilized whites, the Indian, Jefferson felt, had shown admirable examples of primitive genius and real promise.[24]

---

21. Ford, *3,* 246–48.
22. To Henri Grégoire, Feb. 25, 1809 (Ford, *9,* 246). Boorstin's discussion of Jefferson's vacillation is excellent; see *Lost World,* pp. 81–97. As a result of this ambiguity, Jefferson was claimed by both sides in the abolition controversy preceding the Civil War. See Peterson, *Jefferson Image,* pp. 162–89.
23. See *Notes on Virginia,* Query 6 (Ford, *3,* 158–61).
24. See ibid., Query 14 (Ford, *3,* 246).

In 1812 he felt that their promise was already bearing fruit. He pointed to the developments among the Creeks and the Cherokees, showing that they had become "far advanced in civilization. They have good cabins, enclosed fields, large herds of cattle and hogs, spin and weave their own clothes of cotton, have smiths and other of the most necessary tradesmen, write and read, are on the increase in numbers, and a branch of the Cherokees is now instituting a regular representative government."[25] The Cherokees and Creeks had shown progress.

The Concept of Progress

Progress was a powerful theme in the Enlightenment. The work of Newton and Locke had inspired men to go on and discover a science of human nature and human society. Man and his institutions were included in the order of nature and the scope of the recognized scientific method, and in all things the newly invented social sciences were assimilated to the physical sciences.[26] At last, it was felt, mankind held in its own hands the key to its destiny. Man could make the future almost what he would. If he destroyed the foolish errors of the past and returned to a rational cultivation of nature, there were scarcely any limits to human welfare that he might not transcend.[27] There was no uniform theory of progress.[28] Nevertheless, the passion for social reform, the determined application of man's rational powers to this new field, confidence in the ability of man through law and government to bring about an immediate improvement in human affairs, and the combination of these proximate hopes with a still brighter vision of the more distant future—all these hopes became a common pos-

25. To John Adams, June 11, 1812 (Ford, 9, 358).
26. See J. H. Randall, p. 255.
27. See ibid., p. 381.
28. See Roger Lincoln Shinn, *Christianity and the Problem of History* (New York, 1953), p. 106.

session of the mind of Western Europe and America in the eighteenth century.[29]

CONDORCET'S OPTIMISM

One of the most optimistic of the prophets of progress was Condorcet, a French philosophe with whom Jefferson talked and corresponded. Condorcet had insisted that mankind's progress obeyed the same general laws governing individual improvement, and that as generations passed, continuity and growth of the human intellect would inevitably take place.[30] He proclaimed that the improvement of the human faculties would be boundless, that man was indefinitely perfectible, and that no power other than the end of the world could stop the progress of the race.[31] This, he believed, might be slow or fast, but never retrograde.[32] Condorcet, incidentally, penned his credo on human perfectibility during the reign of terror in the French Revolution, just a short time before being captured and put in a prison cell, there to die while awaiting the call to place his neck in the guillotine.

JEFFERSON'S OPTIMISM

In the main, Jefferson was also a prophet of progress. To Joseph Priestley (himself such a prophet as early as 1768) he said that the American people would not endure the idea of looking backward instead of forward for improve-

29. See John Baillie, *The Belief in Progress* (London, 1950), p. 110. See pp. 102–30 for a good summary of the effect of the belief in progress upon 18th-century European thought.

The development of the concept of progress during the Enlightenment is discussed in painstaking detail by J. B. Bury in *The Idea of Progress* (London, 1928), pp. 78–259. The same concept is the central theme of Becker's *Heavenly City*. See also Karl Löwith, *Meaning in History*, 4th ed. (Chicago, 1957), pp. 91–114. Other references given below.

30. See Arthur Alphonse Ekirch, Jr., *The Idea of Progress in America, 1815–1860* (New York, 1944), p. 15.

31. See ibid., p. 15.

32. See Shinn, p. 107; Löwith, pp. 92–93.

ment of the human mind and for what is most perfect in government, learning, and religion.[33] He could say seriously at the beginning of his first administration as President that good principles, wisely and honestly administered, could not fail to attach the American people to the order of things he espoused.[34] The basis of his optimism was religious: "I have no fear but that the result of our experiment will be, that men may be trusted to govern themselves without a master. Could the contrary to this be proved, I should conclude, either that there is no God, or that he is a malevolent being."[35] The human mind could progress. A corresponding progress in government was necessary: "laws and institutions must go hand in hand with the progress of the human mind."[36]

In the New World the idea of progress proved particularly influential. The United States, born in the Age of the Enlightenment, was able far more than Europe to actually make a break with the past and build a rational history.[37] The growing evidence on the frontier of man's ability to convert wilderness into civilization gave the theory of progress the solidity of fact. Jefferson had beheld this and in his insistence that progress had taken place he almost sang his description of the advances he had seen in his own country during his lifetime: "the march of civilization advancing from the sea coast, passing over us like a cloud of light, increasing our knowledge, and improving our condition insomuch as that we are at that time more advanced in civilization here than the seaports were when I was a boy."[38] To

33. Jan. 27, 1800 (Ford, 7, 416).

34. To Gideon Granger, 1800 (N.Y. Public Library, MS II, p. 73). See Saul K. Padover, ed., *Thomas Jefferson on Democracy* (New York, New American Library, 1953), p. 35.

35. To David Hartley, July 2, 1787 (LB, 6, 151).

36. To Samuel S. Kercheval, July 12, 1816 (Ford, 9, 42–43).

37. See Shinn, p. 108.

38. To William Ludlow, Sept. 6, 1824 (LB, 16, 75). See also letter to Dr. Benjamin Waterhouse, March 3, 1818 (Ford, 10, 103–04).

convince John Adams that he was wrong in maintaining
that the human mind would never advance beyond the
wisdom of the fathers, Jefferson did not resort merely to
reason and theory, but used a telling bit of evidence: Adams' own consciousness of science, unknown to his forefathers.[39]

JEFFERSON'S DOUBTS

Jefferson was convinced that progress had undeniably
taken place. Yet for all that, his remarks concerning man's
capacity for improvement are not generally given to the
heedless optimism of Condorcet. He was not, for the most
part, overly sanguine or unduly optimistic about the possibilities of progress. For one thing, it could be slow: "when
we reflect how difficult it is to move or inflect the great machine of society, how impossible to advance the notions of
a whole people suddenly to ideal right, we see the wisdom
of Solon's remark, that no more good must be attempted
than the nation can bear."[40] Progress was not even certain:
"There is a snail-paced gait for the advance of new ideas on
the general mind under which we must acquiesce. A 40
years' experience of popular assemblies has taught me, that
you must give them time for every step you take. If pushed
too hard, they baulk & the machine retrogrades."[41] In one
way or another Jefferson's most optimistic statements about
man's capacity for progress are tempered by the accompanying recognition of the real and ever present possibility of
delay, failure, reverse, and retrogression. He showed this
awareness when explaining the disappointing results of the
French Revolution:

> The generation which commences a revolution rarely
> completes it. . . . The light which has been shed on

39. To John Adams, June 15, 1813 (Ford, 9, 387).
40. To Dr. Walter Jones, March 31, 1801 (LB, 10, 255–56).
41. To Joel Barlow, Dec. 10, 1807 (Ford, 9, 168–69).

mankind by the art of printing, has eminently changed the condition of the world. . . . it continues to spread, and while printing is preserved, it can no more recede than the sun return on his course. A first attempt to recover the right of self-government may fail, so may a second, a third, etc. But as a younger and more in-structed race comes on, the sentiment becomes more intuitive, and a fourth, a fifth, or some subsequent one of the ever renewed attempts will succeed.[42]

The hopefulness of this passage is qualified by the recogni-tion of one past failure and of the real possibility of many failures to come. Similar examples of Jefferson's qualified optimism are the following statements:

Whether the succeeding generation is to be more vir-tuous than their predecessors I cannot say; but I am sure they will have more worldly wisdom, and enough, I hope, to know that honesty is the first chapter in the book of wisdom.[43]

I look to the diffusion of light and education as the source most to be relied on for ameliorating the con-dition, promoting the virtue, and advancing the hap-piness of man. That every man shall be made virtuous, by any process whatever, is no more to be expected, than that every tree shall be made to bear fruit, and every plant nourishment. The brier and the bramble can never become the vine and the olive; but their asperities may be softened by culture, and their prop-erties improved to usefulness in the order and econo-my of the world. And I do hope that, in the present spirit of extending to the great mass of mankind the blessings of instruction, I see a prospect of great ad-vancement in the happiness of the human race; and

42. To John Adams, Sept. 4, 1823 (LB, *15*, 464–65).
43. To Nathaniel Macon, Jan. 12, 1819 (Ford, *10*, 122).

that this may proceed to an indefinite, although not to an infinite degree.[44]

Several things about Jefferson's thought can be seen in the last passage. First, Jefferson's understanding of man was not that of the "typical" Enlightenment philosophe who, according to Carl Becker, knew instinctively that "man in general" was a fine virtuous fellow, generous, humane, tolerant, easily enlightened, reasonable, sensible, by nature a good citizen always ready and willing to accept the restrictions of "good" government (that is, government dedicated to preserving all men's inalienable rights).[45] By contrast, Jefferson knew at least that individuals among men could be briers and brambles, and that this had to be taken seriously, even if their asperities could be softened. Second, Jefferson and Condorcet evidently differed concerning the limits of progress. The statement that progress "may proceed to an indefinite although not to an infinite degree," makes increasingly less logical sense the more it is studied, and yet it does indicate a real reservation in Jefferson's mind. Third, contrary to the position of Condorcet, Jefferson held that under certain conditions the machine will retrogress and that it is by no means beyond the control of every power that would impede it.

Man and Corruption

These doubts and reservations about man's capacity to achieve progress stemmed from Jefferson's refusal to delude himself concerning a fact proved by history and personal observation. Obviously, man was subject to corruption. Throughout his life Jefferson insisted that this was a real and ever-present danger which man ignored at his peril. No amount of progress could guarantee that man, the individual, or "man in general," would become incorruptible.

44. To Cornelius Camden Blatchly, Oct. 21, 1822 (LB, *15*, 399–400).
45. See Becker, *Heavenly City*, p. 103.

He sounded the theme repeatedly in *Notes on Virginia:*

> Mankind soon learn to make interested uses of every right and power which they possess or may assume. . . . The public money and public liberty . . . will soon be discovered to be sources of wealth and dominion to those who hold them. . . . Nor should our assembly be deluded by the integrity of their own purposes, and conclude that these unlimited powers will never be abused, because themselves are not disposed to abuse them. They should look forward to a time, and that not a distant one, when a corruption in this, as in the country from which we derive our origin, will have seized the heads of government, and be spread by them through the body of the people. . . . Human nature is the same on every side of the Atlantic and will be alike influenced by the same causes.[46]

Forty years later the refrain had not changed:

> I hope this generation will preserve for their sons the political blessings delivered into their hands by their fathers. Time indeed changes manners and notions, and so far we must expect institutions to bend to them. But time produces also corruption of principles, and against this it is the duty of good citizens to be ever on the watch, and if the gangrene is to prevail at last, let the day be kept off as long as possible.[47]

SOURCES OF CORRUPTION

The sources of corruption were many. Ignorance, superstition, poverty, and oppression of body and mind had effectively corrupted the masses, but the danger was not limited to them. The regimen of kings was equally a regimen of corruption:

46. Query 13 (Ford, *3*, 224–25).
47. To Spencer Roane, March 9, 1821 (Ford, *10*, 188).

Now take any race of animals, confine them in idleness
and inaction, whether in a stye, a stable, or a state-
room, pamper them with high diet, gratify all their
sexual appetites, immerse them in sensualities, nourish
their passions, let everything bend before them, and
banish whatever might lead them to think and in a
few generations they become all body and no mind.[48]

The wealthy had their own peculiar source of corruption:
"I consider the extravagance which has seized [my country-
men] as a more baneful evil than toryism was during the
war."[49] The danger was truly great in the area of public
service: "Offices are as acceptable here as elsewhere, & whenever a man has cast a longing eye on them, a rottenness begins in his conduct."[50] Corruption could be caused in a
man by any right or power in his possession of which he
could make selfish use, any privilege by which he could
hope to obtain power, profit, and pre-eminence: "Public
money and public liberty . . . will soon be discovered to be
sources of wealth and dominion to those who hold them."
   In this connection, Jefferson's fears of a strong, centralized government are well known. Consolidation had corruption as its necessary consequence.[51] Jefferson closed a
letter to Joseph C. Cabell with the prayer that God would
give public leaders the wisdom to fortify the people against
the degeneracy of government and the concentration of all
its powers in the hands of the one, the few, the wellborn,
or the many.[52] Once corruption had its way with the leaders, they in turn could fasten it on the people:

With money we will get men, said Caesar, and with
men we will get money . . . [The Virginia Assembly]

48. To John Langdon, March 5, 1810 (LB, *12*, 377).
49. To John Page, May 4, 1786 (Boyd, *9*, 445).
50. To Tench Coxe, May 21, 1799 (Ford, 7, 380–81).
51. To Nathaniel Macon, Oct. 21, 1821 (Ford, *10*, 194).
52. Feb. 2, 1816 (Cabell, *Early History*, p. 55).

should look forward to a time when a corruption in this, as in the country from which we have derived our origin, will have seized the heads of government, and be spread by them through the body of the people; when they will purchase the voice of the people and make them pay the price.[53]

Whatever the means a leader might choose to corrupt the people—money; delusion; fastening ignorance, superstition, and poverty upon them; coercing them in their beliefs until they were one half fools and the other half hypocrites; oppressing them mind and body—the damage would be serious. Corruption was exceedingly difficult to remove once it had eaten its way into the fabric of society. The problem of eradicating it tempered Jefferson's joy at the European reception of his Bill for Establishing Religious Freedom in 1786:

I think [the Bill] will produce considerable good even in these countries where ignorance, superstition, poverty, and oppression of body and mind, in every form, are so firmly settled on the mass of the people, that their redemption from them can never be hoped. If all the sovereigns of Europe were to set themselves to work, to emancipate the minds of their subjects from their present ignorance and prejudices, and that as zealously as they now endeavor the contrary, a thousand years would not place them on that high ground, on which our common people are now setting out.[54]

By the same token Jefferson felt that the people of Rome had been so "steeped in corruption, vice, and venality," that their most powerful and benevolent emperors could not have taught them to govern themselves, had they so desired.[55]

53. *Notes on Virginia*, Query 13 (Ford, *3*, 225).
54. To George Wythe, Aug. 13, 1786 (LB, *5*, 395–96).
55. To John Adams, Dec. 10, 1819 (LB, *15*, 233–34).

MAN UNCORRUPTED

By corruption Jefferson did not mean sin. He rejected the doctrine of original sin and called it an artificial system attributed falsely to Jesus by ultra-Christian sects.[56] Corruption was always possible, but never inevitable. There were men who had not been corrupted, among whom were his own countrymen, "separated from their parent stock, and kept from contamination, either from them or the other people of the old world, by the intervention of so wide an ocean."[57] In 1796 he declared, "If ever the morals of a people could be made the basis of their own government, it is our case."[58]

Jefferson felt that farmers as a class tended to be free from the blight. He is well known for the statement:

> Those who labor in the earth are the chosen people of God, if ever he had a chosen people, whose breasts He made His peculiar deposit for substantial and genuine virtue. It is the focus which keeps alive that sacred fire which otherwise might escape from the earth. Corruption of morals in the mass of cultivators is a phenomenon of which no age nor nation has furnished an example. It is a mark set on those, who, not looking up to heaven, to their own soil and industry as does the husbandman, for their subsistence, depend for it on the casualities and caprice of customers.[59]

This statement is an expression of Jefferson's agrarian ideal. He believed firmly that agriculture was man's fundamental

---

56. To William Short, Oct. 31, 1819 (Ford, *10*, 143–45). See Jefferson's footnote. There is, incidentally, nothing in Jefferson's records to show that he had any feelings remotely resembling consciousness of personal sin. See above, p. 32.

57. To George Wythe, Aug. 13, 1786 (LB, *5*, 396).

58. To John Adams, Feb. 28, 1796 (Ford, *7*, 57).

59. *Notes on Virginia,* Query 19 (Ford, *3*, 268–69).

employment, all other economic activities being secondary. This was the natural life for man. It was good, per se, while city life was artificial and bad. Jefferson therefore maintained that the United States ought to be a nation of small family-owned farms.[60] Jefferson's belief in the moral values of a life close to the soil was undoubtedly rooted in his personal experience. There was his boyhood on a Virginia frontier plantation, his personal love of the land, his early reading of the Roman poets and their idealizing of the Arcadian way of life.[61] Most of all, there was Monticello, Jefferson's own example of how an agricultural unit supplying all the necessities for a small community could be set up and maintained.[62]

Jefferson was convinced that free society and the fate of a large class of prosperous tillers of small farms were indissolubly linked. His experience in France confirmed his views of the distinction in quality between the agricultural Americans and the European city mobs. He pointed out the superiority of American common people to John Adams in 1813, and remarked in *The Anas* that George Washington had not been sufficiently aware of it.[63]

PREVENTION OF CORRUPTION

Jefferson never relinquished his belief that man need not be corrupted. Provided corruption was recognized, it could be prevented or at least long delayed. Corruption could be held off, first, by legal means. This was an oft-repeated theme in the *Notes on Virginia:* "The time to guard against corruption and tyranny is before they shall have

60. See Lowry Nelson, *American Farm Life* (Cambridge, Mass., 1954), p. 10; J. H. Randall, *Making of Modern Mind*, pp. 355–56.
61. See Koch, *Philosophy of Jefferson*, p. 133.
62. See Chinard, *Jefferson*, p. 315.
63. To John Adams, Oct. 28, 1813 (Ford, 9, 428–29); *The Anas*, Feb. 4, 1818 (Ford, 1, 168).

gotten hold of us. It is better to keep the wolf out of the fold, than to trust to drawing his teeth and talons after he shall have entered."[64] The careful listing of men's rights in a constitution before there was any possibility of their being usurped was essential: "It can never be too often repeated, that the time for fixing every essential right on a legal basis is while our rulers are honest, and ourselves united."[65] When the Alien and Sedition Acts were passed and the Federalists asked the people to trust them to handle such powers fairly, Jefferson replied in the Kentucky Resolutions, "In questions of power . . . let no more be heard of confidence in man, but bind him down from mischief by the chains of the Constitution."[66]

Besides putting rights on a legal basis beyond the reach of the heads of government and circumscribing carefully the powers those in office might use, Jefferson also felt that corruption might be prevented by general suffrage for all male citizens, since it would "lessen the danger of buying and selling votes, by making the number of voters too great for any means of purchase."[67]

Another major means of attacking corruption and preventing its growth was education. This is the main purpose behind Jefferson's lifelong drive for public education. In Query 14 of *Notes on Virginia,* it was put in these words: "Every government degenerates when entrusted to the rulers of the people alone. The people themselves are its only safe depositories. And to render even them safe, their minds must be improved to a certain degree. . . . An amendment of our constitution must here come in aid of the public education."[68] He also wrote to James Madison: "Educate and inform the whole mass of the people. Enable them to see

64. Query 13 (Ford, *3,* 225).
65. Ibid., p. 266.
66. Nov. 1798 (Ford, 7, 3–5).
67. To Jeremiah Moore, Aug. 14, 1800 (Ford, 7, 454).
68. Ford, *3,* 254.

that it is to their interest to preserve peace and order, and they will preserve them."[69] Jefferson felt so strongly about the powers of education that he wrote the following about the requirement of literacy for full citizenship in the constitution drawn up by Cortes for Spain:

> Of all those [requirements] thought of for securing fidelity in the administration of government, constant ralliance to the principles of the constitution, and progressive amendments with the progressive advances of the human mind, or changes in human affairs, it is the most effectual. Enlighten the people generally, and tyranny and oppressions of body and mind will vanish like evil spirits at the dawn of day.[70]

69. Dec. 20, 1787 (LB, 6, 392).
70. To P. S. Dupont de Nemours, April 24, 1816 (Ford, 10, 24–25).

CHAPTER 4

*G*overnment

Man and Government

JEFFERSON'S IMAGE OF MAN

Thomas Jefferson's concept of government had a direct relationship to his concept of man, which contained some logical inconsistencies. God had created men as material animals endowed with the ability to think in patterns determined by the structure of their brains. Since no two brains were physically identical, identical opinions could not be expected. "As the Creator had made no two faces alike, so no two brains and probably no two creeds."[1] Despite all this, Jefferson also maintained that reason was the enemy of error only and that, given complete freedom, it could lead men through argumentation and debate to the truth.

1. To Timothy Pickering, Feb. 27, 1821 (LB, *15*, 324).

Man was also a social being. Endowed by his Creator with a moral sense, the healthy, free man could distinguish infallibly between right and wrong. This physical faculty served effectively to urge man to do good and eschew evil. The structural determination of reason made it worthless in solving moral problems; the moral sense made it unnecessary. A ploughman could answer a moral question as quickly and validly as a professor.[2] Yet despite all this Jefferson also firmly held to what his eyes plainly showed him, that man's social behavior was appalling. Of all the beasts, man was so ruthless, relentless, and cannibalistic that Jefferson believed the Creator had provided humanity as the means of preventing any species from overpopulating the earth.[3]

This contradictory view of man, innately moral and observably vicious, whose reason is both a guide and a delusion, provides the basis for Jefferson's concept of good government. If the human capacity for morality made democracy possible, the human penchant for corruption made it necessary.

MAN'S TALENTS FOR GOVERNMENT

Jefferson's belief in the benevolence of God and his understanding of God's purpose and manner in creating man undergirded his unwavering opinion that man had the right and ability to govern himself individually and collectively.[4] The variety of human individuals made this possi-

2. To Peter Carr, Aug. 10, 1787 (Boyd, *Papers of Jefferson, 12,* 14–15).

3. To James Madison, Jan. 1, 1797 (Ford, *Writings of Jefferson, 7,* 100–02). Boorstin's comment that this is an example of Jefferson's irrepressible urge to see benevolence in the work of the Creator misses the point. The letter is essentially ironic. The key to this passage lies in Jefferson's closing words: "We both, I believe, join in wishing to see [man] softened." Cf. Boorstin, *Lost World,* p. 50.

4. See letter to David Hartley, July 2, 1787 (LB, *6,* 151); "Opinion . . . whether the seat of government shall be transferred to the Potomac," July 15, 1790 (Ford, *5,* 205–06); letter to Joseph C. Cabell, Feb. 2, 1816 (Cabell, *Early History,* p. 55); and elsewhere.

ble. Jefferson was no equalitarian; he saw that some men were obviously more greatly endowed with virtue and talent than others. The Creator's plan had included a natural human aristocracy to manage the affairs of society. The problem of good government was to provide "the most effectually for a pure selection of these natural aristoi into the affairs of government."[5] The best government, nevertheless, carried within it the seeds of its own destruction: "In every government on earth is some trace of human weakness, some germ of corruption and degeneracy, which cunning will discover, and wickedness insensibly open, cultivate, and improve. Every government degenerates when entrusted to the rulers of the people alone."[6] To prevent this degeneracy, the people must share the responsibility with their rulers.

This was a live option to Jefferson because he believed all men were competent to judge character.[7] Here he was a strict equalitarian. Allowed real freedom, the masses could choose those best qualified to manage the concerns of society. Guided by his own interests, the common man could determine when an office holder was no longer fit to continue in his post. Moreover, only the governed could perform that function. The record proved that there was no such thing as an elite fit simply to rule over the rest of mankind. "Sometimes it is said that man cannot be trusted with the government of himself. Can he, then, be trusted with the government of others? Or have we found angels in the form of kings to govern him? Let history answer this question."[8] The answer of history was "that whenever the people are well-informed, they can be trusted with their own government; that, whenever things get so far wrong as

5. To John Adams, Oct. 28, 1813 (Ford, *9*, 425).
6. *Notes on Virginia*, Query 14 (Ford, *3*, 254).
7. To Dupont de Nemours, April 24, 1816 (LB, *14*, 487–88).
8. First Inaugural Address (LB, *3*, 320). For Jefferson's use of history, see Appendix.

to attract their notice, they may be relied on to set them to rights."[9]

MAN IN AMERICA

Man's capacity for social interrelationships revealed the Creator's benevolence. Society occurred when men drew together to jointly solve common problems and evils beyond their powers as individuals. Morality was part of this capacity for society, the faculty which enabled man to promote the welfare of his neighbors: "[The Creator] has formed us moral agents . . . that we may promote the happiness of those with whom He has placed us in society, by acting honestly towards all, benevolently to those who fall within our way, respecting sacredly their rights, bodily and mental, and cherishing their freedom of conscience as we value our own."[10]

Since morality made self-government possible, the United States of America presented a unique opportunity to develop freedom and self-rule. "If ever the morals of a people could be made the basis of their own government, it is our case."[11] The American common man was an independent, self-reliant pioneer or farmer. He lived close to nature. He was a free husbandman looking for his subsistence to heaven, his own soil, and his industry. His character was both steady and rational. He could understand the issues affecting his interests and those of his society, and make the best choice for all concerned:

> Here every one may have land to labor for himself, if he chooses; or, preferring the exercise of any other industry, may exact for it such compensation as not only to afford a comfortable subsistence, but wherewith to provide for a cessation from labor in his old

9. To Richard Price, Jan. 8, 1789 (LB, 7, 253).
10. To Miles King, Sept. 26, 1814 (LB, *14*, 197–98).
11. To John Adams, Feb. 28, 1796 (Ford, 7, 57).

age. Every one, by his property, or by his satisfactory situation, is interested in the support of law and order. And such men may safely and advantageously reserve to themselves a wholesome control over their public affairs.[12]

This was not the man of the old world, crowded in cities, steeped in vices. This was not the rabble of Europe, in whose hands freedom would be instantly perverted to demolition and destruction.[13] Americans could learn. As a group they could be duped once in a generation, but not more often than that. Allowed freedom of information, opinion, and discussion, they could sift truth from falsehood even when their sources were almost totally corrupt and abandoned to licentiousness. Jefferson proved this to his own satisfaction by refusing to contradict the "thousand of calumnies so industriously propagated against myself" during his presidential administration. On the basis of this "great experiment" to which he "lent myself willingly as a subject," he concluded that the press is impotent when it abandons itself to falsehood.[14] "The printers and the public are very different personages. The former may lead the latter a little out of their track, while the deviation is insensible; but the moment they usurp their direction and that of their government, they will be reduced to their true places."[15] Canny and interested, the American man was just the person to supervise his leaders as they managed his concerns.

12. To John Adams, Oct. 28, 1813 (Ford, *9*, 428–29).

13. See *The Anas*, Feb. 4, 1818 (Ford, *1*, 168).

14. To Thomas Seymour, Feb. 11, 1807 (Ford, *9*, 30–31). In the 1800 campaign Jefferson was accused of atheism, visionary impracticality (his philosophic and scientific interests), maligning other patriots, sympathy with the French Revolution, plotting the destruction of the government, encouraging slave insurrections, maintaining a "Congo harem," siring mulatto children, and of being a moral and personal coward. See Charles O. Lerche, Jr., "Jefferson and the Election of 1800: A Case Study in the Political Smear," *William and Mary Quarterly*, 3rd ser. 5 (1948), 467–91.

15. To James Monroe, May 5, 1811 (Ford, *9*, 324).

PARTIES

His optimism about the steady and rational American character did not lead Jefferson to conclude that the government would function free from politics or factions. Like the poor, these would always be with us. Jefferson attributed political parties ultimately to nature herself: "The terms Whig and Tory belong to natural as well as civil history."[16] Men by their constitutions were naturally divided into two temperaments which had existed through all time.[17] Since the source of party differences was nature itself, the divergence of philosophy and programs could be expected to be irreconcilable.

Far from being dismayed and convinced, as some were, that self-government must founder on this eternal rock of disagreement, Jefferson felt that the natural division of people into parties was of positive value. As a matter of fact, he declared that he would not do without it. It was too precious as a means of supervision: "I am no believer in the amalgamation of parties, nor do I consider it as either desirable or useful for the public. . . . In that form, they are censors of the conduct of each other and useful watchmen for the public."[18]

A government thus supervised could be made to serve man as God had created him, rather than mulct him or attempt to impose upon him a pattern which claimed to be ideal but was actually specious because of its human origin. Jefferson held that man had certain God-given needs, capacities, and potentialities which he had every right to fulfill but could satisfy only when free. With his colleagues of the American Philosophical Society, Jefferson agreed that society was a divinely ordered community based

16. To John Adams, June 27, 1813 (LB, *13*, 279–80).
17. To James Sullivan, Feb. 9, 1797 (LB, *9*, 377); to Henry Lee, Aug. 10, 1824 (LB, *16*, 73–74).
18. To Henry Lee, Aug. 10, 1824 (LB, *16*, 73).

on motives implanted in men by the Creator.[19] Man could not blueprint society; only the Creator could do that. Man could respond to the actual problems of his environment as they came along, and leave the end to God.

INSTITUTIONS

Human institutions were examples of this type of response, valid only in that situation which called them forth. They were at best only expedients by which diverse and feeble minds grapple with transient problems. Men were mistaken in their attempts to erect permanent, ideal, all-encompassing institutions for the ordering of society. These soon lost touch with the needs they were originally intended to satisfy. For this reason there could be no ideal government. Only man could understand his needs and how they should be satisfied. To hinder his response was to thwart the Creator's plan. The best government was therefore the least government, the absolute minimum necessary to protect man from certain unhappy but essential qualities of the human species.[20] All that was necessary, maintained Jefferson, was "a wise and frugal government, which shall restrain men from injuring one another, which shall leave them otherwise free to regulate their own pursuits of industry and improvement, and shall not take from the mouth of labor the bread it has earned."[21]

SELF-GOVERNMENT'S DUAL REQUIREMENTS

Legitimate government had as its sole objects man's freedom, his equal rights, and his happiness.[22] If these were the objectives of government, man should govern himself.

19. See Boorstin, *Lost World*, pp. 171–73.
20. See ibid., pp. 186–90.
21. First Inaugural Address (LB, *3*, 320–21).
22. To Thaddeus Kosciusko, Feb. 26, 1810 (LB, *12*, 369–70); to A. Coray, Oct. 31, 1823 (LB, *15*, 482).

No one could exercise freedom for another; no one could determine the conditions of another's happiness. These things each had to do for himself. This meant, however, that every man had to understand the equal rights of all. Man could govern himself only as long as he could see that it was to his interest and advantage to be restrained, and to restrain others, from trampling the rights of fellow humans. Whoever did not understand this was not ready for self-government, even though he had a natural right to it. The peoples of continental Europe and Spanish America, subjected as they had been for centuries to the abuses of centralized power in a ruthless society, would need to be improved for generations before they could be safely entrusted with the guidance of their own destinies. On the other hand, some peoples were ready. The British to some extent, and the Americans to a great extent, were fully competent to take their own reins and hold them as long as they could forestall the corruption of their leaders or themselves.

Man is fit to govern himself only if he remains self-reliant, on the one hand, and cherishes the rights of his fellows, on the other. He can be corrupted in several ways, however, each of which must be prevented if self-government is to succeed. For instance, he must have no opportunity to imitate tyrannous passions. This provided Jefferson with a strong objection to the institution of slavery:

> The whole commerce between master and slave is a perpetual exercise of the most boisterous passions, the most unremitting despotism on the one part, and degrading submissions on the other. Our children see this, and learn to imitate it; for man is an imitative animal. . . . The parent storms, the child looks on, catches the lineaments of wrath, puts on the same airs in the circle of smaller slaves, gives a loose to the worst of passions, and thus nursed, educated and daily exercised in tyranny, cannot but be stamped by it with odi-

ous peculiarities. The man must be a prodigy who can
retain his morals undepraved by such circumstances.[23]

Measures would have to be taken to correct both the tyranny and the dependency slavery inculcated in men:

> The mind of the master is to be apprized by reflection,
> and strengthened by the energies of conscience, against
> the obstacles of self-interest to an acquiescence in the
> rights of others, that of the slave is to be prepared by
> instruction and habit for self-government, and for the
> honest pursuits of industry and social duty. Both of
> these courses of preparation require time, and the
> former must precede the latter.[24]

Jefferson argued that self-government depended on man
being both independent and careful of others' rights. If
anything, the second is of more immediate concern than the
first. Corruption has far more dangerous consequences
among the powerful than among the weak, and opportunities for corruption increase as men and parties gain power
through office.[25] The main task then is to develop a type
of government which has within it effective safeguards
against corrupted power, which will "restrain men from
injuring one another" whether they be the governors or
the governed.

Forms of Government

TYRANNY

To Jefferson there were only two forms of government,
the one wherein the will of everyone has a just influence,
and the other wherein it does not. The "form" of government in Jefferson's thought was determined by its provisions to safeguard the rights of the governed. If rule was
established at the expense of the rights of any, it did not

23. *Notes on Virginia*, Query 18 (Ford, *3*, 266–67).
24. To David Barrow, May 1, 1815 (Ford, *9*, 516).
25. See *Notes on Virginia*, Query 18 (Ford, *3*, 224).

matter whether the government was technically a monarchy, oligarchy, aristocracy, or a dictatorship of the proletariat. It was still a tyranny, a government of force, "a government of wolves over sheep."[26] By Jefferson's observation most governments in history had been of this form.

DEMOCRACY

Pure democracy. In contrast there was the form of government "wherein the will of everyone has a just influence." Two systems were possible in which this would be true. One was "pure democracy." All of the people in a given society would gather together at stated times and places to make decisions about their common affairs. Historical examples were available in the government of ancient Athens and some of the cantons of Switzerland. Jefferson had two objections to pure democracy. In the first place it was feasible only for small groups occupying small areas. Beyond these limits it became imperial and authoritarian.[27] Secondly, small states are inherently unstable. Here he deliberately differed from Montesquieu and others of the eighteenth century who argued that only small states were fit to be republics, because only among limited numbers of citizens would there be homogeneous interests rather than disrupting factions. For this very reason, however, Jefferson objected. Parties were natural and healthy. Only a variety of points of view could serve as a check to the runaway tendencies of particular interests and thus give stability to a republic.[28]

Representative democracy. Jefferson contended that neither of the shortcomings of pure democracy were present in the system called "representative democracy," which had rendered obsolete almost everything written before on the structure of government: "It seems not to have occurred [to

26. To James Madison, Jan. 30, 1787 (LB, *6*, 64).
27. To Isaac H. Tiffany, Aug. 26, 1816 (LB, *15*, 55–56).
28. To Monsieur D'Ivernois, Feb. 6, 1795 (LB, *1*, 299–300).

the Greeks] that where the citizens cannot meet to transact their business in person, they alone have the right to choose the agents who shall transact it; and that in this way a republican or popular government, of the second grade of purity, may be exercised over any extent of country."[29] Representative democracy was genuinely new. A smidgen of it may have existed formerly in the English constitution but not enough to cause excitement. It was a great experiment taking place for the first time in any fullness on American soil. Never really tried before, it was bound to promote suspicion. The only alternative, however, was tyranny, and as far as Jefferson was concerned the case against that was conclusive. History proved that tyranny as government was madness. Representative democracy might be novel, but it had to be tried.

For this experiment the new American nation provided a golden opportunity. The great body of Americans were unquestionably of democratic temperament. This Jefferson believed even when they seemed to be swept away in the Alien and Sedition Act crisis.[30] They were schooled in self-reliance and cooperation by their efforts to tame a wilderness and hew out of it a living that was natural, free, and happy. They were cut off by an ocean and a successful revolution from the corruption and hoary traditionalisms of Europe. They were equipped by their unique natural, historical, and political environment (if they avoided the dangers under which Europe was laboring) to develop that form of government which would pursue only its legitimate objects, the freedom and happiness of man. And in so doing they would not only bless themselves with the best possible form of government, but set an example to be followed by all mankind.[31]

29. To Isaac H. Tiffany, Aug. 26, 1816 (LB, *15*, 65–66).
30. To John Taylor, Nov. 13, 1798 (Ford, 7, 310).
31. To James Sullivan, Feb. 9, 1797 (Ford, 7, 117–18). See also Chinard, *Jefferson*, pp. ix–x.

Principles of Self-Government

MAJORITY RULE

To be successful, the experiment demanded strict adherence to two principles. First, "the will of the majority is in all cases to prevail."[32] In Jefferson's eyes this "majority" was limited to free, adult males. Children, women, and slaves were not to vote or to participate in government.[33] On the other hand, suffrage was to be extended to *all* free men without regard to birth, possessions, or other qualifications,[34] except literacy, which Jefferson late in life decided should be required.[35]

Above all, the will of the majority was not to be thwarted by the dead. That the earth belongs to the living was one of Jefferson's constant themes. Only the living were sovereign over the earth. They alone were to determine how it was to be used, how they themselves were to be governed, what institutions were to be set up and supported, what laws were to be enacted, enforced, and obeyed. They were under no obligations to decisions, laws, institutions, pacts, and traditions of the past. That was the work of the dead, and since the dead existed no longer, their will was nothing. The living could decide for themselves what of their heritage they would preserve, change, or abolish.[36] It was axiomatic to Jefferson that this was their God-given right.[37] "A generation may bind itself as long as its majority continues in life; when that has disappeared another majority is in

32. First Inaugural Address (LB, *3*, 318).

33. To Samuel Kercheval, Sept. 5, 1816 (Ford, *10*, 45–46 n.); to Angelica Schuyler Church, Sept. 21, 1788 (Boyd, *13*, 623).

34. To Jeremiah Moore, Aug. 14, 1800 (Ford, *7*, 454).

35. To Dupont de Nemours, April 24, 1816 (Ford, *10*, 24–25).

36. See letter to James Madison, Sept. 6, 1789 (Ford, *5*, 121); to John Adams, April 25, 1794 (Ford, *6*, 505); to John Wayles Eppes, June 24, 1813 (Ford, *9*, 389–90); to Samuel S. Kercheval, July 12, 1816 (Ford, *9*, 42–44); to William Plumer, July 21, 1816 (LB, *15*, 46–47); and elsewhere.

37. To Thomas Earle, Sept. 24, 1823 (LB, *15*, 470–71).

place, holds all the rights and powers, their predecessors once held, and may change their laws and institutions to suit themselves. Nothing then is unchangeable but the inherent and unalienable rights of man."[38] Obviously, in this doctrine of rule by the will of the living majority there are important implications for those of us who desire to apply Jefferson's thought, dicta, or practices to contemporary problems. These implications will be explored before the discussion is ended.

MINORITY RIGHTS

Essential as it was, majority rule by itself was no guarantee of democracy. A tyranny of the many was as real a danger as a tyranny of the one, the few, or the wellborn. To prevent oppression, the majority, whose will was sovereign, had nevertheless to recognize a check and adhere willingly to a second great principle. Jefferson's first Inaugural Address emphasized this: "All, too, will bear in mind this sacred principle, that though the will of the majority is in all cases to prevail, that will, to be rightful, must be reasonable, that the minority possess their equal rights, which equal laws must protect, and to violate which would be oppression."[39] Democracy existed only when the people held two seemingly contradictory principles in tension. By itself, one principle led to tyranny, the other to anarchy. Yet together they made self-government a reality. *"To inculcate on minorities the duty of acquiescence in the will of the majority; and on majorities a respect for the rights of the minority,"*[40] this was the essence, the great lesson Americans had to learn.

38. To John Cartwright, June 5, 1824 (LB, *16*, 48).
39. March 4, 1801 (LB, *3*, 318).
40. Italics Jefferson's. To William Bache, Feb. 2, 1800 (MS copy by Nicholas P. Trist, University of Virginia). Quoted in Adrienne Koch, and William Peden, eds., *Life and Selected Writings of Thomas Jefferson* (New York, Random House, 1944) p. 556.

Jefferson's high evaluation of the doctrine of natural rights was based on a twofold faith. First, he believed that only when every man was allowed, within reason, to pursue happiness as he saw fit would the plan of the Creator be fulfilled. This aspect of Jefferson's faith was confirmed by the development of frontier New York and New England in his lifetime:

> But from Saratoga ... to Northampton was then [1791] mostly desert. Now [1825] it is what thirty-four years of free and good government have made it. It shows how soon the labor of men would make a paradise of the whole earth were it not for misgovernment, and a diversion of all his energies from their proper object— the happiness of man—to the selfish interests of kings, nobles, and priests.[41]

God's plan is to be achieved through laissez faire.

Second, he had faith that the preservation of natural rights made for a healthy, active government. They serve as a prophylactic, preventing or quickly curing the diseases of government by providing two salutary conditions. The first is understanding. Unimpeded communication and freedom of thought enable the people to recognize problems as they arise, inform their fellow citizens, and think of solutions. The second condition is the ability to act, preserved in the rights to regulate and control society, and to initiate, alter, or abolish governmental structures and measures in whatever manner seems fitting. As a result, Jefferson declared, the American republic was the strongest government on earth: "I believe it the only one where every man, at the call of the law, would fly to the standard of the law; would meet invasions of public order as his own personal concern."[42]

41. To Ellen Wayles Coolidge, Aug. 27, 1825 (LB, *18*, 341).
42. First Inaugural Address (Ford, *8*, 3).

The Constitutional Ideal

Jefferson conceived of a constitution as a document which defined the various divisions of government and delineated their functions, powers, duties, and interrelationships. It was a compact entered into by all the people of a given society, describing how they would work together to solve common problems. Such an agreement was not to be entered into lightly or abandoned with ease, but it was subject to change as necessity indicated: "I am certainly not an advocate for frequent and untried changes in laws and constitutions. I think moderate imperfections had better be borne with. . . . But I know also that laws and institutions must go hand in hand with the progress of the human mind."[43] In Jefferson's view, the power to frame a constitution or make changes in it properly belonged to the people alone, and not to the government to which the constitution applied, nor to any department within that government.[44]

No particular constitution was a permanent ideal. Any particular provision could be good under some circumstances and evil under others. For this reason Jefferson often resorted to metaphor to describe his concept of good constitutional government. For example, Jefferson expressed this hope for his country: "As to myself I sincerely wish that the whole Union may accommodate their interests to each other, & play into their hands mutually as members of the same family, that the wealth & strength of any one part should be viewed as the wealth & strength of the whole."[45] Two weeks later he used another image:

> I do not think it for the interest of the general government itself & still less of the Union at large, that the

43. To Samuel Kercheval, July 12, 1816 (LB, *15*, 40–41).
44. See *Notes on Virginia*, Query 13 (Ford, *3*, 249–50).
45. To Hugh Williamson, Feb. 11, 1798 (Ford, 7, 201).

State governments should be so little respected as they have been. However I dare say that in time all these as well as their central government, like the planets revolving round their common sun, acting & acted upon according to their respective weights & distances, will produce that beautiful equilibrium on which our Constitution is founded, and which I believe it will exhibit to the world in a degree of perfection unexampled but in the planetary system itself. The enlightened statesman, therefore, will endeavor to preserve the weight and influence of every part, as too much given to any member of it would destroy the general equilibrium.[46]

These images expressed Jefferson's ideal of free government: *the family,* a group of related individuals who worked together, recognizing at all times that the interest of any member was the interest of all; and the divinely created *machine* of the universe, constructed and maintained by the Creator so that its parts always move in balance and harmony. Another figure Jefferson used was that of *partnership:*

It is a fatal error to suppose that either our State governments are superior to the federal, or the federal to the States. The people, to whom all authority belongs have divided the government into two distinct departments, the leading characters of which are *foreign* and domestic, and they have appointed for each a distinct set of functionaries. These they have made coordinate, checking and balancing each other, like the three cardinal departments in the individual States; each equally supreme as to the powers delegated to itself, and neither authorized ultimately to decide what belongs to itself, or to its coparcener in government. . . . a spirit of forbearance and compromise,

46. To Peregrine Fitzhugh, Feb. 23, 1798 (Ford, 7, 210).

therefore, and not of encroachment and usurpation, is
the healing balm of such a constitution.[47]

In a sense, all of Jefferson's subsequent writings upon
government are a commentary on the basic assumptions set
forth in the Declaration of Independence:

> We hold these truths to be self-evident: that all men
> are created equal; that they are endowed by their Crea-
> tor with inherent and unalienable rights; that among
> these are life, liberty, and the pursuit of happiness;
> that to secure these rights, governments are instituted
> among men, deriving their just powers from the con-
> sent of the governed; that whenever any government
> becomes destructive of these ends, it is the right of the
> people to alter or abolish it, and to institute new gov-
> ernment, laying its foundation on such principles and
> organizing its powers in such form as to them shall
> seem most likely to effect their safety and happiness.

The purpose behind framing a constitution was to lay out
a government which would have the power to work for the
benefit of all its citizens while preserving "rightful Liberty"
—that is, "unobstructed action according to our will, within limits drawn around us by the equal rights of others."[48]
It was also to set up a standard to enable the people to judge
whether their government was exercising rightful powers
to perform proper duties. The existence of a constitution
was in itself a force working positively for the correction
of abuses: "It is certain that though written constitutions
may be violated in moments of passion or delusion, yet
they furnish a text to which those who are watchful again

47. To ——— 1821 (quoted in Padover, *Jefferson on Democracy*, pp.
53–54).
48. To Lewis Williams, Feb. 18, 1820 (Jefferson Papers, Library of Congress, *217*, 38713) quoted in Nathan Schachner, *Thomas Jefferson: A Biography*, 2 (New York, Appleton-Century-Crofts, 1951) 970.

rally and recall the people; they fix too for the people the principles of their political creed."[49]

The Varying Formula

This discussion so far has been limited to theory. Was there any specific form of government which Thomas Jefferson felt to be the most democratic? Did he see any particular form of organization to be least susceptible to the dangers of corruption or tyranny? It seems obvious now that at various points in his career he tried to find a formula to guard against whatever dangers he perceived. The insuperable difficulty was that no *unvarying* formula for the proper relations between the nation and its various members could be devised.[50]

Jefferson was constantly aware of the danger that "the natural progress of things is for liberty to yield and government to gain ground."[51] However, this was not a gradual over-all yielding but an occurrence which at any given moment was usually localized in one department of government or another. For this reason, many proposals Jefferson made stand in contradiction to others he made at other times. He shifted ground and changed tactics in response to developments. Generally he opposed the tyranny that seemed most menacing at a particular time. His deeper consistency lay in his continued striving for freedom and repeated advocacy of a balanced government.[52]

STATE AND NATION

This accounts for the differences in the types of governmental changes he demanded over the years. For instance,

---

49. To Joseph Priestley, June 19, 1802 (LB, *10*, 325).
50. See Malone, *Jefferson, 2*, 344.
51. To Edward Carrington, May 27, 1788 (Ford, *5*, 20–21).
52. To Peregrine Fitzhugh, Feb. 23, 1798 (Ford, *7*, 210).

Jefferson's discussion of the Articles of Confederation bears
little resemblance to his later discussion of the Constitution
when he was Secretary of State, Vice-President, and President. As Minister to France he expressed the opinion that
the Confederation was "a wonderfully perfect instrument, considering the circumstances under which it was
formed."[53] Jefferson's praise was based on his willingness
at this stage to accept a doctrine of implied powers: "It has
so often been said . . . that Congress have no power by the
confederation to enforce anything, e.g. contributions of
money. It was not necessary to give them that money expressly; they have it by the law of nature. When two parties
make a compact, there results to each a power of compelling
the other to execute it." Jefferson was saying, in other
words, that the Continental Congress should take whatever
powers it needed to put the states in their places on this
issue. As it turned out, he did have objections to the "wonderfully perfect instrument," but they are quite different
from the kind many people usually associate with Jefferson.
Under it there was imperfect provision for the control of
commerce and lack of unity in foreign affairs. He was se-
verely hampered in his work in Europe by the fragmentiz-
ing results of the independent efforts of the American states.
To him they needed the control of a strong federal bond
which, although not touching their independence in purely
domestic matters, would make them one in everything connected with foreign affairs.[54]

A few years later his goal was the same, but his tack differed. As Secretary of State he had become disturbed by
Hamiltonian federalism, and was casting about for effective
ways to counterbalance it. The independence of the states
was now to be cherished:

53. To M. de Meusnier, Jan. 24, 1786 (Ford, *4*, 141).
54. To Edward Carrington, Aug. 4, 1787 (Ford, *4*, 423–24). See also Claude
G. Bowers, *The Young Jefferson, 1743–1789* (Boston, 1945), p. 501; Malone,
Jefferson, 2, 161–62.

I would rather be exposed to the inconveniences attending too much liberty, than those attending too small a degree of it. Then it is important to strengthen the State governments; and as this cannot be done by any change in the federal constitution, (for the preservation of that is all we need to contend for), it must be done by the States themselves, erecting such barriers at the constitutional line as cannot be surmounted either by themselves or by the general government.[55]

From this point on he never reversed the trend. He tried to counterbalance the federal government's seizure of power in the Alien and Sedition Acts by declaring that the states had the right to declare particular acts of the federal government unconstitutional, null, and void.[56] He called the state governments "the true barriers of our liberty,"[57] and as late as one year before his death was still pondering proper methods for the states to use in opposing federal usurpation of power.[58] For this Jefferson saw state secession as the ultimate measure. He expressed the hope, however, that long before secession became necessary, the watchful would rally the people to force their government once again to adhere to the principles of the Constitution. This in turn reveals a concept basic to all of Jefferson's thought on constitutions. They were intended to return to the people for decision all conflicts between divisions of government over power. This was certainly true of the United States Constitution: "The peculiar happiness of our blessed system is, that in difference of opinion between these different sets of servants, the appeal is to neither, but to their employers peaceably assembled by their representatives in convention."[59]

55. To Archibald Stuart, Dec. 23, 1791 (LB, *18*, 276).
56. See Kentucky Resolutions, Nov. 1798 (Ford, 7, 298–309).
57. To Destutt de Tracy, Jan. 26, 1811 (LB, *13*, 19).
58. To William B. Giles, Dec. 26, 1825 (LB, *16*, 146–48).
59. To ———, 1821 (quoted in Padover, *Jefferson on Democracy*, p. 54).

LEGISLATURE

Another objection Jefferson had to the Articles of Confederation was the lack of any distinction between legislative, executive, and judicial departments. The legislature was the whole of the government. As a member of the Virginia Assembly, as Governor of Virginia, and as member of Congress, Jefferson had learned to fear legislative dominance.[60] He also deplored the governmental ineffectiveness which resulted when a legislature tried to handle all details. He therefore advocated division of the government into three coordinate departments, so as to make the will of the people effective by checking tyranny and increasing efficiency.

JUDICIARY

The development of Jefferson's thought concerning the place of courts in constitutional government is another example of his moving to combat tyranny wherever it posed the most immediate threat. In the discussion connected with framing the Constitution, Jefferson favored giving the federal courts specific and important powers, including a power of veto over legislation similar to the President's.[61] Suggestions such as these, however, were made within a context of understanding that Jefferson emphasized increasingly as events showed him that judicial dominance was not remote but close.[62] He consistently held that the judiciary should be independent of other branches of government but not independent of the will of the people. He argued that the people should participate in the judiciary in two ways. First, juries, not judges, should decide questions of fact and, in some cases, questions of law.[63] Juries, incident-

60. See *Notes on Virginia*, Query 13 (Ford, *3*, 229).
61. To James Madison, Dec. 20, 1787 (Boyd, *12*, 440).
62. See Chinard, *Jefferson*, p. 196; Malone, *Jefferson*, *2*, 161–62.
63. To Abbé Arnoud, July 19, 1798 (LB, *7*, 422–23).

ally, should be elected by the people, not appointed by the judge or sheriff. Second, judges, like legislators and executives, should be elected by the people and subject to periodic reappointment to office.[64]

EXECUTIVE

When Jefferson examined the Constitution in 1787, one of his chief objections was to the lack of provision for compulsory rotation in governmental office. He worried particularly about the Presidency. He was convinced that with repeated re-elections an ambitious Chief Executive could quickly transform the office into royalty. Such an outcome, he maintained, must be prevented positively by constitutional amendment.[65] Basically, he never retreated from that position, but in contrast to his views concerning the judiciary, the danger seemed less urgent to him with passing time. At the end of Jefferson's first term as President, he described his feelings in this manner:

> The service for 8. years with a power to remove at the end of the first four, comes nearly to my principle as corrected by experience. And it is in adherence to that that I determined to withdraw at the end of my second term. . . . General Washington set the example of voluntary retirement after 8. years. I shall follow it, and a few more precedents will oppose the obstacle of

64. To Samuel Kercheval, July 12, 1816 (LB, *15*, 36–37); to William C. Jarvis, Sept. 28, 1820 (LB, *15*, 277); to Thomas Ritchie, Dec. 25, 1820 (LB, *15*, 297); to James Pleasants, Dec. 26, 1821 (Ford, *10*, 198–99); to William T. Barry, July 2, 1822 (LB, *15*, 389 90); and elsewhere.

On the other hand, see his letter to George Wythe, June 7, 1776 (Boyd, *1*, 410–11), in which apparently Jefferson advocates having judges hold office for life. The text is suspect, however. See Boyd's footnote for a listing of reasons why the document may be presumed a forgery. Nevertheless, none of Jefferson's drafts for a constitution in 1776 provides for the election of judges.

65. To James Madison, Dec. 20, 1787 (Boyd, *12*, 440–41); see also Chinard, *Jefferson*, pp. 197–98.

habit to any one after a while who shall endeavor to extend his term. Perhaps it may beget a disposition to establish it by an amendment of the Constitution.

Strange to say, the danger about which Jefferson grows sanguine here seems to be most evident in his next few sentences:

> I had determined to declare my intention, but I have consented to be silent on the opinion of friends, who think it best not to put a continuance out of my power in defiance of all circumstances. There is, however, but one circumstance which could engage my acquiescence in another election, to wit such a division about a successor as might bring in a Monarchist. But this circumstance is impossible.

Ironically, Jefferson's words here give an excellent example of the incipience of the very danger he was determined in his political theory to eliminate.[66]

THE GENERAL EQUILIBRIUM

What Jefferson approved in the Constitution of the United States reveals his desire to establish and preserve a balance of power both on and between all levels of government,[67] and to correct the imbalance inherent in the Articles of Confederation. Too much power had previously been placed in the hands of Congress and the state legislatures. The Constitution's provisions for executive and judicial departments would be good counterbalances. Thus each of the three departments of the federal government would be balanced against the others.

Further, the federal government itself would be balanced against the several states. Ideally, each of them would have similar constitutional government. Every county, too,

66. To John Taylor, Jan. 6, 1805 (Ford, *8*, 339).
67. To James Madison, Dec. 20, 1787 (Boyd, *12*, 439–40).

would be a representative republic containing within its borders the ultimate units of government, the "wards," which would be "pure" democracies.[68] Every citizen was to participate in all branches of government: in local government directly, in others by the election of representatives to all offices. Election provided the means by which the people were to make their will known and settle conflict of opinion on questions facing the government. One of the most important functions of a constitution, therefore, was to preserve the right of suffrage.

WISDOM AND SUFFRAGE

Jefferson's constant objective was "to secure self-government by the republicanism of our Constitution, as well as by the spirit of the people; and to nourish and perpetuate that spirit. I am not among those who fear the people. They, and not the rich are our dependence for continued freedom."[69] Jefferson's belief in the people was qualified by one important reservation, however, put strikingly in a comment concerning the United States Constitution in 1787:

> I like the power given the Legislature to levy taxes; and for that reason solely approve of the greater house being chosen by the people directly. For tho' I think a house chosen by them will be very illy qualified to legislate for the Union, for foreign nations &c. yet this evil does not weigh against the good of preserving inviolate the fundamental principle that the people are not to be taxed but by representatives chosen immediately by themselves.[70]

Thomas Jefferson's statement that a legislature chosen directly by the people should be an "evil," ill qualified to

68. To Samuel Kercheval, July 12, 1816 (LB, *15*, 38–39).
69. Ibid.
70. To James Madison, Dec. 20, 1787 (Boyd, *12*, 440).

legislate for the Union or in international matters, may be unexpected. For years, however, this had been his considered opinion. In his drafts of a constitution for Virginia in 1776, Jefferson had provided for a bicameral legislature in which the members of the upper house would be chosen by the lower house and not by the people at all.[71] This was his explanation:

> I had two things in view: to get the wisest men chosen, and to make them perfectly independent when chosen. I have ever observed that a choice by the people themselves is not generally distinguished for its wisdom. This first secretion from them is usually crude and heterogeneous. But give to those so chosen by the people a second choice themselves, and they will generally chuse wise men. For this reason it was that I proposed the representatives (and not the people) should chuse the Senate, and thought I had notwithstanding that made the Senators (when chosen) perfectly independent of their electors. However I should have no objection to the mode of election proposed in the printed plan of your committee, to wit, that the people of each county should chuse twelve electors, who should meet those of the other counties in the same district and chuse a senator. . . . My reason for fixing them in office for a term of years rather than for life, was that they might have an idea that they were at a certain period to return into the mass of the people and become the governed instead of the governors which might still keep alive that regard to the public good that otherwise they might be induced by their independence to forget. Yet I could submit tho' not so willingly to an appointment for life, or to anything rather than a mere creation by and dependence on the people.

71. See Boyd, *1*, 341, 348, 358.

This is a strong statement which can easily be interpreted to mean that Jefferson doubted the people's ability to govern themselves and would like to have restricted their suffrage and voice in government. A few lines farther on in the same letter, however, Jefferson argues favorably "for extending the right of suffrage (or in other words the rights of a citizen) to all who had a permanent intention of living in the country." That intention alone, as far as Jefferson was concerned, should suffice to qualify a man to vote. "Whoever intends to live in a country must wish that country well, and has a natural right of assisting in the preservation of it."[72]

Despite his lifelong effort to extend suffrage to the broadest possible base, Jefferson never relinquished his reservation about the wisdom of the people. The doubt cropped up in one of his letters half a century after the Revolutionary War:

> Men by their constitution are naturally divided into two parties. 1. Those who fear and distrust the people, and wish to draw all powers from them into the hands of the higher classes. 2. Those who identify themselves with the people, have confidence in them, cherish and consider them as the most honest and safe, although not the most wise depository of the public interests.[73]

Jefferson's purpose in making the Virginia senate "perfectly independent" of the people is clear. He hoped in this way to let wisdom have its full effect on the deliberations of government.

However, for the purpose of assuring that wisdom would have its proper effect in the councils of government, Thomas Jefferson had more than one string to his bow. The people were still "the most honest and safe depository of the public interests." If they were not the most wise, some-

72. To Edmund Pendleton, Aug. 26, 1776 (Boyd, *1*, 503–04).
73. To Henry Lee, Aug. 10, 1824 (LB, *16*, 73–74).

thing had to be done. Educate them. All of them! Public
education was not a constitutional matter, but it was essential to the survival of self-government. I shall come back
to this question in due time.

RIGHTS AND FENCES

One other function that Jefferson felt must be served by
a constitution should be noted. If a constitution described
the powers each division of government was to have, it also
listed those powers which were not to be given to any department or official. A most important purpose of any constitution was to declare, and in so doing protect, man's
inalienable rights.

Jefferson strongly protested against the omission of a bill
of rights in the United States Constitution.[74] The rights he
demanded were essentially those he had included in all
three of his drafts of a constitution for the state of Virginia
in 1776.[75] The primary purpose of government to Jefferson
was to enforce men's natural rights. This was the object for
which society was formed and municipal laws established.[76]
That such protection called for joint action and joint responsibility he fully recognized. If man had natural rights,
in the state of society he also had natural duties. But even
these were motivated by the need to preserve the rights of
others. In this sense the task of government was to see to
it that both were observed and to go no further.[77]

Experience had shown that one of the chief problems in
government was that official leaders seemed incapable of
learning this. Some rights might be delegated to branches
of government to facilitate the preservation of the rights of
all. This was to be done only by the specific consent of the

74. To James Madison, Dec. 20, 1787 (Boyd, *12*, 440).
75. See Boyd, *1*, 337–64.
76. To James Monroe, Sept. 7, 1797 (LB, *9*, 422).
77. To Francis W. Gilmer, June 7, 1816 (Ford, *10*, 32).

governed. There were certain rights, however, such as free-dom of religion, which no individual had to cede in order to make government effective and yet on which govern-ments were constantly encroaching. There were also certain "fences" (such as trial by jury, habeas corpus laws, and a free press), proved by experience to be peculiarly efficacious against wrong and rarely obstructive of right, which gov-erning powers had always been disposed to weaken and re-move.[78]

In his efforts to prevent governmental leaders from being able to encroach upon the rights of individuals, he called for devices such as universal suffrage, limitation of the term of office for President, the ward system of local government in Virginia, frequent elections, and trial by jury in all ju-diciary cases. Preventing encroachment was behind his doc-trine of strict construction and his contention that the fa-thers intended Congress to pass only legislation indispens-able to carrying its specifically enumerated powers into effect. He maintained that "as an axiom of eternal truth in politics, whatever power in any government is independent, is absolute also."[79] The problem was to prevent that inde-pendence, to say effectively, "Thus far, and no farther!" through specific limitations, "fences," and "chains."

Yet no matter how numerous and ingenious, these limi-tations would never work by themselves. The people had to make them work. To be effective these devices needed the vigilance of the people they were designed to protect. Otherwise there was always the possibility of subversion, even in the best of society.[80] Only one precaution could safeguard the people against this danger, their own constant vigilant and distrustful superintendence. Unless the devices

78. To Noah Webster, Dec. 4, 1790 (Ford, 5, 254–55, and LB, 8, 112–13).
See also Chinard, Jefferson, pp. 80–85, and Koch, Philosophy of Jefferson,
p. 142.
79. To Spencer Roane, Sept. 6, 1819 (Ford, 10, 141).
80. To Mann Page, Aug. 30, 1795 (Ford, 7, 24–25).

limiting official power were backed by an enlightened suspicion of those in office, freedom could easily be lost.[81]

Jefferson's somewhat gory point, that from time to time the tree of liberty must be refreshed with the blood of patriots and tyrants, was simply an extension of his belief that without the people's jealousy, liberty would not survive. The people had a right to information concerning their government. If they did not get it or if it did not satisfy them, they had a right to take action.[82] To secure natural rights was the duty of the people, and they needed proper education in order to carry it out.

Jefferson in Power

The doctrine of strict construction, which Jefferson maintained against Hamilton throughout the decade the Federalists were in power, was essentially a negative use of the Constitution as a shield against despotism. As early as 1791, however, Jefferson was probably beginning to realize that it was an imperfect shield. An effective defense against Hamiltonianism required more aggressive tactics and weapons than arguments concerning constitutional construction.[83] Jefferson proceeded over the years to develop positive counterbalances, to increase the weight and influence of hitherto neglected groups and develop their effective participation in the deliberations of government. Nor did these groups remain as mere checks against the positive action of others. Before long, Jefferson and his followers were in power themselves. Government was not limited at that point to the securing of natural rights. That Jefferson's philosophy of government included much more than what he insisted upon when he was a member of the opposition can be seen partly in his activities as party politician.

81. See Kentucky Resolutions (Ford, 7, 303–05).
82. To William S. Smith, Nov. 13, 1787 (LB, 6, 372–73).
83. See Malone, *Jefferson*, 2, 350.

LEADERSHIP AND THE PRESIDENCY

To get some idea of how Jefferson thought constitutional government should work, one must observe his practice in the years preceding and during his presidential administration. During his term of office Jefferson fully maintained in practice the Federalist conception of executive power. His role as President was that which Washington and the Federalists had adopted, although his methods were more subtle and indirect, suited both to his own personality and to the character of his party. He would have preferred to have Congress function as his "coparcener" in government. However, when he was confronted with the hard choice either of allowing faction to wreck his program (and perhaps fatally weaken his party) or of taking charge of the management of Congress, he chose the latter course. His whole system of administration seemed to have been founded on the principle of carrying through legislative measures by personal or official influence. By party devices such as the congressional floor leader, the party caucus, intimate personal relations with members of Congress, and suggested drafts for important bills, Jefferson built up a highly centralized political system, operated for the most part by conference, consultation, and free discussion rather than by harsher means of leadership. The constitutional relations between the two branches of government were not changed in the slightest. The Presidency under Jefferson maintained fully the authority and prestige that it had earned under Washington and Adams.[84]

THE FUNCTION OF PARTY

All of this may provide an important insight into the nature of legitimate, positive, governmental action accord-

84. See Leonard D. White, *The Jeffersonians: A Study in Administrative History, 1801–1829* (New York, 1951), pp. 52–53, chaps. 3–4.

ing to Jefferson. Such positive action depended not so much upon the Constitution as it did upon party politics. The beginning of the party system that is with us today was one of Jefferson's major contributions to functioning American government. His concept of an active Presidency was an extension of that party system.

The party system developed by Jefferson and the Republicans was a device intended to determine the will of the people and to apply it effectively in governmental deliberations. It was an attempt to channel power without removing constitutional chains and fences, to discover what the people desired by means of caucuses and carefully centralized party machinery, to create a political will in the people by means of political instruction and propaganda, and to get out the vote. The election results would show whether the party's interpretation was right or wrong.[85]

ANTICIPATION OF THE POPULAR WILL

Jefferson's assumptions of power in matters such as the Louisiana Purchase and the Embargo must be seen in this light. The President had to function not only as a constitutional theorist but also as a party member, a member of a group concerned with the task of determining the will of the people and implementing it. Circumstances made it impossible, however, to ferret out the will of the people in advance of making certain decisions. Thus the Louisiana Purchase (an unprecedented executive act having no specific constitutional sanction), the Embargo of 1807–08 (a massive attempt to use governmental power to stop all movements of American ships to foreign ports), and other aspects of Jefferson's administration reveal an aspect of his philosophy of government which he later formulated in this manner:

85. See William A. Robinson, *Jeffersonian Democracy in New England* (New Haven, 1916), chap. 4.

The question . . . whether circumstances do not sometimes occur, which make it a duty in officers of high trust, to assume authorities beyond the law, is easy of solution in principle, but sometimes embarrassing in practice. A strict observance of written law is doubtless *one* of the highest duties of a good citizen, but it is not the *highest*. The laws of necessity, of self-preservation, of saving our country when in danger, are of higher obligation. To lose our country by a scrupulous adherence to written law, would be to lose the law itself, with life, liberty, property and all those who are enjoying them with us; thus absurdly sacrificing the ends to the means.[86]

By itself this formulation allows for exactly the sort of subversion Jefferson inveighed against in the Kentucky Resolutions and the violation of natural rights that he inveighed against in the Declaration of Independence. It would seem to let all the governmental abuses he had fought against come in the back door after he had kicked them out the front. The problem is that theory of government may never be equal to the task of determining practice in all circumstances. The Constitution did not indicate what means were both legitimate and effective in enforcing the Embargo. The philosophy of natural rights could not answer the question of whether or not to purchase Louisiana. Action was demanded in response to events which had not been anticipated in 1787. The action Jefferson took certainly made the Constitution elastic. But this approach did not remove the trammels upon government. The will of the people remained sovereign. Election results, by which the party and its members would stand or fall, were to show whether the people's will had been rightly interpreted. What had to be decided without consulting the people was nevertheless to be ratified or rejected by them. According

86. To John B. Colvin, Sept. 20, 1810 (Ford, *9*, 279).

to this standard there can be no doubt that the purchase of Louisiana was in accord with the will of the majority, and that the powers used to enforce the Embargo were not. Jefferson finally became aware of both decisions and abided by them.

Context makes a difference, and the context Jefferson had in mind here was the American people. As we have seen, he felt that the safeguarding of natural rights depended ultimately not upon legislation but upon the distrustful and vigilant superintendence by the people. Nothing he said or did was to be considered as an attack upon their superintendence or upon the means by which they exercised it. Provided their freedoms were maintained, the people could recognize and check any threat to their rights; as long as they were zealous to prevent encroachment, their liberty would be safe.

CHAPTER 5

$\mathcal{S}$ectarianism

Thomas Jefferson had an intense concern for right religious belief. Despite his numerous protests of tolerance for the opinions of others in the realm of religion, he was never indifferent to his own faith, nor to its implications. The value he placed on man's search for right belief is expressed typically in his advice to Peter Carr: "Religion. Your reason is now mature enough to examine this object. In the first place, divest yourself of all bias in favor of novelty and singularity of opinion. Indulge them in any other subject rather than that of religion. It is too important, and the consequences of error may be too serious."[1]

Jefferson never admitted, however, that there need be any conflict between concern for right religious belief on the one hand and concern for freedom of opinion, on the other.

1. Aug. 10, 1787 (LB, 6, 258).

The ability to maintain both of these concerns was something he honored in Joseph Priestley[2] and strove consciously to develop in himself. He considered it a lie and a slander to say that the government was without religion simply because he had not used his office of President of the United States to proclaim days of fast or thanksgiving, or to indicate in other ways how the people might engage in religious activities.[3]

The Source of Variety of Opinion

The rationale behind Jefferson's efforts to bring about freedom of opinion is not always clear; ultimately it seems to be based on two conflicting motives. The first goes back to the hypothesis, which Jefferson evidently accepted in common with members of the American Philosophical Society, that ideas are determined by the structure of the brain and that since each man's brain is to some extent physically unique, his opinions must be expected to be so too.[4] To Jefferson thinking, like gravity and magnetism, was a property or mode of action of matter. Thought was therefore determined by the structure of the thinking organ.[5]

In line with this, Jefferson made remarks such as, "Our opinions are not voluntary"; "Differences of opinion . . . like differences of face, are a law of nature, and should be viewed with the same tolerance";[6] and, "As the Creator made no two faces alike so no two minds and probably no

2. To John Adams, June 15, 1813 (Ford, *Writings of Jefferson, 9,* 386).
3. To DeWitt Clinton, May 24, 1807 (Ford, *9,* 62–64).
4. See Boorstin, *Lost World,* pp. 112–28.
5. To John Adams, Aug. 15, 1820 (LB, *15,* 274). This view was similar to that of Priestley, who held that thought and sensation were found only in connection with an organized system of matter, that the brain was the seat of thought, and that there was no recorded instance of thought surviving the destruction of the brain. See Basil Willey, *The Eighteenth Century Background* (London, 1940), p. 173.
6. To William Duane, July 25, 1811 (LB, *13,* 67).

two creeds."⁷ Jefferson held the view that this variety of opinion, determined as it was by the physical variety of minds, was desirable on aesthetic grounds, and that uniformity of opinion could only result in an undesirable moral monotony.⁸ If we develop this whole position to its logical end, however, we are left with the conclusion that variety of opinion is desirable because the Creator made men in different molds, but that no man's reasoning can lead him surely to truth, and that similarly no certainty or truth can result from the conflict of opinion. Tolerance was not a means of promoting free discussion by which men could approach truth. It was merely an acceptance of the Creator's intention that all men think differently.

The Consensus Gentium

Yet in his battle for religious freedom Jefferson also develops the position which seems ruled out by his understanding of the nature and structure of the human mind, the position that freedom of thought is a *sine qua non* for the development of true religion. He put it succinctly in *Notes on Virginia:* "Reason and free inquiry are the only effectual agents against error. Give a loose to them, they will support the true religion by bringing every false one to their tribunal, to the test of their investigation."⁹ And this, of course, is simply a rewording of the contention in the Bill for Establishing Religious Freedom that "truth is great and will prevail if left to herself; that she is the proper and sufficient antagonist to error, and has nothing to fear from the conflict unless by human interposition disarmed of her natural weapons, free argument and debate."¹⁰

7. To Timothy Pickering, Feb. 27, 1821 (LB, *15*, 324).
8. To Charles Thomson, Jan. 29, 1817 (Ford, *10*, 76).
9. Query 17 (Ford, *3*, 263).
10. Boyd, *Papers of Jefferson, 2,* 546.

These conflicting positions—that reason was too weak and uncertain not to lead to different results,[11] and that truth would prevail under the conditions of free discussion and debate—were not simply an attempt to have the argument both ways, nor an inconsistency into which Jefferson slipped when his intellectual guard was down. He consciously believed that despite men's different opinions, there were certain things upon which they could be expected to agree, even in the field of religion, and that, "What all agree in, is probably right. What no two agree in, most probably wrong."[12] This was an acceptable criterion in the Enlightenment for determining right and wrong,[13] and Jefferson used it often to settle his doubts. As we have seen, for example, he based his own belief in God rather strongly on the argument from *consensus gentium*. In other words, he did not feel that the field of religion was entirely a welter of conflicting opinions without any standards by which to separate truth from error. "All" did agree on some things. Since what "all" agreed on was probably right, the proper approach was to make this the basis of religious belief, rather than the points at which men differed. It was part of the climate of Jefferson's age to believe that true religion was actually the common residuum of all historic religions.[14] In contemporary terms we might say that Jefferson believed there was a "common core" of religious belief, a group of tenets on which all sects could be expected to agree. Obviously this common core did not include creed or dogma, but it did most certainly embrace the field of morality and also the rational or philosophic proofs of the existence of God.

11. To Abigail Adams, Sept. 11, 1804 (LB, *11*, 52).
12. To John Adams, Jan. 11, 1817 (Ford, *10*, 73); and elsewhere.
13. See Hazard, *European Thought*, p. 30.
14. See Bryson, *Man and Society*, p. 13.

MORALITY

Jefferson's opinion that morality was common to all men, a thing upon which they naturally agreed, was based upon his belief in the existence of the moral sense. He held that man had been endowed with the need and capacity for social living, and with the physical faculty of conscience, the "moral instinct" that prompts men to sympathize with their fellows and succor them in their distress. It did not necessarily follow from this that all men would have the same moral customs. Since Jefferson believed that nature had constituted utility as the criterion of virtue for specific acts, the same act could be either virtuous or vicious depending entirely upon the circumstances in which it took place.[15] The principle of utility was nevertheless common to all, as was the sense of morality, and on the basis of these Jefferson concluded that the moral branch of religion also was the same for all peoples. The evidence he considered supported him, for he observed that all religions forbade murder, theft, false witness, and other crimes,[16] and likewise all inculcated honesty, truth, temperance, gratitude, and love of man.[17] Like other philosophers of his era, Jefferson went further and maintained that morality was normally so much a part of man's nature that the idea that it depended upon a belief in God was completely erroneous. The virtuous and moral lives led by avowed atheists such as Condorcet, Diderot, d'Holbach, d'Alembert, and Grimm utterly disproved that notion. Morality was the justification of Jefferson's own religion. "Its evidence before the world is to be sought in my life; if that has been honest and dutiful to society, the Religion which has regulated it cannot be a bad one."[18] Religion was not only to be seen in the life a

15. To Thomas Law, June 13, 1814 (LB, *14*, 138–44).
16. To James Fishback, Sept. 27, 1809 (LB, *12*, 314–16).
17. See First Inaugural Address, March 4, 1801 (LB, *3*, 320).
18. To Charles Thomson, Jan. 29, 1817 (Ford, *10*, 75–76).

person led,[19] but indeed true religion was morality.[20] In holding to this belief Jefferson was being very much a man of his time.[21] The common emphasis of eighteenth-century Quakers upon morality rather than upon dogma drew Jefferson's respect.[22]

One of his great and abiding interests was in the development of a system of morality. As a young man Jefferson approved Bolingbroke's dictum that such a system would be better based on materials drawn from moralists of ancient Greece and Rome, such as Xenophon, Epictetus, Seneca, and Cicero.[23] This faded away before the conviction in his later years of the unquestionably superior social value of the moral teachings of Jesus. Jefferson's reply to every question concerning abstract theological or metaphysical speculation was that he confined his religious reading to the moral branch. That this reply was not simply an attempt to avoid argument and the embarrassment that accompanies conflict of opinion is shown by his request to James Madison for help in selecting books for a library to be willed to the University of Virginia: "The good moral writers, Christian as well as Pagan, I have set down; but there are writers of celebrity in religious metaphysics . . . whom you can suggest."[24]

NATURAL THEISM

In addition to his belief that part of the common core of religion upon which all men agreed was morality, Jeffer-

19. To John Adams, Jan. 11, 1817 (Ford, *10*, 73); and elsewhere.

20. To John Adams, May 5, 1817 (LB, *15*, 427).

21. E.g. Voltaire: "I understand by natural religion the principles of morality common to the human race," *Oeuvres* (1883–85), *22*, 419, as quoted by Becker, *Heavenly City*, p. 44; cf. Chinard, *Jefferson*, pp. 523–24. See also Cassirer's discussion of Bayle, Voltaire, and Diderot in *Philosophy of the Enlightenment*, pp. 166–71.

22. To William Canby, Sept. 18, 1813 (LB, *13*, 377).

23. To Robert Skipwith. See Aug. 3, 1771 (Boyd, *1*, 79–80).

24. To James Madison, Aug. 8, 1824 (Madison Papers, Library of Congress, quoted in Koch, *Jefferson and Madison*, p. 279).

son also expressed the opinion that if man were allowed to observe and to use his reason freely, he would be led "irresistibly" to a belief in the existence of God:

> And when the atheist descanted on the unceasing motion and circulation of matter through the animal, vegetable and mineral kingdoms, never resting, never annihilated, always changing form, and under all forms gifted with the power of reproduction; the theist pointing "to the heavens above, and to the earth beneath; and to the waters under the earth," asked, if these did not proclaim a first cause, possessing intelligence and power; power in the production, and intelligence in the design and constant preservation of the system; urged the palpable existence of final causes; that the eye was made to see, and the ear to hear, and not that we see because we have eyes, and hear because we have ears; an answer obvious to the senses, as that of walking across the room, was to the philosopher demonstrating the non-existence of motion.[25]

This restatement of arguments typical of the time expresses Jefferson's conviction that all men, generally, agree on the existence of God.[26] The few individual atheists were exceptions that no more disproved the rule than did the fact that a few individuals were born without a moral sense prove that the moral sense was not a human attribute:

> It is impossible, I say, for the human mind not to believe, that there is in all this, design, cause and effect, up to an ultimate cause. . . . So irresistible are these evidences of an intelligent and powerful Agent, that of the infinite numbers of men who have existed through all time, they have believed in the proportion of a

25. To John Adams, April 8, 1816 (LB, *14*, 469).
26. See J. H. Randall, *Making of Modern Mind*, "The Arguments of Natural Theology," pp. 294–97.

million at least to a unit, in the hypothesis of an eternal
pre-existence of a Creator, rather than in that of a self-
existent universe. Surely this unanimous sentiment
renders this more probable, than that of the few in
the other hypothesis.[27]

Supernatural Revelation

USELESSNESS

Morality and the rational deduction of God's existence
from observable phenomena were thus two areas in religion
upon which men could agree. These to Jefferson, as to the
philosophes of the eighteenth century generally, were the
essentials of the Christian faith to which nothing more need
be added.[28] Revelation, on the other hand, caused nothing
but schisms and all of the evils attendant upon men's dis-
agreeing violently. Jefferson's concept of revelation seemed
to be limited to the affirmation of events and opinions
which by every other test are totally incapable of proof.
Thus to Jefferson the Bible was a history book. Its testimony concerning events was to be accepted as the events in
any other history were to be believed, on the basis of the
writer's affirming them, provided the accounts did not fly
into the face of reason or of what was known in the eighteenth century concerning natural law. Miracles, such as
Joshua's causing the sun to stand still, were obviously impossible. The biblical writer demanded the reader's belief
in them on the basis of his claim to divine inspiration; this
was revelation in action and it was obviously something to
be avoided as totally irrational.[29] No such problem existed
when one considered the biblical account of the creation
of the world. This was an account which Jefferson accepted
because he saw it as a sensible hypothesis capable of rational

27. To John Adams, April 11, 1823 (LB, *15*, 427–28).
28. See J. H. Randall, p. 286–94.
29. To Peter Carr, Aug. 10, 1787 (LB, *6*, 258–61).

and scientific demonstration. Revelation, then, was of no
real use in man's quest for knowledge. At best it was a fifth
wheel. More often it was a screen for obscurantism or superstition. Whatever was susceptible of demonstration made
the claims of revelation concerning it superfluous. Whatever could not be demonstrated was best ignored as unimportant. If it was plainly irrational, as so many "revealed"
doctrines were, it was best condemned.[30]

Jefferson consciously ruled out revelation as a fit source
of knowledge concerning God. He went so far as to say that
whoever insisted on the necessity of revelation for the sufficient proof even of the existence of God was simply "giving
a handle to atheism." In reply, the leading atheists of the
seventeenth and eighteenth centuries could, according to
Jefferson, call on the philosophical principle of simplicity
or economy. They could insist that it makes better sense to
believe in the eternal uncreated existence of the universe
as it can be observed "than to believe in the eternal pre-
existence of an ulterior cause, or Creator of the world, a
Being whom we see not and know not, of whose form, substance and mode, or place of existence, or of action, no

30. The argument over the utility of revelation went back to John Locke.
For a description of his position and those of subsequent English philosophers with whom Jefferson was familiar, see Stephen, *English Thought*, Vol.
I, chap. 3.
Concerning the claims of revelation, Jefferson tended to be more extreme
than his colleagues of the A.P.S. (see Boorstin, pp. 151 ff.) but not as drastic
as many French *philosophes* (see Koch, *Philosophy of Jefferson*, pp. 104 ff.)
Jefferson and Priestley, for instance, differed on the question of what was
authentic in Scripture. Priestley was a leader in the movement for the restoration of "primitive Christianity" by purging it of all "corruptions" such as
the doctrines of the Trinity, Virgin Birth, Original Sin, Predestination,
Atonement, and Plenary Inspiration of Scripture. Yet he retained his belief
in the Final Resurrection, and in the miracles and resurrection of Jesus
Christ. These fit into his philosophical and metaphysical system, and he was
able to justify them as being originally scriptural, not corruptions. (See
Willey, *Eighteenth Century Background*, pp. 188–93.) Jefferson took one of
his rare departures from Priestley on these points. For Jefferson's position
concerning Christ's miracles and resurrection read *The Morals and Life
of Jesus of Nazareth* (LB, end of Vol. XX).

sense informs us, no power of the mind enables us to deline-
ate or comprehend."[31] To Jefferson the deist position concerning the creation of the world was susceptible of much
stricter demonstration.

DANGERS

Revelation, then, was worthless for two reasons: it was
undemonstrable and it was superfluous. It depended for
its authority on the unsupported claims of private individuals to divine inspiration, but could not be publicly tested,
observed, or proved. With a few insignificant exceptions, all
men had come (or would have come) to a belief in God
without its aid. But Jefferson felt it was worse than worthless; it was a source of real and dangerous evil, because the
contents of revelation were invariably irrational (almost by
definition to Jefferson) and therefore unacceptable to most
people, except under coercion. The reason why the contents
of Christian revelation had been accepted by such a small
minority of the world's people, and why it would probably
gain no more adherents if freedom of thought were protected, was that the undemonstrable cannot win the free assent
of the mind.

The difficulty Jefferson had in reconciling the ideas of
trinity and unity—"articles which I never had sense enough
to comprehend"—and his belief that comprehension must
precede assent are expressed in his writings many times.[32]
To him the dogmas of religion, as distinguished from its
moral principles, were unintelligible abstractions absolutely beyond the comprehension of the human mind:[33] "Ideas
must be distinct before reason can act upon them; and no
man ever had a distinct idea of the trinity."[34]

31. To John Adams, April 11, 1823 (LB, *15*, 426–27).

32. The earliest example in print is his letter to J. P. P. Derieux, July
25, 1788 (Boyd, *13*, 418). See Boyd's footnote, p. 419.

33. To Mathew Carey, Nov. 11, 1816 (Ford, *10*, 76–78).

34. To F. A. Van der Kemp, 1816 (quoted in Padover, *Jefferson on Democracy*, p. 118).

For all the unacceptability of revealed dogma, its pro-
claimers invariably demanded that all men accept it, as
Jefferson saw the matter. Since the very lack of rationality
in these incomprehensible articles of faith made it impossible for most men to assent freely to such propositions, the
adherents of revealed religious dogmas always resorted to
coercion in its worst forms—quarreling, fighting, burning,
and torturing—in order to have their way. Persecution, oppression, the worst outrages of physical and mental tyranny,
any means at all were not only acceptable but positively desirable to make all men within reach subscribe to their articles.

The most obvious result of these actions is a monstrous
phenomenon: the denial and violation of that very common
core of morality which all religions teach and upon which
they all agree, however much they may differ in dogmatic
abstractions. "Christians" destroy truth, honesty, temperance, gratitude, and love of man, in the name of him who
had taught these principles in their sublimest form. Murder, theft, false witness, and other crimes which religion
had forbidden they encourage as a service to God. Although
Jefferson expressed horror over this, he did not show surprise. It was easily accounted for. It was not to be traced
to honest men who differed in opinions, but was the work
of greedy conspirators, "priests," mountebanks, charlatans,
rogues guided in their words and actions solely by self-
interest and an eye for easy, parasitical living at the expense
of the common people.

Jefferson summed up his view of this conspiracy in pun-
gent words:

> But a short time elapsed after the death of [Jesus] be-
> fore his principles were departed from by those who
> professed to be his special servants, and perverted into
> an engine for enslaving mankind, and aggrandizing
> their oppressors in Church and State: that the purest

system of morals ever before preached to man has been adulterated and sophisticated by artificial constructions, into a mere contrivance to filch wealth and power to themselves: that rational men, not being able to swallow their impious heresies, in order to force them down their throats, they raise the hue and cry of infidelity, while themselves are the greatest obstacles to the advancement of the real doctrines of Jesus, and do, in fact, constitute the real Anti-Christ.[35]

The ecclesiastical conspiracy accounted for the doctrine of the Trinity, "mere Abracadabra of the mountebanks calling themselves the priests of Jesus. If it could be understood it would not answer their purpose. Their security is in their faculty of shedding darkness."[36] By contrast, to Jefferson,

> The mild and simple principles of the Christian philosophy would produce too much calm, too much regularity of good, to extract from its disciples a support for a numerous priesthood, were they not to sophisticate it, ramify it, split it into hairs, and twist its texts till they cover the divine morality of its author with mysteries, and require a priesthood to explain them.[37]

A strong position strongly expressed, it was nevertheless characteristic of the intellectual circle and climate in which Jefferson was at home and of much of the thought of his age. It must be admitted also that there was some truth to the position, for in the eighteenth century the suspicion was often vindicated that appeals to mystery, darkness, or authority to justify arbitrary behavior were often alibis

---

35. To Samuel Kercheval, Jan. 19, 1810 (LB, *12*, 345–46).

36. To F. A. Van der Kemp, 1816 (quoted in Padover, *Jefferson on Democracy*, p. 118).

37. To Elbridge Gerry, March 29, 1801 (Ford, *8*, 42–43). See also letter to Thomas Leiper, Jan. 21, 1809 (Ford, *9*, 238); to John Adams, July 5, 1814 (Ford, *9*, 463–64); and to George Logan, Nov. 12, 1816 (Ford, *10*, 68).

concealing self-interest, intellectual indolence, or stupidity.[38]

But as far as Jefferson was concerned, the toll exacted by the priests was not limited to the expense of providing support for human parasites. It included damage to men's minds and characters. The effect of coercion in religious belief, as Jefferson had remarked in *Notes on Virginia,* was to make one half the world fools and the other half hypocrites.[39] This, he felt, was the aim of the priests, the goal of their "fulminations against endeavors to enlighten the general mind, to improve the reason of the people, and to encourage them in the use of it,"[40] and the success of their efforts could be seen, he noted, in New England where their sway was indeed formidable and "no mind beyond mediocrity dares there to develop itself."[41]

Moral Superiority of the Consensus Gentium

When contrasted with these horrifying and detestable results, the superior advantages of a religion based on reason, nature, common sense, and man's innate moral sense are obvious. To begin with, differences of opinion in a religion based on reason and man's natural faculties are readily solved by demonstration; whatever cannot be readily demonstrated can be ignored as insignificant or probably untrue. For example, the existence of God was a demonstrable matter; anyone could read it in the wonders of the universe:

> the theist pointing "to the heavens above, and to the earth beneath, and to the waters under the earth," asked, if these did not proclaim a first cause, possessing intelligence and power; power in the production and

38. See Berlin, *Age of Enlightenment,* p. 29.
39. See Query 17 (Ford, *3,* 265).
40. To William Short, April 13, 1820 (LB, *15,* 246–47).
41. To Horatio Spafford, Jan. 10, 1816 (Ford, *10,* 12–13).

intelligence in the design and constant preservation of the system; urged the palpable existence of final causes; that the eye was made to see, and the ear to hear, and not that we see because we have eyes, or hear because we have ears; an answer obvious to the senses . . .[42]

To this undeniable demonstration of first and final causes, Jefferson maintained, thinking men have always given free assent. By an overwhelming numerical superiority, men have always been theists rather than atheists, and rational Christians or pagan theists rather than supernatural revelationists.[43] Nor should it be forgotten that the demonstration thus finds itself reinforced by the argument from consensus gentium: "What all agree in, is probably right. What no two agree in, most probably wrong."[44]

This overwhelming numerical superiority also favored the concept that true religion is morality and not sectarian dogma, on which no two agree but everyone differs.[45] We have seen that Jefferson believed man had a moral faculty, that his moral principles were innate, part of his physical constitution, so completely a part of man that they could not be effaced by the subtleties of his brain, and so completely independent of dogma that even atheists had led wholly moral lives.[46] Thus assent was given to morality by all thinking men just as overwhelmingly and as freely as it was given to theism. Another great advantage possessed by a religion based on reason, common sense, the moral faculty, and nature was that it could be tested by what it proclaimed and inculcated, the fruits of men's lives, while

42. To John Adams, April 8, 1816 (LB, *14*, 468–69).

43. To John Adams, April 11, 1823 (LB, *16*, 427).

44. To John Adams, Jan. 11, 1817 (Ford, *10*, 73).

45. To John Adams, May 5, 1817 (LB, *15*, 427); to Thomas Leiper, Jan. 21, 1809 (Ford, *9*, 238).

46. To James Fishback, Sept. 27, 1809 (LB, *14*, 141); to John Adams, May 5, 1817 (LB, *15*, 427); and elsewhere.

it demoted undemonstrable abstractions to their proper secondary place. Coercion of belief, in other words, would be unnecessary, since all men freely accept a belief in God and in the need to lead moral lives. More than that, such coercion would be undesirable. A religion based on morality and common sense would not countenance the vile inconsistency of trying to preserve the morality it was dedicated to engender, develop, and protect, by using methods which could only violate and destroy it.

TRINITARIANISM

Against this background we can see Jefferson's professed "Unitarianism." He had a great love for rational clarity and precision. To Benjamin Rush he once remarked, "Having to conduct my grandson through his course of mathematics, I have resumed that study with great avidity. It was ever my favorite one. We have no theories here, no uncertainties remain on the mind; all is demonstration and satisfaction."[47] In the light of this personal demand for clarity and demonstration, one can see why he rejected the doctrine of the Trinity. "It is too late in the day for men of sincerity to pretend they believe in the Platonic mysticisms that three are one, and one is three; and yet that the one is not three, and the three are not one."[48] It was a mathematical monstrosity, a rational impossibility, a combination of ideas which he claimed to have been unable to reconcile from very early in life.[49] He could conceive of the doctrine having come into existence only as an unintelligible system of heathen mysteries (particularly the works of Plato), compounded by priests anxious to gain a living by interpreting the incomprehensible. The doctrine was engrafted upon and disfigured the simple religion of Jesus, which in its

47. Aug. 17, 1811 (Ford, 9, 327–28).
48. To John Adams, Aug. 22, 1813 (Ford, 9, 409–10). See also letter to James Smith, Dec. 8, 1822 (LB, 15, 409).
49. To J. P. P. Derieux, July 25, 1788 (Boyd, 13, 418).

original purity would bring peace to mankind but would never support a priesthood.[50] Trinitarianism was deliberately irrational and deliberately fraudulent.

DANGERS OF TRINITARIANISM

Trinitarianism brought with it all of the faults which accompanied any doctrine based on "supernaturalism,"[51] "spiritualism," or "immaterialism." First, it gave a handle to atheism, or rather something much worse. As Jefferson once explained to John Adams:

> I can never join Calvin in addressing *his* God. He was indeed an atheist, which I can never be, or rather his religion was daemonism. If ever a man worshiped a false God, he did. The being described in his five points, is not the God whom you and I acknowledge and adore, the Creator and benevolent governor of the world, but a daemon of malignant spirit. It would be more pardonable to believe in no God at all, than to blaspheme him by the atrocious attributes of Calvin.[52]

The advocates of Trinitarianism were irrational and also tyrannous. "Fanaticism, it is true, is not sparing of her invectives against those who refuse blindly to follow her dictates in abandonment of their own reason."[53] Invective was all the law allowed the Christian clergy in his day, said Jefferson, but they were "ready at the word of the lawgiver, if such could be now obtained, to put the torch to the pile. . . . They pant to reestablish, *by law,* that holy inquisition which they can now only infuse into *public opinion.*"[54]

50. To Dr. Benjamin Waterhouse, Oct. 13, 1815 (Ford, *9,* 533); to Charles Thomson, Jan. 9, 1816 (Ford, *10,* 5–6); and elsewhere.

51. See Koch, *Philosophy of Jefferson,* pp. 99–100.

52. To John Adams, April 11, 1823 (LB, *15,* 426). Italics Jefferson's.

53. To William Carver, Dec. 4, 1823 (Ford, *10,* 284–85).

54. To Attorney General Levi Lincoln, Aug. 26, 1801 (Ford, *8,* 84) italics Jefferson's. See also letter to William Short, April 13, 1820 (LB, *15,* 246–47).

UNITARIANISM

Unitarianism, in Jefferson's opinion, stood in direct contrast to this in every respect. To begin with, it was not an artificial system engrafted upon and disfiguring the precepts of Jesus, but the basic, original, primitive Christian philosophy itself. Jefferson came to this conclusion after reading the works of Middleton, Waterland,[55] and Priestley, whose arguments, he held, "have never been answered, nor can be answered by quoting historical proofs as they have done."[56] Jefferson was convinced that Jesus was a great religious reformer who tried to correct the vicious ethics of the deism of the Jews, and received for his efforts a reformer's reward. The moral code Jesus bequeathed to mankind, although incomplete because of his premature death, was to Jefferson the most sublime ever constructed. On the other hand, there was no valid evidence that Jesus ever meant "to impose himself on mankind as the son of God, physically speaking," although "he might conscientiously believe himself inspired from above," since "the whole religion of the Jew . . . was founded in the belief of divine inspiration," and "he might readily mistake the coruscations of his own fine genius for inspirations of an higher order."[57]

The drive of Jefferson's approach can be seen in the short title to his harmony of the gospels, *The Morals of Jesus*. His aim was to humanize the deified concept of Christ. Like the early deists, he stressed his belief that primitive Christianity was free from mystery, and asserted that Judaic and Greek sources were responsible for the intrusion of the idea that mystery is that which transcends reason.[58]

55. For the position of Conyers Middleton on Christianity, and particularly on Scripture and Orthodox Dogmas, see Stephen, *English Thought, 1,* 253–57, and 261–73; for Waterland, pp. 257–61.
56. To John Adams, Aug. 22, 1813 (Ford, *9,* 418).
57. To William Short, Aug. 4, 1820 (LB, *15,* 261).
58. See Koch, *Philosophy of Jefferson,* p. 25.

UNITARIANISM'S MORAL SUPERIORITIES

In addition to being a restoration of the religion of Jesus himself, Unitarianism was Jefferson's idea of the only rational belief and, as such, the one belief to which all men could be counted on to give assent. Originally they had done so, "nor was the unity of the Supreme Being ousted from the Christian creed by the force of reason, but by the sword of civil government wielded at the will of the fanatic Athanasius." Its power to win adherents among people free to think was plainly evident:

> a strong proof of the solidity of the primitive faith, is its restoration, as soon as a nation arises which vindicates to itself the freedom of religious opinion, and its external divorce from civil authority. The pure and simple unity of the Creator of the Universe is now all but ascendant in the Eastern States; it is dawning in the West, and advancing towards the South; and I confidently expect that the present generation will see Unitarianism become the general religion of the United States.[59]

Its power could be seen even in countries where freedom of belief was not protected by law: "I remember to have heard Dr. Priestley say, that if all England would candidly examine themselves, they would find Unitarianism was really the religion of all."[60]

To Jefferson, Unitarianism, in contrast to Trinitarianism, was not demonistic but benevolently theistic. Jesus, he maintained, had "corrected the Deism of the Jews, confirming them in their belief of only one God, and giving them juster notions of his attributes and government." Instead of developing coercion and tyranny, Jesus' doctrines,

59. To James Smith, Dec. 8, 1822 (LB, *15*, 408).
60. To John Adams, Aug. 22, 1813 (Ford, *9*, 409).

according to Jefferson, led to the development of a wise morality:

> His moral doctrines, relating to kindred & friends, were more pure & perfect than those of the most correct of the philosophers, and greatly more so than those of the Jews; and they went far beyond both in inculcating universal philanthropy, not only to kindred and friends, to neighbors and countrymen, but to all mankind, gathering all into one family, under the bonds of love, charity, peace, common wants, and common aids. . . .
>
> He pushed his scrutinies into the heart of man; erected his tribunal in the region of his thoughts, and purified the waters at the fountain head.
>
> He taught emphatically, the doctrines of a future state . . . and wielded it with efficacy, as an important incentive, supplementary to the other motives to moral conduct.[61]

Four years before his death Jefferson prophesied the early victory of this sublime religion in the free nation he had helped to found: "I rejoice that in this blessed country of free inquiry and belief, which has surrendered its creed and conscience to neither kings nor priests, the genuine doctrine of only one God is reviving and I trust that there is not a *young man* now living in the United States who will not die an Unitarian." But when all was said and done, even Jefferson's sunny hopes for the success of that truly rational and truly moral primitive Christianity, Unitarianism, were not completely unclouded:

> But much I fear, when this great truth shall be reestablished, its votaries will fall into the fatal error of fabricating formulas of creed and confessions of faith,

---

61. "Syllabus of an Estimate of the Merit of the Doctrines of Jesus Compared with Those of Others," April 1803 (Ford, *8*, 227–28).

the engines which so soon destroyed the religion of
Jesus, and made of Christendom a mere Aceldama;
that they will give up morals for mysteries, and Jesus
for Plato. How much wiser are the Quakers, who,
agreeing in the fundamental doctrines of the gospel,
schismatize about no mysteries, and, keeping within
the pale of common sense, suffer no speculative differences of opinion, any more than that of feature, to
impair the love of their brethren. Be this the wisdom of
the Unitarians, this holy mantle which shall cover
within its charitable circumference all who believe in
one God, and who love their neighbor.[62]

A fly might fall even into this ointment; the possibility of
corruption existed even here, and had to be understood
and counteracted.

Jefferson's Sectarianism

On several counts Jefferson may fairly be charged with
being as sectarian as the Trinitarians whom he opposed.
For one thing, he was fired by a missionary zeal. Like many
another prophet, Jefferson did his best to bring his fervent
hopes to fruition. Of course, he never ceased to protest that
he cherished the rights of others to freedom of opinion,
and is not known to have engaged in direct evangelizing or
proselytizing. Jefferson, nevertheless, gave support and en-
couragement to Unitarians actively engaged in seeking converts, and advised those whose position in public life enabled them to help his favorite belief. For example, he once
commented, "The genuine and simple religion of Jesus
will one day be restored: such as it was preached and practiced by himself. Very soon after his death it became muffled

---

62. To Benjamin Waterhouse, June 22, 1822 (Ford, *10*, 220), italics Jefferson's. See also letter to Benjamin Waterhouse, July 19, 1822 (Ford, *10*,
220–21 n.); to James Smith, Dec. 18, 1822 (LB, *15*, 408).

up in mysteries and has been ever since kept in conceal-
ment from the vulgar eye. To penetrate and dissipate these
clouds of darkness, the general mind must be strengthened
by education."[63] The last sentence has great implications,
which I shall explore when I consider Jefferson's specific
measures concerning religion in public education.

A second aspect of Jefferson's sectarianism was his inability to take seriously the beliefs of those with whom he
disagreed. He set his rule concerning what all men believe,
and rode roughshod over evidence to the contrary. He cate-
gorized such evidence as meaningless exceptions which by
no means disprove the rule, and often explained it away
as part of that great conspiracy of the fraudulent and greedy
priests. Jefferson refused to wrestle with the fact that there
were men of sincerity who meant what they said when they
averred a belief in the Trinity.[64] If he admitted their sincerity, he explained away their beliefs as determined by the
structure of their brains. Even when he recognized that the
same argument applied to his own opinions, he still held
that he was right and the Trinitarians and atheists wrong.
Despite his belief that men's thoughts were beyond their
own control, he also maintained that they could verify *his*
opinions scientifically!

Third, Jefferson's beliefs were by no means limited to
"what all men agreed on." Even if it could be proved that
all men were naturally theists and moralists (as we have
seen, Jefferson could cling to this position only by over-
riding evidence to the contrary), Jefferson advocated a good
deal more than this. He had his excess metaphysical bag-
gage in the form of a doctrine of materialism. Insisting that
this was not metaphysical did not make it any less so. Jefferson could thus be said to be guilty of exactly what he
accused the early Christians of doing: adulterating and so-

63. To F. A. Van der Kemp, 1820 (quoted in Padover, *Jefferson on Democracy*, p. 118).
64. To John Adams, Aug. 22, 1813 (Ford, 9, 409–10).

phisticating his doctrine with artificial constructions.[65] Because of his inability to see it, this sectarianism was to cause Jefferson some hindrance in his efforts to develop the University of Virginia, as we shall see in due course.

We must remember that missionary zeal played its part in Jefferson's lifelong efforts to bring about the condition of free opinion. Under religious freedom, true religion could be expected to grow on its own merit, and sectarianism, lacking the sanction of force, would die out. But what was "religious freedom" to Thomas Jefferson? When did he think it existed?

65. To Samuel S. Kercheval, Jan. 19, 1810 (LB, *12*, 345).

CHAPTER 6

Religious Freedom

The History of the Alliance of Church and State

History had provided Jefferson with his argument against
despotism in any form. The record showed that tyranny
was always governmental madness, that it always made the
people wretched, that it always lost sight of legitimate government's sole object: popular happiness. So also did history
provide Jefferson with his argument against the establishment of religion and the alliance of church and state. He
summed up his thesis in a few sentences copied from Locke:

> Why have [Christians] been distinguished above all
> people who have ever lived for persecutions? is it be-
> cause it is the genius of that religion? no it's genius is
> the reverse. It is refusing *toleration* to those of a differ-
> ent [opinion] which has produced all the bustles and
> wars on account of religion. It was the misfortune of

mankind that during the dark centuries the [Christian] priests following their ambition and avarice and combining with the magistrate to divide the spoils of the people could establish the notion that Schismatics might be ousted of their possessions and destroyed.[1]

JESUS AND ISRAEL

Jefferson's attention was limited to Judaeo-Christian history. The earliest of the examples of religious intolerance, which he discussed frequently, was the relationship of Jesus to the Jews. The nation of ancient Israel, according to Jefferson, worshiped an unjust, vindictive God through meaningless ceremonies and mummeries lacking social utility or incentive to virtue, but calculated rather to produce hostility between that nation and all others. Jesus attempted to reform this "vicious deism" by giving the Jews "juster" notions of God. "Jesus, taking for His type the best qualities of the human head and heart, wisdom, justice, goodness, and adding to them power, ascribed all of these, but in infinite perfection, to the Supreme Being, and formed Him really worthy of their adoration."[2] Jesus exposed the futility of Jewish ceremonials. He taught the most sublime of all moral codes, inculcating philanthropy, universal charity, and benevolence. He also taught explicitly that there would be a future life of rewards and punishments, and thereby gave men a powerful incentive to goodness.

Jefferson's concept of Jesus was almost that of an Enlightenment philosophe presenting a nonsectarian, nonspeculative, moral view of God.[3] The God of Jesus was to be imitated, not defined or metaphysically explored.[4] But the priests of the Jews, bloodthirsty, cruel, and remorseless like their own vindictive Jehovah, would have none of this.

1. Chinard, *Commonplace Book*, p. 383.
2. To William Short, Aug. 4, 1820 (LB, *15*, 260).
3. See Boorstin, *Lost World*, p. 159.
4. To Ezra Styles, June 25, 1819 (LB, *15*, 203–04).

They constantly laid snares to entangle Jesus in the web of the law. Despite his strenuous efforts to avoid their traps, they very quickly caught him and, thanks to their alliance with the state, were able to destroy him:

> According to the ordinary fate of those who attempt to enlighten and reform mankind, he fell an early victim to the jealousy & combination of the altar and the throne, at about 33. years of age, his reason having not yet attained the *maximum* of its energy, nor the course of his preaching, which was but of 3. years at most, presented occasions for developing a complete system of morals.[5]

As Jefferson saw the matter, the unholy alliance of Jewish church and Roman state had destroyed the world's leading moralist and benevolent reformer.

CHRISTIANITY CORRUPTED

After Jesus' death, his teachings were rapidly corrupted. They were fragmentary to begin with, because Jesus had not time to complete his system. Nor had he committed anything to writing. When his unlettered followers tried to record his life and teachings, they included frequent mutilations and misrepresentations because of lapse of memory or lack of understanding.[6] Worse than this, other "followers" deliberately perverted the record. Jesus' teachings "have been still more disfigured by the corruptions of schismatizing followers, who have found an interest in sophisticating & perverting the simple doctrines he taught, by engrafting on them the mysticisms of a Grecian sophist [Plato], frittering them into subtleties & obscuring them with jargon, until they have caused good men to reject the

---

5. "Syllabus of Doctrines of Jesus" (Ford, *Writings of Jefferson*, 8, 226-27).
6. To John Adams, Oct. 13, 1813 (LB, *13*, 390).

whole in disgust, & to view Jesus himself as an impostor."[7]
Jefferson knew where to fix the blame for this: "Of this
band of dupes and impostors, Paul was the great Coryphae-
us, and the first corruptor of the doctrines of Jesus."[8] To
put Jefferson's analogy in contemporary terms, Paul was the
conductor, the choir director, the one who called the ob-
scurantist tune.

During the first centuries of the Christian era, Jefferson
held, these rogues professing to be the special servants of
Jesus corrupted his doctrines by engrafting upon them the
metaphysical and philosophical opinions of the heathen
world.[9] Having thus perverted his pure and simple moral
doctrines into an engine for enslaving mankind, they con-
tracted an alliance with the civil government to get the
best use out of it.[10] This was the accomplishment of the
Council of Nicaea. The true and rational moral beliefs of
primitive Christianity were ousted "by the sword of civil
government wielded at the will of the fanatic Athanasius."[11] The way was made clear throughout the Middle Ages
in Europe for kings, nobles, and priests, the members of
this unholy alliance, to filch for themselves power, profit,
and pre-eminence. A pattern had been set that was destined
to recur many times.

CHRISTIANITY AND THE COMMON LAW

Jefferson's acceptance of the Whig interpretation of English history and his belief in the "Saxon myth" were basic

7. "Syllabus of Doctrines of Jesus" (Ford, *8*, 227–28).

8. To William Short, April 13, 1820 (LB, *15*, 245). Although "Old Bailey
theology" was not the whole of 18th-century English thought, it was true,
nevertheless, that "the Apostles are being tried once a week for the capital
crime of forgery!" One of the favorite books of the time was Sherlock's *Trial
of the Witnesses.* See Pattison, *Essays and Reviews,* pp. 314, 366.

9. Jefferson read Joseph Priestley's *History of the Corruptions of Christianity* many times. Good discussion in Willey, *Eighteenth Century Background,* pp. 188–93.

10. To Samuel Kercheval, Jan. 19, 1810 (LB, *12*, 345).

11. To James Smith, Dec. 8, 1822 (LB, *15*, 408–09).

to his understanding of the history of church and state in England.[12] Here he saw the development of another conspiratorial alliance. According to the "Saxon myth," the Anglo-Saxons had reached England in the fifth century, bringing with them their common law, containing a code of moderate *humane* penalties for specific criminal acts. It was an unwritten constitution embodying the individual's natural rights. It could be changed only by legislative act. This was a completely pagan institution, Jefferson pointed out, because Christianity did not enter England before the seventh century. Periodically, one of the kings of England would have the common law reduced to writing. Jefferson traced the perversion of the common law to one of these reductions after Christianity's arrival, in which someone "monkishly" prefaced the laws of King Alfred with four chapters of Exodus. Still later, in Jefferson's view, the words *ancien scripture,* meaning the ancient written laws of the church, were falsely interpreted to mean *holy scripture.* Since *ancien scripture* had received its sanction from English common law, the way was open for lawyers and judges to argue for the mistaken notion that *holy scripture,* and therefore Christianity, was part of the common law, although no primary sources were ever quoted. In 1728 the Court *assumed* that Christianity was the law of England, and Blackstone included the notion in his Commentaries without critical reconsideration. But, argued Jefferson, no part of Holy Scripture or Christianity had ever actually been made part of the English common law in the only legitimate way, by legislative act.[13] This, said Jefferson, was a sample "of the pious disposition of the English judges, to connive at the frauds of the clergy, a disposition of which has often rendered them faithful allies in practice."[14] The

12. See Appendix.
13. See "Whether Christianity is Part of the Common Law" (Ford, *1,* 360–67).
14. To Thomas Cooper, Feb. 10, 1814 (Ford, *1,* 360–61 n.).

judges had perverted the common law (which had never been concerned with opinion) into an engine for the extirpation of heresy, blasphemy, profaneness, and other purely religious offences:

> In truth, the alliance between church and state in England, has ever made their judges accomplices in the frauds of the clergy; and even bolder than they are . . . And thus they incorporate into the English code, laws made for the Jews alone, and the precepts of the gospel, intended by their benevolent author as obligatory only *in foro conscientiae;* and they arm the whole with the coercions of municipal law.[15]

THE REFORMATION

The history of the Reformation provided Jefferson with another example of the baneful effects of the alliance of church and state. This movement, initially just an attempt to purge Rome of her centuries-old abuses, rapidly degenerated and became responsible for crimes as heinous as any laid at Rome's door. To Jefferson the arch-villains of the Reformation were John Calvin and his myrmidons, the Presbyterians. Jefferson speaks with horror of "the flames in which their oracle Calvin consumed the poor Servetus, because he could not find in his Euclid the proposition which has demonstrated that three are one and one is three, nor subscribe to that of Calvin, that magistrates have a right to exterminate all heretics to Calvinistic Creed." Jefferson charged that his contemporary Calvinists would love to continue the oppression and persecution: "The Presbyterian clergy are the loudest; the most intolerant of all sects, the most tyrannical and ambitious; ready at the word of the lawgiver, if such a word could now be obtained, to put the torch to the pile . . . They pant to re-establish, *by law,* that

15. "Whether Christianity is Part of the Common Law" (Ford, *1,* 367).

holy inquisition, which they can now only infuse into *public opinion.*"[16]

THE COLONY OF VIRGINIA

The history of religions in the colony of Virgina also presented examples of civil persecution for unorthodox opinion. The Church of England had always been established in the colony:

> The first settlers of this colony were Englishmen, loyal subjects to their king and church, and the grant to Sr. Walter Raleigh contained an express Proviso that their laws "should not be against the true Christian faith, now professed in the church of England." As soon as the state of the colony admitted, it was divided into parishes, in each of which was established a minister of the Anglican church, endowed with a fixed salary ...a glebe house, and land.... To meet these expenses all the inhabitants of the churches were taxed whether they were or not, members of the established church.[17]

Evidently this establishment remained secure even during the interregnum. The colony at first showed resistance to Cromwell's government, but in 1651 accepted its jurisdiction and authority after having secured a covenant guaranteeing certain civil rights. Among these was a stipulation that the Book of Common Prayer would continue to be used for at least a year as the basis of worship, and that parish ministers would continue to receive their customary support wherever the majority desired.[18]

After the Restoration, establishment in Virginia was le-

16. To William Short, April 13, 1820 (LB, *15*, 246).
17. *Autobiography* (Ford, *1*, 52).
18. See *Notes on Virginia,* Query 13 (Ford, *3*, 218–19). There is an implication here, however (which Jefferson does not spell out) that in this semi-Erastian agreement lies a germ of a tradition of freedom of worship in Virginia.

gally as cruel and abusive as any example of it in New England or on the Continent. The Quakers were the objects of particularly vicious laws and penalties, but other sects were likewise oppressed: "If no execution took place here, as did in New England, it was not owing to the moderation of the church, or the spirit of the legislature, as may be inferred from the law itself; but to historical circumstances which have not been handed down to us."[19]

For a while the Anglicans retained full religious possession of the colony. Monopoly destroyed the ministers' incentive to become effective pastors: "The established clergy, secure for life in their glebes and salaries, adding to these generally the emoluments of a classical school, found employment enough, in their farms and schoolrooms for the rest of the week and devoted Sunday only to the edification of their flock. . . . Their other pastoral functions were little attended to."[20] As a result, when zealous and industrious preachers of other sects came into the field later, they found it wide open and undisputed:

> Other opinions began to creep in, and the great care of the government to support their own church, having begotten an equal degree of indolence in its clergy, two-thirds of the people had become dissenters at the commencement of the . . . revolution. The laws, indeed, were still oppressive on them, but the spirit of one party had subsided into moderation, and the other had risen to a degree of determination which commanded respect.[21]

Jefferson was personally acquainted with the deleterious effect establishment had upon the competence and industry

---

19. *Notes on Virginia*, Query 17 (Ford, *3*, 261–62). Albert J. Nock lists additional examples of legal cruelty in colonial Virginia in *Jefferson* (New York, Harcourt, Brace, 1926), pp. 6–7.

20. *Autobiography* (Ford, *1*, 52–53).

21. *Notes on Virginia*, Query 17 (Ford, *3*, 262).

of the clergy. Security made the ministers drones and worse. He had been counsel in the case of the insufferably crude and profligate Patrick Lunan, who "cared not of what religion he was so he got the tobacco, nor what became of the flock so that he could get the fleece."[22] Jefferson also knew men of merit, such as James Ogilvie, who were hindered by the duplicity of Episcopal bureaucrats from entering a ministry which could only benefit from their presence.[23]

NEW ENGLAND

The history of religions in New England presented no better picture. In Connecticut and Massachusets, where the church was established, the record was cruelty and oppression. It differed in one way from Virginia. The salaries of the clergy were not fixed by law in New England, and ministers could be dismissed from their pulpits. As a result, they were apparently a good deal more zealous in the prosecution of their pastoral duties. Behind this, however, Jefferson saw only an attempt to mold the minds of the people to guarantee the continuance of clerical privileges deriving from the alliance of church and state. Witness that peculiar New England phenomenon of elective offices seeming to be the hereditary possession of a few leading families:

> it has proceeded from . . . strict alliance of Church and State. These families are canonised in the eyes of the people on common principles, "you tickle me, and I will tickle you." In Virginia we have nothing of this. Our clergy, before the revolution, having been secured

22. Report of Cases in the General Court, Oct. 1771 (Ford, *1, 400 n.*).

23. For the case of James Ogilvie, Jefferson's correspondence in Boyd, *Papers of Jefferson,* Vol. I, gives almost the complete story. See letter from James Ogilvie, March 28, 1770, p. 38; to Thomas Adams, July 11, 1770, p. 48; to Peyton Randolph, July 23, 1770, p. 49; to Thomas Adams, Feb. 20, 1771, p. 61; to James Ogilvie, Feb. 20, 1771, p. 62; from James Ogilvie, April 26, 1771, p. 71.

against rivalship by fixed salaries, did not give themselves the trouble of acquiring influence over the people.[24]

JEFFERSON'S CONCLUSION

This view of history was part of Jefferson's thought when he wrote the Bill for Establishing Religious Freedom. The case was conclusive: the alliance of church and state was an unmitigated evil. Whenever the state had enforced belief in any one doctrine, it had always destroyed true religion: "The impious presumption of legislators and rulers, civil as well as ecclesiastical . . . hath established and maintained false religions over the greatest part of the world and through all time." Whenever the church looked to the state for support, it inevitably became a parasite on the people. "Even forcing [a man] to support this or that teacher of his own religious persuasion . . . is withdrawing from the ministry those temporal rewards, which proceeding from an approbation of their personal conduct, are an additional incitement to earnest and unremitting labors for the instruction of mankind."[25]

Despite the claims of those who advocate establishment, no improvements in the morals of society have ever been shown to take place: "All attempts to influence [the mind] by temporal punishments, or burthens, or by civil incapacitations, tend only to beget habits of hypocrisy and meanness . . . [and] to corrupt the principles of that very religion [they are] meant to encourage, by bribing, with a monopoly of worldly honors and emoluments, those who will externally profess and conform."[26] The result was corruption of both government and religion, the death of progress, the stifling of truth. And all for the purpose of attaining uni-

24. To John Adams, Oct. 28, 1813 (Ford, 9, 426).
25. Bill for Establishing Religious Freedom (Boyd, 2, 545).
26. Ibid., pp. 545–46.

formity of opinion, which by nature is neither possible nor desirable.[27]

The only condition in which true religion could thrive, held Jefferson, was absolute freedom of conscience. This included not only the right of people to "be free to profess, and by argument to maintain, their opinions in matters of religion," but also their right to refuse to answer any questions concerning religious beliefs, and the right not to be questioned at all: "I never will, by any word or act, bow to the shrine of intolerance, or admit a right of inquiry into the religious opinions of others."[28]

> I am moreover averse to the communication of my religious tenets to the public; because it would countenance the presumption of those who have endeavored to draw them before the tribunal, and to seduce public opinion to erect itself into that inquisition over the rights of conscience, which the laws have so justly proscribed. It behoves every man who values liberty of conscience for himself, to resist invasions of it in the case of others; or their case may, by change of circumstances, become his own. It behoves him, too, in his own case, to give no example of concession, betraying the common right of independent opinion, by answering questions of faith, which the laws have left between God & himself.[29]

To limit the mind in any way was "a departure from the plan of the Holy Author of our religion, who being Lord both of body and mind, yet chose not to propagate it by coercion on either, as was in his Almighty power to do."[30] Reason and free enquiry were the natural enemies of error

27. See *Notes on Virginia* (Ford, *3*, 264–65).
28. To Edward Dowse, April 19, 1803 (LB, *10*, 378).
29. To Benjamin Rush, April 21, 1803 (Ford, *8*, 224 n.).
30. Bill for Establishing Religious Freedom (Boyd, *2*, 545).

only, and truth would always receive willing assent and support in a society of truly free men.

Furthermore, human progress also depended on freedom of thought. Science was constantly being hamstrung in states where the government defended the faith. A people could progress only when their government refused to become involved in religious matters:

> Galileo was sent to the inquisition for affirming that the earth was a sphere; the government had declared it to be as flat as a trencher, and Galileo was obliged to abjure his error. This error however at length prevailed, the earth became a globe, and Descartes declared it was whirled round its axis by a vortex. The government in which he lived was wise enough to see that this was no question of civil jurisdiction, or we should all have been involved by authority in vortices. In fact the vortices have been exploded, and the Newtonian principle of gravitation is now more firmly established, on the basis of reason, than it would be were the government to step in and to make it an article of necessary faith. Reason and experiment have been indulged, and error has fled before them.[31]

Establishing Religious Freedom

Jefferson's views on religious freedom, like his views on religion and on government, remained relatively stable throughout his life. Just as all of Jefferson's subsequent political writings are in a sense commentary upon the Declaration of Independence, so all of his subsequent writings on the problem of religious liberty are commentary upon the Bill for Establishing Religious Freedom. Jefferson worked consistently to make liberty of conscience an explicit rule wherever he could work it legitimately into his gov-

31. *Notes on Virginia*, Query 17 (Ford, *3*, 264).

ernmental and political activities. It was his custom, for instance, when drafting a treaty between the United States and any foreign power, to include a clause protecting the religious freedom of the citizens of either party when in the territory of the other.[32] In his efforts to have a bill of rights added to the Constitution he invariably listed freedom of religion as one of the essentials.[33] He considered the passing of the First Amendment as great news, but could not rest satisfied as long as states such as Connecticut and Massachusetts did not have what he considered to be complete freedom of religion.

If Jefferson's views concerning the necessity of religious freedom for all people remained consistent, his practice in attempting to implement these beliefs about freedom of conscience is, by contrast, startlingly varied. Obviously the first step in regaining religious liberty in any nation in Jefferson's time was to end the unholy alliance between church and state. That alliance had always caused religious persecution. It had to go. This usually meant the disestablishment of a particular church, but it did not rest there. As the provisions of the Virginia Statute for Religious Freedom show, Jefferson intended all forms of church establishment, both single and multiple, to be ruled out. The only permissible form of establishment was to be the establishment of religious freedom.

Jefferson believed that the religion clause of the first amendment to the Constitution affirmed for the federal government what the Statute for Religious Freedom proclaimed for Virginia, that no religion was to be the established belief or practice of the state. He wanted the American people to know that this was the meaning he attached to that clause. When an opportunity came to make them

32. E.g. see the draft of a treaty to be proposed to London and Versailles, enclosed in a letter of July 28, 1785, to John Adams (Boyd, *8*, 319); and elsewhere.

33. E.g. letter to James Madison, Dec. 20, 1787 (Boyd, *12*, 440).

aware of how he interpreted the First Amendment, he
seized it and used it in deadly earnestness.

"THE WALL OF SEPARATION"

The document in which Jefferson went on record was the
Reply to the Danbury Baptists. Its brevity should not lead
anyone to underestimate the deliberateness with which he
composed and sent it.[34] At the beginning of his second year
in the Presidency, he was asked by the Danbury Baptist
Association in Connecticut to designate a day of fasting
in connection with the nation's past ordeals.[35] Jefferson
wrote a reply, but decided to check first with the Attorney
General, Levi Lincoln, to whom he sent it enclosed with
this note:

> Averse to receive addresses, yet unable to prevent them,
> I have generally endeavored to turn them to some ac-
> count, by making them the occasion, by way of answer,
> of sowing useful truths & principles among the people,
> which might germinate and become rooted among
> their political tenets. The Baptist address, now en-
> closed, admits to a condemnation of the alliance of
> Church and State, under the authority of the Constitu-
> tion. It furnishes an occasion, too, which I have long
> wished to find, of saying why I do not proclaim fastings
> & thanksgivings, as my predecessors did.
>
> The address, to be sure, does not point at this, & it's
> introduction is awkward. But I foresee no opportunity
> of doing it more pertinently. I know it will give great
> offence to the New England clergy; but the advocate of

34. O'Neill tried to minimize its importance by repeatedly calling it "a
little letter of courtesy" or a "little address of courtesy" (*Religion and Education*, pp. 78–86).

35. See Norman Cousins, ed., *In God We Trust* (New York, 1958), p. 134;
Schachner, *Jefferson*, 2, 701. But cf. O'Neill, pp. 80–81: "a reply which Jefferson made as President . . . to an address of congratulations and good
wishes."

religious freedom is to expect neither peace nor for-
giveness from them. Will you be so good as to examine
the answer, and suggest any alterations which might
prevent an ill effect, or promote a good one among the
people? You understand the temper of those in the
North, and can weaken it, therefore, to their stomachs:
it is at present seasoned to the Southern taste only. I
would ask the favor of you to return it, with the address, in the course of the day or evening. Health &
affection.[36]

Levi Lincoln was not only Attorney General but also a
Massachusetts Republican, whose advice was therefore not
to be dismissed lightly. He was against sending the reply,
which he felt would probably offend not only Federalists
and clergy but also Republicans in New England.[37] Jefferson sent the document, neverthelesss:

Gentlemen.—The affectionate sentiments of esteem
and approbation which you are so good as to express
towards me, on behalf of the Danbury Baptist Association, give me the highest satisfaction. My duties dictate
a faithful and zealous pursuit of the interests of my
constituents, and in proportion as they are persuaded
of my fidelity to those duties, the discharge of them
becomes more and more pleasing.

Believing with you that religion is a matter which
lies solely between man and his God, that he owes account to none other for his faith or his worship, that
the legislative powers of government reach actions
only, and not opinions, I contemplate with sovereign
reverence that act of the whole American people which
declared that their legislature should "make no law respecting an establishment of religion, or prohibiting
the free exercise thereof," thus building a wall of sepa-

36. Jan. 1, 1802 (Ford, 8, 129).
37. See Schachner, 2, 701.

ration between Church and State. Adhering to this expression of the supreme will of the nation on behalf of the rights of conscience, I shall see with sincere satisfaction the progress of those sentiments which tend to restore to man all his natural rights, convinced he has no natural right in opposition to his social duties.

I reciprocate your kind prayers for the protection and blessing of the common Father and Creator of man, and tender you for yourselves and your religious association, assurance of my high respect and esteem.[38]

This was the origin of the phrase "wall of separation between church and state." It took root among the political tenets of the American people, just as Jefferson intended, and has become a rallying cry whenever American citizens have felt their right to freedom of belief to be encroached upon by the government. To many it has become equated with the religion clause of the First Amendment. Jefferson's use of the phrase to interpret that clause in the Reply would seem to indicate that he, too, made the same equation. The religion clause is too important, however, and the phrase "wall of separation" has proved too powerful in subsequent discussion, for us to be satisfied with what Jefferson *would seem* to indicate. Let us try to find out what he *did* mean by this phrase.

SEPARATION IN THEORY

To begin with, the phrase "wall of separation between Church and State" is a metaphor. We have already seen, when we were considering Jefferson's concept of the Constitution,[39] that he used metaphor to communicate his concept of an ideal relationship about which his thought remained consistent throughout his political career. Yet his specific recommendations and practice sometimes varied

38. To the Danbury Baptist Association, Jan. 1, 1802 (LB, *16*, 281–82).
39. See above, pp. 76–78.

to the point of apparent inconsistency. No particular form of organization of government was permanently invulnerable to the dangers of corruption or tyranny. No unvarying formula could be found for the proper specific relations between the nation and its members. Jefferson did his best, rather, to guard against whatever specific dangers he perceived.

The same pattern holds for his thought on the proper relationships of church and state in a democracy. These institutions were not to be allied but separated in any nation where the citizens were to have freedom of conscience. In this view Jefferson remained utterly consistent, and "the wall of separation" expresses his lifelong view of the ideal relationship. In the specific practices by which he attempted to implement this policy, however, he shows great variety. Superficially, his actions over a period of years appeared at times to show many inconsistencies because his practices concerning this, like those concerning free government, were not doctrinaire but flexible, adapted to specific situations, reflecting his own astute resourcefulness.

Religious Liberty in Practice

RELIGIOUS HOLIDAYS

A good example of apparent inconsistency is Jefferson's attitude to governmental proclamation of religious holidays. He evidently intended in the Reply to the Danbury Baptists to state "why I do not proclaim fasts and thanksgivings, as my predecessors did."[40] Actually he included no direct allusion to that question, although he did include an emphatic condemnation of the alliance of Church and State. On other occasions, however, he did go on record, and as a result, it is fairly well known even today that Jefferson as President of the United States refused to proclaim

---

40. To the Attorney General, Jan. 1, 1802 (Ford, *8*, 129).

days of fast, thanksgiving, or other religious observance, or even to recommend them as desirable to the nation:

> In matters of religion, I have considered that its free exercise is placed by the constitution independent of the powers of the general government. I have therefore undertaken, on no occasion, to prescribe the religious exercises suited to it; but have left them, as the constitution found them, under the direction or discipline of State or Church authorities acknowledged by the several religious societies.[41]

It is not generally known, however, that his practice was quite different before and during the Revolutionary War. In his account of the Virginia patriots' reaction to news of the closing of the port of Boston, both the nature of his activities and the tone of his discussion may give some readers a jolt:

> We were under conviction of the necessity of arousing our people from the lethargy into which they had fallen as to passing events; and thought that the appointment of a day of general fasting & prayer would be most likely to call up & alarm their attention. . . . With the help therefore of Rushworth, whom we rummaged over for the revolutionary precedents & forms of the Puritans of that day, preserved by him, we cooked up a resolution, somewhat modernizing their phrases, for appointing the 1st day of June, on which the Port bill was to commence, for a day of fasting, humiliation & prayer, to implore heaven to avert from us the evils of civil war, to inspire us with firmness in support of our rights, and to turn the hearts of the King & parliament to moderation & justice. To give greater emphasis to

41. Second Inaugural Address, March 4, 1805 (Ford, *8,* 341). For a fuller statement of Jefferson's position see his letter to Samuel Miller, Jan. 23, 1808 (Ford, *9,* 174–76).

our proposition, we agreed to wait the next morning on Mr. Nicholas, whose grave & religious character was more in unison with the tone of our resolution, and to solicit him to move it.[42]

Jefferson seems proud of having used religion blithely for purely political purposes. Some may object that this wedding of church and state was in 1774, and that in the next two years Jefferson's thinking must have changed radically. Surely, they may hold, when he wrote the Bill for Establishing Religious Freedom, Jefferson must have dropped this practice and stumped for the most rigid separation. But as a matter of fact, he did not. In the Revisal several other bills follow the Bill for Establishing Religious Freedom. Among them are the Bill for Punishing Disturbers of Religious Worship and Sabbath Breakers, and the Bill for Appointing Days of Public Fasting and Thanksgiving.[43] The latter states specifically that the general assembly, and in its absence the governor, has the power and authority to proclaim days of fast and thanksgiving. Jefferson put real teeth into this one: "Every minister of the gospel shall on each day so to be appointed, attend and perform divine service and preach a sermon, or discourse suited to the occasion, in his church, on pain of forfeiting fifty pounds for every failure, not having a reasonable excuse."[44]

THE CLERGY AND PUBLIC OFFICE

Standing together as these bills do in a group dealing with religion and the state, they serve to point up a problem

---

42. *Autobiography* (Ford, *1*, 9–11).

43. See Boyd, *Papers of Jefferson*, 2, 555, 556. Also worth noticing are the Bill for Saving the Property of the Church Heretofore by Law Established (Boyd, 2, 553); the Bill for Prescribing the Oath of Fidelity, and Oaths of Certain Public Officers, and the Bill Permitting Those Who Will Not Take Oaths to be Otherwise Qualified (Boyd, 2, 638).

44. Boyd, 2, 556. But cf. letter to William Short, April 13, 1820 (LB, *15*, 246–47).

we must not forget: if separation of church and state was Jefferson's aim, there is no way of deciding surely from Jefferson's practice just when separation of church and state actually exists. This complete lack of certainty stands fully revealed in his vacillation concerning whether ministers of the gospel should be legally qualified to hold public office. In 1783 Jefferson wrote a draft of a constitution for the state of Virginia which guaranteed freedom of religious opinion in a clause fairly similar to the enacting clause of the Bill for Establishing Religious Freedom.[45] It also said this about the legislature: "Of this General assembly the Treasurer, Attorney General, Register, Ministers of the Gospel . . . [aliens, felons, candidates convicted of election bribery, etc.] shall be incapable of being members." When asked why the clergy were included among others whose exclusion from the legislature could be more easily understood, Jefferson replied that it was a proper use of the principle of separation of church and state:

> The clergy are excluded, because, if admitted into the legislature at all, the probability is that they would form it's majority. For they are dispersed through every county in the state, they have influence with the people, and great opportunities of persuading them to elect them into the legislature. This body, tho shattered, is still formidable, still forms a *corps,* and is still actuated by the *esprit de corps.* The nature of that spirit has been severely felt by mankind, and has filled the history of ten or twelve centuries with too many atrocities not to merit a proscription from meddling with government.[46]

There is no record of whether Jefferson ever noticed that from another point of view this might be a violation of re-

45. See Boyd, *6,* 297–98; LB, 2, 286–87.
46. To François Jean de Chastellux, Sept. 2, 1785 (Boyd, *8,* 470).

RELIGIOUS LIBERTY IN PRACTICE   137

ligious freedom, an attempt to influence the mind "by temporal punishments or burthens, or by civil incapacitations." Madison saw it, however. He attempted to bring it to Jefferson's attention by including in his observations on the draft some penetrating questions:

> Does not the exclusion of Ministers of the Gospel as such violate a fundamental principle of liberty by punishing a religious profession with the privation of a civil right? Does it not violate another article of the plan itself which exempts religion from the cognizance of Civil power? Does it not violate justice by at once taking away a right and prohibiting a compensation for it? And does it not in fine violate impartiality by shutting the door against the Ministers of one religion and leaving it open for those of every other?[47]

No answer by Jefferson is on record, but his later practice implies a shift in position. In 1790 he wrote a letter to the Reverend Charles Clay approving the latter's candidacy for election as United States congressman and wishing him hearty success.[48] Ten years later Jefferson declared that he had changed his mind about this phase of the draft of 1783:

> I observe however in the same scheme of a constitution, an abridgement of the right of being elected, which after 17. years more of experience & reflection, I do not approve. It is the incapacitation of a clergyman from being elected. The clergy, by getting themselves established by law, & ingrafted into the machine of government, have been a very formidable engine in many

47. "Madison's Observations on Jefferson's Draft of a Constitution for Virginia," Oct. 1788 (Boyd, 6, 311).

48. See Ford, 5, 142. Jefferson remarks, incidentally, that he has no idea whom Clay was running against. Two years later he declined to give Clay a public endorsement, although he still urged Clay personally to run; see letter to Charles Clay, Sept. 11, 1792 (Ford, 6, 110–11).

countries & even in some of these United States. Even
in 1783, we doubted the stability of our recent measures for reducing them to the footing of other useful
callings. It now appears that our means were effectual.
The clergy here seem to have relinquished all preten-
sion to privilege and to stand on a footing with lawyers,
physicians &c. They ought, therefore, to possess the
same rights.[49]

This was not Jefferson's final position concerning the right
of ministers to hold elective office. It shifted again, as we
shall see when we consider his work as an educator. Meanwhile, enough of a sample of his practice in this area has
been given to enable us to draw some important conclusions.

SEPARATION'S RELATIONSHIP TO FREEDOM

The principle of separation of church and state is a very
slippery concept. We cannot at all be sure just when it actually exists. This is true because church members are never
simply church members but also members of society. They
are entitled to all the rights possessed by their fellows without respect to their religious affiliation or to the role they
play in their church. Whereas to remove a particular religious organization from a position of direct influence upon
government is to promote freedom of opinion, to prohibit
members of that organization from influencing government
in ways open to all other citizens is religious persecution.
This we must remember, because in America we have tended to believe that the opposite of religious persecution is
"strict separation of church and state."

At this point we should note something about Jefferson.
Constitutional limits were not ideals to him but means to
an end: a government wherein the will of every person has

---

49. To Jeremiah Moore, Aug. 14, 1800 (Ford, 7, 454-55).

a just influence. So, too, the principle of separation of church and state was intended to bring about an end much greater than itself. Jefferson's chief interest was in establishing religious freedom. Separation of church and state was not to be equated with that any more than a particular pattern of government was to be equated with representative democracy. Jefferson approached the ideal of religious freedom pragmatically. His moves grew out of his understanding of the particular situation. He did not attempt to define separation of church and state, and then apply it politically. Rather, he tried to develop the best device available to insure freedom for all under whatever circumstances obtained. If he felt that a particular group was conspiring against the freedom of opinion of the individuals in his society, then he found it justifiable to deprive such a group of the privilege of serving in public office. When they ceased to have such ambitions, he felt that they should be allowed to exercise all their natural rights. The principle of separation could be relaxed here because freedom of religious opinion for all was not threatened.

The device was to be used only when it served to promote religious freedom, and not otherwise. This must be kept in mind, because not only is the principle of separation in itself no guarantee of religious freedom, but too rigid an application of the principle may even become religious persecution. We would do well, therefore, not to forget that the man who first used the words "wall of separation between church and state" also declared, "I have sworn upon the altar of God, eternal hostility against every form of tyranny over the mind of man."[50]

Jefferson clearly saw that the church, although separated from the state, could still wed other powers, such as public opinion, to produce an oppression as evil as any.[51] There

50. To Benjamin Rush, Sept. 23, 1800 (Ford, 7, 461).
51. To Benjamin Rush, April 21, 1803 (Ford, 8, 224 n.); to William Short, April 13, 1820 (LB, 15, 246).

was also the possibility that separation of church and state might be interpreted to provide for the persecution of those who have religious beliefs by those who claim they have none. In the light of both these possibilities more attention should be paid to the Bill for Punishing Disturbers of Religious Worship and Sabbath Breakers, which, as we have seen, comes second after the Bill for Establishing Religious Freedom. This is not just a blue law but a positive recognition of government's responsibility to protect freedom of worship. It provides that services of divine worship shall not be subject to interference from public officials or private citizens. In other words, the government shall not attack citizens in the peaceful expression of their religious beliefs, nor permit others to do so. Similar laws today have been criticized as violations of the principle of separation. If they are, this only proves that Jefferson's ultimate aim was not separation of church and state but the fullest possible freedom of religious belief and opinion.

The device was important, but it was not foolproof. Like every other device Jefferson tried to develop in order to safeguard free government and free men, it had to be applied zealously and intelligently by those whom it was designed to protect, if it was to achieve its purpose. It could only be made effective by a people who had tasted freedom and were able to maintain it through vigilant, distrustful superintendence of their officials. Jefferson knew that the American people had tasted freedom. He had faith that they would never willingly return to despotism. But he also knew that their jealousy and vigilance could never be left to chance. They had to be trained in the art of self-government, all of them. They had to be taught to discern the signs of the times and to act together in intelligent response to their needs. For this task there was only one answer, a system of public education designed to develop in each man his fullest intellectual power.

CHAPTER 7

*E*ducation in General

To understand fully the role Jefferson felt education must play in the preservation of a democracy, we must first come to know something of his philosophy of education apart from its political and governmental uses. We must do this because, as we shall see, to Jefferson democratic public education is not qualitatively distinct from any other education, but is rather education brought into important public service.[1] Leaving the problem of safeguarding freedom and

1. The treatment of Jefferson's philosophy of education per se seems to have been skipped. The typical approach has been to delve immediately into his whole plan for public education. See, e.g., C. F. Arrowood, *Thomas Jefferson and Education in a Republic*, New York, 1930; R. J. Honeywell, *The Educational Work of Thomas Jefferson*, Cambridge, Mass., 1931; and K. Lehmann, *Thomas Jefferson, American Humanist* (New York, 1947), chap. 12. Bowers, Chinard, Kimball, and other biographers also use this tack. That this may lead to confusion should be obvious. Certainly some of the misconceptions concerning the role of religion in public education stem from a lack of consideration of Jefferson's thought concerning education itself.

A good treatment of the sources—both established and highly probable—of Jefferson's educational ideas can be found in Arrowood, pp. 33–58, 63–64, 73–75.

natural rights to one side, then, what did Jefferson believe to be the proper aim and method of education? What kind of man should education produce? How was this ideal to be approached?

Jefferson's Aim

EDUCATION IN VIRGINIA COLONY

Good education was one of Jefferson's lifelong concerns. His letters show that he was often asked to give specific advice concerning the education of a number of young people. The demand for his services along this line was due partly to his obvious qualifications and willingness to give of his time and thought, and partly also to the haphazard state of education in colonial and post-Revolutionary Virginia. The church schools were usually inadequately supervised; their teachers were licensed by the Bishop of London or the Governor of Virginia, often with little regard to academic qualifications. A few grammar schools and private tutors offered meager and often temporary opportunity to those who could afford it of learning Latin and a few other subjects. William and Mary College was limited in both faculty and curriculum. Virtually no coordination existed between elementary schools and grammar schools, or between grammar schools and the college. The elementary schools did not prepare for the grammar schools, nor did grammar schools do as well preparing for the college as did the private tutors. Graduates of the college were not prepared for a profession (except that of minister in the Church of England), nor for learning a profession, nor for their likely career of Virginia planter. There was neither graduate school nor university.[2]

JEFFERSON AS MENTOR

This haphazard "system" of education was the best available in colonial Virginia, and even that was beyond the

2. See Honeywell, *Educational Work*, pp. 9–10.

reach of any but the well-to-do. Nor had the situation greatly improved by the time Jefferson retired from the Presidency of the United States. To make up for these deplorable
conditions, Jefferson throughout his adult life made it a
practice to take young people under his wing and give them
specific and detailed advice on how to educate themselves
properly. Whenever he could provide such supervision personally, he would,[3] but when distance made this impossible
he would nevertheless write long letters either to them or
to their parents, discussing aims, comparing the merits of
different educational centers, recommending professors,
listing books to read, outlining schedules to be followed by
the day and by the year. A number of these survived.[4]
There are also many letters he wrote to his daughters,
Martha and Maria. The insight they provide shows Jefferson's fundamental philosophy of education to be clear and
consistent.

EDUCATIONAL VALUES

Men. In these letters Jefferson repeatedly emphasizes
three important values to be achieved through education:

3. To Thaddeus Kosciusko, Feb. 26, 1810 (LB, *12*, 369–70).

4. They include: one to Bernard Moore (undated, Ford, *Writings of
Jefferson*, *9*, 480–85 n.); one to John Banister, Jr. (Oct. 15, 1785, Boyd, *Pa-
pers of Jefferson*, *8*, 536); three to Peter Carr (Aug. 19, 1785, LB, *5*, 82–87;
Aug. 10, 1787, LB, *6*, 256–62; and May 28, 1788, *LB*, *7*, 43); one to John
Wayles Eppes (July 28, 1787, LB, *6*, 190); two to Thomas Mann Randolph,
Jr. (July 6, 1787, LB, *6*, 165–68, and May 30, 1790, LB, *8*, 31–32); two to
John Garland Jefferson (June 11, 1790, Ford, *5*, 179, and April 14, 1793, LB,
19, 103–05); one to Ralph Izard (July 17, 1788, LB, *7*, 70–73); and one to
John Minor (Aug. 30, 1814, Ford, *9*, 480). To these should be added Jeffer-
son's letter to John Brazier (Aug. 24, 1819, LB, *15*, 207–11), which differs
from the others in that it is not personal advice but discussion between
two authorities.

   An excellent discussion of this aspect of Jefferson's life is provided by
Marie Kimball, in *Jefferson: The Scene in Europe* (New York, Coward-Mc-
Cann, 1950), pp. 253–60. Mrs. Kimball correctly included Jefferson's instructions to young Americans traveling in Europe as part of his advice on education.

morality, health, and knowledge. He places unmistakable stress upon the cultivation of virtue, the strengthening of the moral sense, and the repetition of right moral choices until they become absolutely habitual: "The defect of these virtues can never be made up by all the other acquirements of body and mind. Make these, then, your first object. Give up money, give up fame, give up science, give up the earth itself and all it contains, rather than do an immoral act."[5] He insists on the importance of health, and extols early rising and retiring, clean living, and regular daily exercise: "The time necessary to secure [health] by active exercise, should be devoted to it in preference to every other pursuit. I know the difficulty with which a studious man tears himself from his studies, at any given moment of the day. But his happiness, and that of his family, depend on it. The most uninformed mind, with a healthy body, is happier than the wisest valetudinarian."[6]

Finally, most of every letter is naturally devoted to the subjects to be studied, the books to be used as texts, and the relative amounts of time to be spent in each field. Vocational and general utility form the standards which determine these matters. To Jefferson the worth of knowledge is that it makes the individual useful to himself and his society:

> I can assure you that the possession of [knowledge] is, what (next to an honest heart) will above all things render you dear to your friends, and give you fame and promotion in your own country. When your mind shall be well improved with science, nothing will be necessary to place you in the highest points of view, but to pursue the interests of your country, the interests of your friends, and your own interests also, with the purest integrity, the most chaste honor.[7]

5. To Peter Carr, Aug. 19, 1785 (LB, 5, 83).
6. To Thomas Mann Randolph, Jr., July 6, 1787 (LB, 6, 168).
7. To Peter Carr, Aug. 19, 1785 (LB, 5, 82–83).

Jefferson's aim in education is already clear. The properly educated man was to be moral, healthy, and above all useful, capable of understanding the interests of his neighbors, his countrymen, and himself, and of working for their development. Education could advance individuals to happiness "by improvements in their minds, their morals, their health, and in those conveniences which contribute to the comfort and embellishment of life."[8] From education, society should receive its leaders, politicians, lawyers, physicians, or engineers. But no matter how extended their training, these professionals should also be able to solve their own personal problems and by no means be ignorant and helpless as to the common necessities of life. The properly educated American should be equal to any task, from leading his country in time of war to adjusting a broken saddle girth.[9]

Women. At no point does the utilitarianism of Jefferson's philosophy of education and this goal of the practical person ready for any contingency stand out more clearly than in the letters concerning education for women. We must not be misled by Jefferson's remark: "a plan for female education has never been a subject of systematic contemplation with me. It has occupied my attention so far only as the education of my own daughters occasionally required."[10] This does not mean that he gave little thought to the matter, but rather that he had not written out systematic plans of education for girls, as he had so often for young men and for his country.[11] Still, he had decided ideas about the kind of

8. To David Williams, Nov. 14, 1803 (L.B, *10, 428*).
9. See Boyd, *8, 412* n.
10. To Nathaniel Burwell, March 14, 1818 (Ford, *10, 104*).
11. Jefferson is seriously misinterpreted by Nock, who says, "Woman's duty being so incomplex, and the grasp of it needing so little brains, the education of women was correspondingly simple; so simple, indeed, that one would not think much about it" (*Jefferson,* p. 97). Jefferson's statement that "female education has never been the subject of systematic contemplation" does not mean that he did "not think much about it," nor does Jefferson's statement, "It has occupied my attention so far only as the education of my daughters occasionally required," mean that he was perfunctory about it.

training that was suitable for women. The vocations of men were not open to them. They could not be expected to become physicians, lawyers, or politicians. They were not even to concern themselves with political problems.[12]

But this did not mean that women had no vocation. Indeed, the *American* woman had not one but two, and the education she received might determine her success or failure at either. First, she had to be housewife and mother. This was so obvious that Jefferson felt no need to discuss it in detail:

> I need say nothing of household economy, in which the mothers of our country are generally skilled, and generally careful to instruct their daughters. We all know its value, and that diligence and dexterity in all its processes are inestimable treasures. The order and economy of a house are as honorable to the mistress as those of the farm to the master, and if either be neglected, ruin follows, and children destitute of the means of living.[13]

Jefferson took great care to foster in his daughters diligence and dexterity in all the processes of household economy. He repeatedly asked Martha and Maria how well they were doing: "Tell me . . . how many hours a day you sew? . . . whether you know how to make a pudding yet, to cut out a beefsteak, to sow spinach? or to set a hen?"[14]

In addition to this, however, the American woman had to be prepared to take up another equally demanding vocation, that of a competent educator. Concerning his daughters, Jefferson remarked: "Considering that they would be placed in a country situation, where little aid could be obtained from abroad, I thought it essential to give them a

12. To Angelica Schuyler Church, Sept. 21, 1788 (Boyd, *13*, 623).
13. To Nathaniel Burwell, March 14, 1818 (Ford, *10*, 104–05).
14. To Maria Jefferson, April 11, 1790, quoted in Henry S. Randall, *Life of Thomas Jefferson, 1* (New York, 1858), 622.

solid education, which might enable them, when become mothers, to educate their own daughters, and even to direct the course for their sons, should their fathers be lost, or incapable, or inattentive."[15] A moment's thought will show that this aim makes the education of women just as complex a problem as that of men. Woman did not need man's preparation for professions such as law, medicine, or science, but she did need an intelligent grasp of the subjects upon which such preparation was based. The fact that his daughters might have both to instruct their sons and to supervise their educations accounts for Jefferson's inclusion of subjects far removed from domestic economy, such as drawing, "a qualification not to be neglected in one who is to become a mother and an instructor," and French, "the general intercourse of nations . . . the depository of all science . . . an indispensable part of education for both sexes."

This also accounts for the fact that in letters concerning the education of Jefferson's daughters we find all of the elements which are present in his advice to young men. There is a clearly articulated goal or aim for them, which he believed suitable for any American woman of the time. The themes of morality, health, and practical knowledge are all stressed. In addition, Jefferson constantly urged them to develop the "American" virtues of industry, resolution, independence, and ingenuity:

> It is your future happiness which interests me, and nothing can contribute more to it (moral rectitude always excepted) than the contracting a habit of industry and activity. . . . Idleness begets ennui, ennui the hypochondria, and that a diseased body. . . . Exercise and application produce order in our affairs, health of body, cheerfulness of mind, and these make us precious to our friends. It is while we are young that the habit of industry is formed. If not then, it never is afterwards.

15. To Nathaniel Burwell, March 14, 1818 (Ford, *10*, 104).

The fortune of our lives, therefore, depends on employing well the short period of youth.

We are always equal to what we undertake with resolution. . . . It is part of the American character to consider nothing as desperate—to surmount every difficulty by resolution and contrivance. . . . Remote from all other aid, we are obliged to invent and execute; to find means within ourselves, and not to lean on others. Consider, therefore, the conquering your Livy as an exercise in the habit of surmounting difficulties; a habit which will be necessary to you in the country where you are to live, and without which you will be thought a very helpless animal, and less esteemed.

My expectations from you are high—yet not higher than you may attain. Industry and resolution are all that are wanting. . . . But great exertions are necessary, and you have little time left to make them. Be industrious, then, my dear child. Think nothing unsurmountable by resolution and application and you will be all that I wish you to be.[16]

Basically, then, Jefferson's aim in education for both men and women was the same (an aim that has become for many people an American ideal), the moral, healthy, capable man or woman, both independent and cooperative, whose success and worth can be attributed to personal industry and practical resourcefulness.

Curriculum

THE EDUCATIONAL LADDER

This being the goal, how was it to be reached? Implicit in these letters is a four-step educational ladder, which becomes explicit in the several plans Jefferson proposed for public education. In private education the outlines of the

16. To Martha Jefferson, March 28, 1787 (Ford, *4*, 371–74).

ladder are blurred, because his advice is tailor-made to suit each individual's particular case. For example, if lost time had to be made up, subjects normally separated would be studied together, and two steps would then overlap. Again, Jefferson might at one time lay out a program of studies for several years ahead, and thus cover two phases in one letter.[17] The lack of any real system of education in Virginia at the time tended to make unique the case of each student Jefferson advised.

For all of this, the phases are fairly clear cut. The first is elementary or primary schooling. The objects of primary education were:

> To give every [pupil] the information he needs for the transaction of his own business;
> To enable him to calculate for himself, and to express and preserve his ideas, his contracts and accounts, in writing;
> To improve, by reading, his morals and faculties;
> To understand his duties to his neighbors and country, and to discharge with competence the functions confided to him, by either . . .
> And, in general, to [teach him to] observe with intelligence and faithfulness all the social relations under which he shall be placed. . . .[18]

In order to have these basic personal attainments, somewhere between the sixth and ninth years, he must learn reading, writing, simple arithmetic, "the first elements of morality," and some geography and history.

The second or grammar-school level would extend from there into the student's fifteenth or sixteenth year. The chief purpose of this stage was to prepare the student for college. Since Jefferson felt that the pupil's memory was

17. To Peter Carr, Aug. 19, 1785 (LB, 5, 82–87); to Thomas Mann Randolph, Jr., July 6, 1787 (LB, 6, 165–68).
18. Rockfish Gap Report (Cabell, *Early History*, p. 434).

at its best during this period, now was the time to emphasize heavily the study of languages, particularly those which would be needed in the third and fourth stages of schooling. Other "tools of learning"—disciplines necessary to do effective work in higher education—would be grammar, geography, history, advanced arithmetic (including subjects such as surveying and navigation), and elementary science. Advanced mathematics and abstruse sciences were to be postponed, as Jefferson felt these were too difficult for students under fifteen years of age.

Higher education comprised the next two steps:

> To develop the reasoning faculties of our youth, enlarge their minds, cultivate their morals, and instill into them the precepts of virtue and order;
>
> To enlighten them with mathematical and physical sciences, which advance the arts, and administer to the health, the subsistence, and the comforts of human life;
>
> And, generally, to form them to the habits of reflection and correct action, rendering them examples of virtue to others, and of happiness within themselves.
>
> These are the objects of that higher grade of education. . . .[19]

The third or collegiate stage occurred in the student's late teens, and was intended to give him a broad grasp of all the sciences, philosophy, and history.[20] This was an essential base for any later professional training.

The fourth phase was postcollegiate or postgraduate studies, usually training for one of the professions, such as law, medicine, or engineering. But from this point on, the educated man who did not want to enter a profession could

19. Ibid., pp. 434–35.
20. To John Wayles Eppes, July 28, 1787 (LB, *6*, 190); to Bernard Moore, undated (Ford, *9*, 480–85 n.).

study fine arts and belles lettres, and also continue to study history, philosophy, and all the sciences, for which a proper foundation had been laid in college:[21]

> The learned class may . . . be subdivided into two sections: 1. Those who are destined for learned professions as a means of livelihood; and, 2. The wealthy, who, possessing independent fortunes, may aspire to share in conducting the affairs of the nation, or to live with usefulness and respect in the private ranks of life. Both of these sections will require instruction in all the higher branches of science; the wealthy to qualify them for either public or private life; the professional section will need those branches, especially, which are the basis of their future profession, and a general knowledge of the others, as auxiliary to that, and necessary to their standing and association with the scientific class.[22]

None of the steps of this educational ladder were mutually exclusive. A student at the secondary level would continue with morality and arithmetic while studying languages. All of these would be continued in the curriculum of the student mastering the sciences in college. Nevertheless, first things first. Jefferson apprehended real danger to the student who tackled certain matters prematurely. He warned his protégés not to attempt to learn the "difficult sciences" until the grammar school stage was completely finished. Even necessary traveling alone should be postponed until the young American student had become thoroughly mature.[23] A subject was to be studied only when it was suited to the maturity of the student.

21. To Thomas Mann Randolph, Jr., July 6, 1787 (LB, 6, 165).
22. To Peter Carr, Sept. 7, 1814 (LB, 19, 214–15).
23. To Peter Carr, Aug. 19, 1785 (LB, 5, 85), and Aug. 10, 1787 (LB, 6, 261–62); to Ralph Izard, July 17, 1788 (LB, 7, 70–73).

SUBJECTS OF STUDY

Standard of practical value. The curriculum was also determined by utilitarian or vocational considerations. Whether a subject was to be admitted or rejected depended upon its practical value. The languages Jefferson favored most were French, because of its value in studying the sciences, and Spanish, because he felt that the United States must inevitably develop close relationships with Latin America.[24] Ancient languages had less value, he felt, although he was still willing to include them, because nothing that starts the human mind going to good purpose must be rejected out of hand.[25] Similarly, with respect to fiction, Jefferson felt that a proper selection of works of imaginative literature would provide good schooling in morality, although there was a risk that trashy novels might pervert taste, imagination, and judgment in the real business of life.[26]

On the basis of utility many subjects are included which at first glance might seem to us to be irrelevant. Every study is evaluated on the basis of whether or not it can be of use to the person for whom Jefferson is planning. The mastery of apparently peripheral subjects can mean the difference between success and failure in one's chosen profession. Thus Jefferson advises the would-be politician:

> I have proposed to you, to carry on the study of law with that of politics and history. Every political measure will, forever, have an intimate connection with the

24. To Thomas Mann Randolph, Jr., July 6, 1787 (LB, *6*, 168); to John Wayles Eppes, July 28, 1787 (LB, *6*, 190); to Nathaniel Burwell, March 14, 1818 (Ford, *10*, 104–06).

25. To John Brazier, Aug. 24, 1819 (LB, *15*, 207).

26. To Robert Skipwith, Aug. 3, 1771 (Boyd, *1*, 176–77); to Nathaniel Burwell, March 14, 1818 (Ford, *10*, 104).

laws of the land; and he who knows nothing of these will always be perplexed, and often foiled by adversaries having the advantage of that knowledge over him. Besides, it is a source of infinite comfort to reflect, that under every chance of fortune, we have a resource in ourselves from which we may derive an honorable subsistence.[27]

Ornament. None of this meant that studies could never be ornamental, or that the individual was to avoid whatever had no immediate function in helping him prepare for his vocation: "I deem luxury in science to be at least as justifiable as in architecture, painting, gardening, or the other arts."[28] This was Jefferson's justification for the study of the classics. When Jefferson's nephew expressed a desire to fix on politics for his career, Jefferson advised him, "Mathematics, Natural Philosophy, Natural History, Anatomy, Chemistry, Botany, will become amusements for your hours of relaxation, and auxiliaries to your principal studies. Precious and delightful ones they will be. As soon as such a foundation is laid in them, as you may build on as you please, thereafter, I suppose you will proceed to your main objects, Politics, Law, Rhetoric, and History."[29] Although he calls them amusements for hours of relaxation, these studies are hardly trivia. They were truly auxiliaries to a politician in a nation facing the task of subduing a continent, and to a man who would undoubtedly spend in agriculture whatever time he did not give over to public service. This is typical of Jefferson. He never suggests a study as an ornament or luxury unless it would be thoroughly practical under some other condition.

27. To Thomas Mann Randolph, Jr., July 6, 1787 (LB, *6*, 166–67). See also letter to John Garland Jefferson, June 11, 1790 (Ford, *5*, 179).
28. To Joseph Priestley, Jan. 27, 1800 (Ford, *7*, 413).
29. To Thomas Mann Randolph, Jr., July 6, 1787 (LB, *6*, 165–66).

Dangers in Education

Whatever its limitations, so much of Jefferson's aim in education seems like common sense that it would be well for us not to forget that in his day he was striving to effect a major reform. Positive miseducation was going on. In one way or another, those who could afford to take advantage of the limited facilities were being corrupted rather than improved in body and mind. Young people were actually being trained into immorality, poor health, and uselessness.

SOCIAL CORRUPTION

The elimination of some types of miseducation depended not on the change of aim or improvement of pedagogical techniques, but required a change in the structure of society. Jefferson nevertheless sounded the warning that situations existed which were leading to serious consequences. In Virginia, for instance, children in most well-to-do families were being subjected to deleterious, unconscious conditioning. This was the effect of the slave-owning parent upon the behavior of his children. In his despotism, "the parent storms, the child looks on, catches the lineaments of wrath, puts on the same airs in the circle of smaller slaves, gives a loose to the worst of passions, and thus nursed, educated, and daily exercised in tyranny, cannot but be stamped by it with odious peculiarities. The man must be a prodigy who can retain his manners and morals undepraved by such circumstances."[30]

Another example of education leading to corruption, completely ruining whatever potentialities men might have for good, was that given to European royalty. Jefferson saw the results of royal education for himself when he met the Prince of Wales.[31] His Highness was an ignorant, coarse,

30. *Notes on Virginia*, Query 18 (Ford, *3*, 266–67).
31. To John Jay, Jan., 1789 (Ford, *5*, 60–63).

profligate boor. His training had made him that. According to the Linnaean biological theories held by Jefferson, royal education over the centuries had produced a human variant pretty well beyond hope of salvation.[32]

EUROPEAN EDUCATION

Other types of miseducation could be avoided, however, if recognized. For instance, with respect to American youth, Jefferson believed that European education on the whole could lead only to corruption. His main objections were two. First, he felt that in Europe men received the "education that made men ignorant and helpless as to the common necessities of life." To illustrate this, Jefferson liked to tell a homely story of a young man, educated in Europe, who was helpless in the face of a saddle girth broken at the buckle, and who had to be told by a "plain country man" that the problem could be solved by loosening the girth one or two notches from the other side. His second objection, an early suspicion later confirmed by personal observations, was that European education could corrupt young Americans morally. Any American visiting Europe before his thirties had better be chaperoned.[33] Jefferson often wrote to friends in America urging them to educate their sons at home, if at all possible. After one particularly long and detailed description of the deplorable results of English and Continental education, he concluded: "It appears to me, then, that an American, coming to Europe for education, loses in his knowledge, in his morals, in his health, in his habits, and in his happiness. I had entertained only doubts on this head before I came to Europe: what I see and hear, since I came here, proves more than I had even suspected.[34]

32. To John Langdon, March 5, 1810 (LB, *12*, 377).
33. See Boyd, *8*, 412 n.
34. To John Banister, Jr., Oct. 15, 1785 (Boyd, *8*, 636). See also letter to Charles Thomson, Nov. 11, 1784 (Ford, *4*, 14–15); to Walker Maury, Aug. 19, 1785 (Boyd, *8*, 409–10); to Ralph Izard, July 17, 1788 (LB, *7*, 70–73).

AMERICAN EDUCATION

But even American education had pitfalls. Jefferson believed dissipation and moral corruption were as possible for American youth in their own cities as in Europe.[35] The fad for premature educational specialization without a broad foundation in all the branches of knowledge had developed in America. He blamed this partly on the folly of a generation that believed it could reject knowledge acquired in past ages and start anew from grounds of intuition. He also attributed it to petty academies starting up all over the United States and offering a deficient curriculum: "They commit their pupils to the theatre of the world, with just taste enough of learning to be alienated from industrious pursuits, and not enough to do service in the ranks of science."[36] This could only result in "Blackstone lawyers, Sangrado physicians, a ranting clergy, & a lounging gentry, who render neither honor nor service to mankind."[37] Jefferson was the absolute foe of the miseducation which brought about these wretched results.[38]

METAPHYSICAL SPECULATION

Perhaps the most dangerous of all the corruptions produced by a perverted education, according to Jefferson, was in the area of metaphysics, the field of speculation on the nature of things immaterial and transcendental. He was a materialist. He accepted the evidence of his senses concerning the existence of matter and the conclusion of his reason that whatever was not matter was *no thing,* or *nothing,* and therefore did not exist. Whenever he felt tempted into scepticism concerning the existence of the material world or of himself, or whenever he was tempted to posit some

35. To William Short, Oct. 31, 1819 (Ford, *10*, 145).

36. To John Adams, July 5, 1814 (Ford, *9*, 464).

37. To W. C. Rives, Sept. 18, 1811 (W. C. Rives Papers, Library of Congress, quoted in Koch, *Jefferson and Madison,* pp. 262–63).

38. Ibid. See also letter to Joseph C. Cabell, Feb. 23, 1824 (Cabell, p. 291).

immaterial existence to explain a phenomenon such as thought, he returned to his "habitual anodyne," as he called it: "I feel, therefore I exist."

> Rejecting all organs of information, therefore, but my senses, I rid my self of the pyrrhonisms [hopeless scepticisms] with which an indulgence in speculations hyperphysical and antiphysical, so uselessly occupy and disquiet the mind. A single sense may indeed be sometimes deceived, but rarely; and never all our senses together, with their faculty of reasoning. They evidence realities, and there are enough of these for all the purposes of life, without plunging into the fathomless abyss of dreams and phantasms. I am satisfied, and sufficiently occupied with the things which are, without tormenting or troubling myself about those things which indeed may be, but of which I have no evidence.[39]

Jefferson took this position for several reasons. For one thing, he found metaphysical speculation and scepticism personally disturbing. Earlier in the letter just quoted he explained that he had recurred to his habitual anodyne, "I feel, therefore I exist," because John Adams' sceptical speculations had literally robbed him of sleep![40] He was uneasy in the presence of uncertainty. This explained his love of mathematics: "We have no uncertainties there, no uncertainties remain on the mind; all is demonstration and satisfaction."[41] Jefferson also objected to metaphysical speculation because he felt it to be antiscientific. Based upon the principle that experience was the source and test of human knowledge, science was utterly materialistic. Research, the method of science, resulted in real knowledge, especially human self-knowledge, on which could be based prediction, control of events, and progress. This was invaluable. "Knol-

39. To John Adams, Aug. 15, 1820 (LB, *15*, 275–76).
40. Ibid., p. 274.
41. To Benjamin Rush, Aug. 17, 1811 (Ford, *9*, 327–28).

ege is power . . . knolege is safety . . . knolege is happiness."[42]

By contrast the metaphysicians, the "spiritualists," and the immaterialists denied that human experience was the source and test of real knowledge, and thereby undercut the foundations of science and all the blessings that could result from research. Belief in the immaterial destroyed progress and substituted instead an opening of all avenues to mysteries, miracles, and incomprehensible "logomachies." The mystification engendered by these made man distrust his own mind just when reason, intelligence, or conscience should have been operating freely.[43]

To Jefferson the mysteries and ambiguities of metaphysical speculations obviously made them potential weapons for designing men against the welfare of the people. Used as weapons in the hands of the Platonists, Athanasians, medieval Scholastics, Calvinists, and such, speculation had resulted in evil enough of this sort. Worse than that, however (and, in fact, most dangerous of all), was the damage that metaphysical speculation could do to reason itself. It could ruin the mind beyond all hope of recovery: "Man, once surrendering his reason, has no remaining guard against absurdities the most monstrous, and like a ship without rudder, is the sport of every wind. With such persons, gullibility which they call faith, takes the helm from the hand of reason, and the mind becomes a wreck."[44] Since the proper purpose of education was to free the man, education which wrecked the mind was obviously worse than none at all.

Any student who speculated on metaphysics was courting disaster, in the eyes of Jefferson. As we have seen, what we would call "theology" he called "religious metaphysics." This being so, let us now explore one aspect of his educational philosophy in detail. What was his concept of the proper or ideal role of religion in education?

42. To George Ticknor, Nov. 15, 1817 (Ford, *10*, 96).
43. See Koch, *Philosophy of Jefferson*, pp. 99–100.
44. To James Smith, Dec. 8, 1822 (LB, *15*, 410).

CHAPTER 8

Religion in Education

Religion and the Aim of Education

To Jefferson the aim of education was to produce moral, healthy individuals whose thorough acquaintance with all useful science made them capable of both independent and cooperative action. The question of whether Jefferson felt that religion had any place in a system of education dedicated to this aim will depend upon his concept of morality, what connection he saw between religion and morality, and how he proposed to have education produce the moral individual.

THE ACCEPTABILITY OF MORALITY

Jefferson perceived an intimate connection between religion and morality. His concept of morality was grounded in his religious belief. He believed that the benevolent

Creator had made man a moral agent in order to promote the happiness of men in society.[1] To Jefferson, then, the essence of religion was the imitation of the benevolence of God. The value of faith or belief lay in the guidance it gave to human behavior. Religion, he insisted, "is more than an inner conviction of the existence of the Creator; true religion is morality. . . . the moral precepts, innate in man, and made part of his physical constitution, as necessary for his social being . . . the sublime doctrines of philanthropism and deism taught us by Jesus of Nazareth, in which we all agree, constitute one religion."[2] On this basis alone he could say that both Trinitarianism and Unitarianism had good in them; they had both made honest men.

The distinction between religion and morality was false. That religion was morality, the response of healthy and reasonable men to needs determined by general interest and social utility, was a view Jefferson held in common with many of his friends.[3] His own short title for *The Life and Morals of Jesus of Nazareth* was *Morals of Jesus*.[4] If an aim of education was to produce moral adults, "true religion" had to be included. The exposition and inculcation of the benevolence of God was essential.

Repeatedly in his letters of advice to young people concerning their education Jefferson emphasized the need for unremitting moral behavior. The virtues of truth and industry were to be diligently exercised.[5] The advice given to his namesakes was invariably religious,[6] a brief summation of his views on the Christian religion resulting from a life of inquiry and reflection. Religion was how man acted, and

1. To Miles King, Sept. 26, 1814 (LB, *14*, 197–98).

2. To John Adams, May 5, 1817 (LB, *15*, 427).

3. To J. P. P. Derieux, July 25, 1788 (Boyd, *Papers of Jefferson*, *13*, 418).

4. See the facsimile reproduction, *Life and Morals of Jesus of Nazareth* (Washington, D.C., 1904), p. vii and binding.

5. To Martha Jefferson, April 7, 1787 (Ford, *Writings of Jefferson*, *4*, 375–76).

6. To Thomas Jefferson Smith, Feb. 21, 1825 (Ford, *10*, 340–41).

education was really a perversion if it did not provide for the development of morality through religion.

THE DANGERS OF DOGMAS

Jefferson was fully aware, on the other hand, that to many people religion included a number of dogmas, doctrines, assertions, and beliefs having no direct connection with morality. Since, in addition, these were not subject to rational or experimental proof, he lumped them together as mysteries, beliefs transcending reason. He could not bring himself to accept these "articles which I never had sense enough to comprehend" for "it has always appeared to me that comprehension must precede assent."[7]

A wrecked mind. Having no direct connection with morality, these dogmas were not essential in education. More than that, they could work positive harm. They were for the most part metaphysical or quasi-metaphysical abstractions. They denied experience as the source and test of human knowledge, and troubled the mind, causing the reason to mistrust the evidence of the senses.[8] This was a positive danger, to be ignored at one's peril, for "Man, once surrendering his reason . . . the mind becomes a wreck."[9] Religious dogmas drove men mad, held Jefferson. To take them seriously, or to cause others to do so, was to add to the number of bedlamites.[10] An example of their damage was the deplorable "religious phrensy" inspired in students at Hampden-Sydney College.[11] A mind not totally crazed by these unintelligible assertions would nevertheless be unlikely to develop beyond mediocrity.[12] They had no place in healthy education.

7. To J. P. P. Derieux, July 25, 1788 (Boyd, *13*, 418).
8. To John Adams, Aug. 15, 1820 (LB, *15*, 273–76).
9. To James Smith, Dec. 8, 1822 (LB, *15*, 408–10).
10. To Mathew Carey, Nov. 11, 1816 (Ford, *10*, 67–68).
11. To William Short, Dec. 14, 1789 (Ford, *5*, 136).
12. To Horatio Gates Spafford, Jan. 10, 1816 (Ford, *10*, 12–13).

Immorality. Worse than all this, religio-metaphysical abstractions made men immoral. James Madison had pointed out to Jefferson that, even at its coolest, religion was much more often a motive to oppression than restraint from it. When kindled into enthusiasm, religion could produce the worst of mob passions: "The conduct of every popular assembly, acting on oath, the strongest of religious ties, shows that individuals join without remorse in acts against which their consciences would revolt, if proposed to them separately in their closets."[13] Jefferson heartily agreed. He knew numerous examples of this kind of immorality among religious dogmatizers.[14] "On the dogmas of religion, as distinguished from moral principles, all mankind, from the beginning of the world to this day, have been quarreling, fighting, burning, and torturing one another, for abstractions unintelligible to themselves and to all others, and absolutely beyond the comprehension of the human mind."[15] This was the result of making the mind accept what it could not understand. Jefferson refused to do that: "I never submitted the whole system of my opinions to the creed of any party of men whatever, in religion, in politics, or in anything else, where I was capable of thinking for myself. Such an addiction is the last degradation of a free and moral agent."[16] To him the aim of education was to produce free and moral agents, to train men to be capable of thinking for themselves. Dogma had no place in it.

True Religion in the Curriculum

THE SPECIFIC AIM

The methods Jefferson intended to use and the specific curriculum provisions he made for teaching religion are

13. From James Madison, Oct. 24, 1787 (Boyd, *12*, 278).

14. To John Adams, June 15, 1813 (Ford, *9*, 386); to Samuel Kercheval, Jan. 19, 1810 (LB, *12*, 345–46).

15. To Mathew Carey, Nov. 11, 1816 (Ford, *10*, 67–68).

16. To Francis Hopkinson, March 13, 1789 (Ford, *5*, 76).

interdependent implementations of his total rationale concerning religion and education. Basic to his thought was his belief that man had a moral sense, a physical faculty to guide him in all moral decisions.[17] The educational task was to strengthen that faculty until it was almost irresistible, to employ it regularly in specific problems until right moral decision became habitual. In other words, not the content of moral law but the processes of moral behavior must be developed. The content of the moral law to Jefferson was no problem at all. "I have ever found one, & only one rule, *to do what is right*, & generally we shall disentangle ourselves without almost perceiving how it happens."[18] Unless it resulted from excess and oversubtle reasoning, there could be no difficulty concerning the principles of right and wrong. They were writ large and plainly legible to everyone.[19] To follow them was the task, to make the moral sense strong enough to consistently overcome man's other tendency to make interested use of whatever opportunity came his way.

Since the moral sense, like all physical faculties, was strengthened by exercise, the solution was to give it exercise aplenty. Life itself provided many opportunities for this. Jefferson, therefore, was quick to advise his protégés to use every opportunity for moral decision to develop strong habits of truth, honesty, good humor, and industry. The trick was repetition. Every opportunity must be seized, because every right decision helped. Even the opportunities provided for others could be of use to the student. Inculcating moral habits in others would help to strengthen

17. To Maria Cosway, Oct. 12, 1786 (LB, *5*, 442–45); to James Fishback, Sept. 27, 1809 (LB, *12*, 349–51); to Thomas Law, June 13, 1814 (LB, *14*, 138–44).

18. To Wilson Cary Nicholas, March 26, 1805 (Ford, *8*, 349). Italics Jefferson's.

19. *Summary View of the Rights of British America*, July 26, 1774 (Boyd, *1*, 134).

one's own. Concerning his younger daughter Maria, Jefferson advised her elder sister Martha:

> Teach her always to be true. . . . Teach her never to be angry. . . . And teach her industry and application to useful pursuits. I will venture to assure you, that if you inculcate this in her mind, you will make her a happy being herself, a most inestimable friend to you, and precious to all the world. In teaching her these dispositions of mind, you will be more fixed in them yourself, and render yourself dear to all your acquaintances. Practice them, then, my dear, without ceasing. If ever you find yourself in difficulty, and doubt how to extricate yourself, do what is right, and you will find it the easiest way of getting out of the difficulty.[20]

Behind this lies Jefferson's belief that thought was a mode of action of matter.[21] Imagination, in other words, could substitute for reality in giving the moral sense its exercise.

ELEMENTARY SCHOOL

This provided a method of teaching morality in the school, thought Jefferson. Opportunities closely similar to those of life itself could be found in reading. Jefferson made this an explicit aim of elementary education: "to improve by reading the student's morals and faculties."[22] Here, Jefferson felt, properly selected fiction was of great value:

> A little attention . . . to the nature of the human mind evinces that the entertainments of fiction are useful as well as pleasant. . . . everything is useful which contributes to fix in us the principles and practice of virtue. When any signal act of charity or of gratitude, for

20. To Martha Jefferson, April 7, 1787 (Ford, *4*, 375–76).
21. To John Adams, Aug. 15, 1820 (LB, *15*, 273–74).
22. Rockfish Gap Report (Cabell, *Early History*, p. 434).

instance, is presented either to our sight or imagination, we are deeply impressed with its beauty and feel a strong desire in ourselves of doing charitable and grateful acts, also. On the contrary when we see or read of any atrocious deed, we are disgusted with its deformity and conceive an abhorrence of vice. Now every emotion of this kind is an exercise of our virtuous dispositions; and dispositions of the mind, like limbs of the body, acquire strength by exercise. But exercise produces habit; and in the instance of which we speak, the exercise being of the moral feelings, produces a habit of thinking and acting virtuously.[23]

Jefferson was constantly on the lookout for the kind of fiction that would produce a proper moral reaction in the child.[24] There was real danger, he felt, that too much fiction, or the wrong kind, could result in an inordinate passion for novels, and thus deprave the mind, causing it to revolt against wholesome reading, reason and fact, plain and unadorned.[25] Properly selected, however, fiction could provide interesting and useful vehicles for developing sound morality.

The first elements of morality could also be taught by an open and utilitarian appeal to reason. This would involve the demonstration that happiness did not depend on the condition of life in which chance had placed one, but was always the result of good conscience, good health, occupation, and freedom in all just pursuits.[26] This would depend in part for its effectiveness on the child's acquaintance with facts. In the earliest stage of education, therefore, time

23. To Robert Skipwith, Aug. 3, 1771 (Boyd, *1*, 76–77).

24. He recommended a book "of the instructive kind and fit for children" to his London book seller. "It is entitled 'a complete course of instructions and anecdotes by Father Berenger,' 2.v. 12 mo." To John Stockdale, July 17, 1787 (Boyd, *11*, 597).

25. To Nathaniel Burwell, March 14, 1818 (Ford, *10*, 104–06).

26. See *Notes on Virginia*, Query 14 (Ford, *3*, 252–53).

must be set aside to store children's memories with useful facts from geography and history.

Involved in this was Jefferson's belief that the very use to which reason was put became in itself a moral issue. Since every man's reason was physically as unique as his face, reason by itself was no infallible guide to truth. Man was responsible, therefore, not so much for the rightness of his rational conclusions as for the uprightness with which he came to them.[27] This in turn depended upon his dealing with facts, the evidence of his physical senses, the raw material of all knowledge, rather than with systems, which were merely human abstractions.

The uprightness of reason, then, was its insistence on being guided by the senses. Man had to make this uprightness habitual for his mind, as he had to make the reactions of honesty and gratitude habitual in his dealings with society. To deal with systems instead of facts at too early an age might ruin any possibility of developing an honest and upright reason later: "Instead, therefore, of putting the Bible and Testament into the hands of children at an age when their judgments are not sufficiently matured for religious inquiries, their memories may here be stored with the most useful facts from Grecian, Roman, European, and American history."[28] The development of morality, in other words, required the child to avoid considering human systems (including sectarian beliefs) before he was fully mature.[29]

27. To Peter Carr, Aug. 10, 1787 (LB, 6, 261); to Elbridge Gerry, Jan. 26, 1799 (LB, 10, 85); to William Carver, Dec. 4, 1823 (Ford, 10, 284–85).

28. *Notes on Virginia*, Query 14 (Ford, 3, 252–53). See also Boorstin, *Lost World*, chap. 3, sec. 3.

29. In connection with this, note what Jefferson had to say about the Convent de Panthemont, a school having one of the best reputations in Europe at the time of his residence in Paris. He had placed both daughters there, and by so doing caused some disturbance of mind among several close acquaintances and relatives in Virginia. See letter from James Maury, Sept. 18, 1786 (Boyd, 10, 389), and to James Maury, Dec. 24, 1786 (Boyd, 10, 628).

Thus in the earliest stage of education Jefferson wished, first, to develop the student's moral sense by giving it exercise in making moral decisions both in daily life and by reaction to events in fiction. Second, he wanted the student to develop the habit of reasoning uprightly, that is, on the basis of facts or of the evidence of the senses rather than on the basis of abstract human systems. Third, the value of moral behavior was to be demonstrated rationally. All of this made a good beginning in education aimed at developing the moral or "truly religious" man.

SECONDARY SCHOOL

On the secondary or grammar school level of education, Jefferson felt, this process was to be continued without radical change,[30] but supplemented by a natural and proper development of another part of the curriculum. Languages were the proper study of a student between eight and fifteen years of age, maintained Jefferson, because at this time the mind was best suited for memory work. The learning of a language was chiefly a work of memory. The books used in language study could serve simultaneously to store the mind with useful facts and good principles.[31] In addition to this, the future study of religion would benefit immensely from the study of ancient languages, such as Hebrew, Greek, and Latin, "the depositories of the originals, and of the earliest and most respected authorities of the faith of every sect."[32] To Jefferson language was not science but an instrument for the attainment of science.[33] As such it

---

Concerning the convent, Jefferson's reply was both disarming and revealing: "It is a house of education altogether the best in France, and at which the best masters attend. There are in it as many Protestants as Catholics, and not a word is ever spoken to them on the subject of religion." (To Mary Jefferson Bolling, July 23, 1787, Boyd, *11*, 612.)

30. To Peter Carr, Aug. 19, 1785 (LB, *5*, 82–84).
31. See *Notes on Virginia* (Ford, *3*, 253–54).
32. Report of Board of Visitors, Oct. 7, 1822 (Cabell, pp. 473–74).
33. See *Notes on Virginia* (Ford, *3*, 253–54).

would be invaluable in the proper study of religion once the student had reached maturity.

HIGHER EDUCATION

Practice of morality. In higher education the development of the truly moral, truly religious man depended on continuing those educational methods which had begun at the start of schooling, but with some expansion to take advantage of the increasing maturity of the student.[34] The practice of morality, the ceaseless repetition of the act of making right decisions, was still basic to all else. No amount of reasoning could substitute for the individual's simple decision to do the right thing when faced with any moral choice. Reasoning could indeed be dangerous here; the student facing a practical situation might be led away from the right choice by artificial rules.

Where the dilemma might be particularly difficult, or the wrong choice particularly tempting, Jefferson advocated using a simple process which had always worked for him:

> I had the good fortune to become acquainted very early with some characters of very high standing, and to feel the incessant wish that I could ever become what they were. Under temptations and difficulties, I would ask myself what would Dr. Small, Mr. Wythe, Peyton Randolph do in this situation? What course in it will insure me their approbation? I am certain that this mode of deciding on my conduct tended more to correctness than any reasoning powers I possessed. Knowing the even and dignified line they pursued, I could never doubt for a moment which of two courses would be in character for them. Whereas, seeking the same object through a process of moral reasoning, and with the jaundiced eye of youth, I should often have erred.

34. Discussed briefly by Honeywell, *Educational Work,* pp. 124–26.

. . . these little returns into ourselves, this self-catechis-
ing habit, is not trifling nor useless, but leads to the
prudent selection and steady pursuit of what is right.[35]

With this advice Jefferson hoped to shield his favorite
grandson from the dangers of living alone in Philadelphia,
where the young man had gone to finish his education. Although more specific in method, it is of a piece with advice
he gave to many other young men and women. Earlier examples tend to be direct: "Above all things, lose no occasion
of exercising your dispositions to be grateful, to be generous, to be charitable, to be humane, to be true, just, firm,
orderly, courageous, &c. Consider every act of this kind,
as an exercise which will strengthen your moral faculties
and increase your worth."[36] In later examples the direct
advice is fairly brief: "Adore God. Reverence and cherish
your parents. Love your neighbor as yourself and your
country more than yourself. Be just. Be true. Murmur not
at the ways of Providence." But to these few words Jefferson
usually added "A Decalogue of Canons for Observation in
Practical Life," and Brady and Tate's version of Psalm 15,
which he significantly entitled, "The portrait of a good man
by the most sublime of poets, for your imitation."[37]

Reading. Behind all of this stands Jefferson's lasting conviction that attending lectures in morality was a waste of
time, and that too much reading or reasoning in the field
could be dangerous.[38] This does not mean that Jefferson
felt the student should do no reading in morality at all.

35. To Thomas Jefferson Randolph, Nov. 24, 1808 (LB, *12*, 197–98).

36. To Peter Carr, Aug. 10, 1787 (LB, *6*, 257–58). See also letter to Martha
Jefferson, March 28, 1787 (Ford, *4*, 371–74).

37. To Thomas Jefferson Smith, Feb. 21, 1825 (Ford, *10*, 340–41). See also
letter to Thomas Jefferson Grotjan, Jan. 10, 1824 (Ford, *10*, 287); and to
Isaac Engelbrecht, Feb. 25, 1824 (LB, *16*, 16–17).

38. To Peter Carr, Aug. 10, 1787 (LB, *6*, 257). See also letter to Thomas
Cooper, Aug. 14, 1820 (LB, *15*, 264–65).

He felt that the writings of Sterne formed the best course
in morality ever written, and periodically he recommended
other books, among which usually appear Plato's Socratic
dialogues, Xenophon's Memorabilia, and relevant works of
Epictetus, Seneca, Cicero, Antoninus, Bolingbroke, Locke,
Lord Kames, and Dugald Stewart.[39]

Obviously, then, Jefferson's opinion was that although
the indispensable way to develop morality was by exercising
the moral sense, the student's moral and religious development in higher education could be profitably supplemented
by reading the works of the ancient Stoics and Epicureans,
and of the seventeenth- and eighteenth-century empiricists.
This was accompanied, however, by warnings against the
dangers of oversubtle rationalization. It is also possible that
Jefferson may have stressed the concrete moral advantages
of studying the ancient and contemporary moralists as a
demonstration that an adequate moral theory and practice
could really exist outside the pale of dogmatic or sectarian
religion.[40]

Proofs of God's existence. In higher education Jefferson
believed that reason could play another role in the learning
of morality. At this level the student should be confronted
with the rational or philosophical arguments for the "being
of a God, the creator, preserver, and supreme ruler of the
universe."[41] Jefferson, of course, believed that these were
proofs—not merely arguments—resulting irresistibly from
any open-eyed consideration of the evidence presented by
the universe. Reason used uprightly in conjunction with

39. Ibid.; to Robert Skipwith, Aug. 3, 1771 (Boyd, *1*, 79–80); to Peter
Carr, Aug. 19, 1785 (LB, *5*, 82–87); to John Minor (to Bernard Moore), Aug.
30, 1814 (Ford, *9*, 481 n.).

40. See Koch, *Philosophy of Jefferson*, p. 7. As Miss Koch points out, Jefferson was of the opinion toward the end of his life that the moderns had
superseded the ancients in the science of ethics. See letter to John Brazier,
Aug. 24, 1819 (LB, *15*, 207–11).

41. Rockfish Gap Report (Cabell, pp. 441–42).

the senses came to the incontestable conclusion that God did exist.[42]

Jefferson believed also that the moral implications of these proofs were similarly inescapable. Such philosophical arguments demonstrated the existence of God not only as creator, preserver, and supreme ruler of the universe but also as "author of all the relations of morality and of the law and obligations these infer."[43] Jefferson explicitly linked his cosmology and his ethics: "Assuming the fact, that the earth has been created in time, and consequently the dogma of final causes, we yield, of course, to this short syllogism. Man was created for social intercourse; but social intercourse cannot be maintained without a sense of justice; then man must have been created with a sense of justice."[44] The philosophical proofs of God's existence, then, were not mere metaphysical speculation, in Jefferson's eyes, but had practical, social value for the student as a basis and an incentive for moral action.

Value of morality. Reason could also aid the moral sense by demonstrating the utilitarian value of correct moral action. This was the final development of those elements of morality taught first on the primary level.[45] The utilitarian argument is never absent from Jefferson's advice to his many young charges: "A determination never to do what is wrong, prudence, and good humor, will go far towards securing you the estimation of the world."[46] "Be good, be learned, and be industrious, and you will not want the aid of travelling, to render you precious to your country, dear to your friends, happy within yourself."[47]

42. To John Adams, April 8, 1816 (LB, *14*, 468–69); to John Adams, April 11, 1823 (LB, *15*, 426–28).

43. Rockfish Gap Report (Cabell, pp. 441–42).

44. To Frances W. Gilmer, June 7, 1816 (LB, *15*, 25).

45. See *Notes on Virginia*, Query 14 (Ford, *3*, 253).

46. To Thomas Jefferson Randolph, Nov. 24, 1808 (LB, *12*, 197).

47. To Peter Carr, Aug. 10, 1787 (LB, *6*, 262).

Jefferson believed this utilitarian argument had unusual power. It would always tend to strengthen the normal moral sense in any student, of course; but the rational demonstration that just and upright behavior was always in one's own interest could be used even to develop virtue in students whose moral sense was badly deficient or nonexistent:

> When it is wanting, we endeavor to supply the defect by education, by appeals to reason and calculation, by presenting to the being so unhappily conformed, other motives to do good and eschew evil, such as the love, or the hatred, or the rejection of those among whom he lives, and whose society is necessary to his happiness and even existence; demonstrations by sound calculation that honesty promotes interest in the long run; the rewards and penalties established by the laws; and ultimately the prospects of a future state of retribution for the evil as well as the good done while here. These are the correctives supplied by education . . . and they lead into a course of correct action all those whose disparity is not too profound to be eradicated.[48]

All of these together, the practice of correct decision, reading in the great ancient and contemporary moralists, learning the rational proofs for the existence of God and their implications for moral behavior, and studying the utilitarian arguments for just and upright living served properly to approach one of the great objects of higher education. All four methods of teaching morality to the university student can be seen in the statement: "To develop the reasoning faculties of our youth, enlarge their minds, cultivate their morals, and instill into them the precepts of virtue and order . . . And, generally, to form them to habits of reflection and correct action, rendering them examples

48. To Thomas Law, June 13, 1814 (LB, *14*, 142–43).

of virtue to others, and of happiness within themselves. These are the objects of that higher grade of education."[49]

Approach to Dogma

BEFORE MATURITY

Sectarian doctrines were another matter. Jefferson obviously felt that the dogmas upon which everyone disagrees should be one of the last subjects considered by the student in any sound system of education. Just as he felt that the student's traveling alone should be postponed until moral maturity was beyond all doubt (which to Jefferson could mean after the age of thirty-five), so he had the opinion that the study of religious beliefs should be postponed until the student's rational maturity placed him safely beyond the dangers of a corrupted, wrecked, and ruined reason.[50]

IN MATURITY: JEFFERSON'S REPLY
TO PETER CARR

Jefferson held that the Bible should not be placed in the hands of children at the primary level because they were "at an age when their judgements are not sufficiently matured for religious inquiries."[51] It may well be asked when he thought their judgments would be "sufficiently matured." Only once in all his letters of advice on education to students or their parents did Jefferson give positive, specific advice about studying religious doctrine, and this was in response to Peter Carr's pointed question concerning what to read in the field: "And now Sir I should be glad of your advice on the subject of religion; as I think it time to be

49. Rockfish Gap Report (Cabell, p. 435).

50. At one point in Jefferson's correspondence these motives joined. He advised Ralph Izard to postpone for two or three years his younger son's intended trip to Paris to learn engineering, so that young Izard would be more able to resist attempts to make him change his religion. (To Ralph Izard, July 17, 1788, LB, 7, 70–73.)

51. *Notes on Virginia,* Query 14 (Ford, *3,* 252).

fixed on a point which has had so many advocates and opponents, and still seems to be dubious. I should wish your advice as to the books I should read, and in what order."[52] Perhaps Jefferson never otherwise suggested the study of doctrinal religion to his students because he felt this form of metaphysical speculation to be so dangerous to human reason that it was best completely avoided. Carr's question was specific, however, and Jefferson may have found it difficult to avoid giving an answer.

The answer was long.[53] It was a brilliant attempt by Jefferson to combine a competent study of religious doctrines with safeguards against those dangers he most feared. It begins with stern warnings: "Religion. Your reason is now mature enough to examine this object. In the first place, divest yourself of all bias in favor of novelty and singularity of opinion. Indulge them in any subject rather than that of religion. It is too important, and the consequences may be too serious." The "consequences" Jefferson referred to were undoubtedly a corrupted mind and moral sense. He continued: "On the other hand, shake off all the fears and servile prejudices, under which weak minds are servilely crouched. Fix reason firmly in her seat, and call to her tribunal every fact, every opinion. Question with boldness even the existence of God; because if there be one, he must more approve of the homage of reason, than that of blindfolded fear."

The alternative of reason or fear is typical of Jefferson's thought concerning religious doctrine. The choice he presents is always between reason and something unacceptable to any thinking man: reason or novelty, reason or singularity of opinion, reason or superstition, reason or fear, reason or fraud. His specific suggestions to Peter Carr illustrate this tendency nicely. Read the Bible as a history book, accepting whatever cannot otherwise be disproved and re-

52. From Peter Carr, April 18, 1787 (Boyd, *11*, 299).
53. To Peter Carr, Aug. 10, 1787 (LB, *6*, 256–62; or Boyd, *12*, 14–19).

jecting whatever is irrational or contradictory to the laws
of nature. Decide whether the "personage called Jesus" was
a divinely sired wonder-worker with powers to suspend or
reverse the laws of nature, or a benevolent illegitimate who
deceived himself into believing he was divine and who was
executed for treason. Decide whether a gospel writer's pre-
tension to divine inspiration entitles him to belief when he
makes statements that by any natural standard must be
termed impossible. Do not avoid a conclusion because you
find it personally unpalatable or because it conflicts with
the opinions of others. Let reason be your guide:

> Do not be frightened from this inquiry from any fear
> of its consequences. . . . I repeat, you must lay aside all
> prejudice on both sides, and neither believe nor reject
> anything, because any other persons, or descriptions of
> persons, have rejected or believed it. Your own reason
> is the only oracle given you by heaven, and you are
> answerable not for the rightness, but for the upright-
> ness of the decision.

Jefferson consistently holds the position of a dogmatic
rationalist. Throughout this letter he can be seen strug-
gling mightily to keep young Peter Carr's reason uncon-
taminated by its subject of study. The sum of his advice
is to avoid bias, consider all possible opinions, judge them
as best he can, and then make the best of them his own.
On the surface this is a perfectly fair approach, but Jefferson's presentation is slanted so that it is almost impossible
not to come to his own conclusion. The apparent alterna-
tives are so stated that there is only one possible choice for
a sensible man. When Jefferson says, "You must lay aside
prejudice on both sides," he believes that prejudice is involved in one side only. Mystery, the irrational, the naturally impossible clearly cannot be accepted. To Jefferson his
own religious persuasion, primitive Christianity, was free
from those defects. It was reasonable. Although Jefferson

does not say his position is the right one, he believes that it is the only position a truly rational man can hold.

Jefferson's approach virtually assures that Peter Carr will not find himself facing a fair and open conflict of opinion. The reading suggestions enclosed in the letter bear this out. Listed under "Religion" are Locke, Conyers Middleton, Bolingbroke, Hume, Voltaire, and James Beattie, the same authors who in other lists are either placed under "Ethics" or "Morality," or, if found under "Religion," are lumped together indiscriminately with the rest of the great moralists.[54] No mention is made of theologians with whom Jefferson disagreed, such as Calvin, Aquinas, Augustine, or Paul. They may never have occurred to Jefferson, or he may have felt they were worthless. He did believe they had corroded other human minds. Certainly theology was one area that Jefferson, the voracious reader, deliberately neglected, repeatedly claiming, as he did, to confine himself to "the moral branch in which all sects agree."[55] There is no evidence to the contrary. Yet this was the same man who, in reaction to a particularly heinous example of religious censorship in Philadelphia, had cried out: "It is an insult to our citizens to question whether they are rational beings or not, and blasphemy against religion to suppose it cannot stand the test of truth and reason. . . . for God's sake let us freely hear both sides, if we choose."[56]

In his approach to the problem of religious beliefs Jefferson was in the vanguard of the critical thought of his time.

54. Boyd, *12*, 18–19. Cf. letter to Robert Skipwith, Aug. 3, 1771 (Boyd, *1*, 79–80); to John Minor (to Bernard Moore), Aug. 30, 1814 (Ford, *9*, 481 n.).

55. To Thomas Leiper, Jan. 21, 1890 (Ford, *9*, 238). This claim was more than pretense. In 1824 when working up a list of books for a new library to be willed to the University of Virginia, Jefferson had to turn to Madison for advice on what to include in the field of divinity: "The good moral writers, Christian as well as Pagan, I have set down; but there are writers of celebrity in religious metaphysics . . . whom you can suggest." (To James Madison, Aug. 8, 1824, Madison Papers, Library of Congress, quoted in Koch, *Jefferson and Madison*, p. 279.)

56. To Nicholas Gouin Dufief, April 19, 1814 (LB, *14*, 126–27).

He was involved in the Enlightenment's quest for religious authority. Like other *philosophes*, he was trying to establish religion on a rationally, morally, and empirically valid basis. There is no reason to believe that he ever deliberately attempted to choke off discussion or prevent a point of view he disagreed with from getting a hearing. Yet he was tripped up here by his distaste for personal controversy, his belief that arguments never changed anyone's opinion, and his conviction that there was no hope of reasoning with anyone subscribing to a creed. These attitudes, incidentally, are those of a sectarian: whoever holds them prevents free discussion by closing his ears. These factors affected his advice to his protégés concerning the study of religion. They account for his omitting consideration of denominational beliefs in his letters and for his careful control of the approach when the subject could not be avoided. Surely he never intended to prevent the creeds from having their day in court, but he probably never realized that, just as surely, he never chose to "freely hear both sides." If doctrinal religion was to be studied, it was to be approached only from the point of view of strict dogmatic rationalism, and only by those whose fully matured reasons would give them the maximum possible invulnerability to sectarian doctrinal corruption.

CHAPTER 9

Democratic Public Education

The full experiment of government democratical, but representative, was and still is reserved for us. . . . My most earnest wish is to see the republican element of popular control pushed to the maximum of its practical exercise. I shall then believe that our government may be pure and perpetual.[1]

Education's Role in Democracy

As Jefferson saw it, the requirement of this full experiment in representative democracy made two conditions absolutely necessary: local control whenever feasible, and general education to enable every man to judge for himself what would secure or endanger his freedom.[2] Jefferson cam-

1. To Isaac H. Tiffany, Aug. 26, 1816 (LB, *15*, 66).
2. To John Tyler, May 26, 1810 (LB, *12*, 393; and Ford, *Writings of Jefferson, 9,* 277 n.).

paigned continually for both these conditions: to have government divided into "hundreds" or "wards," the ultimate units of pure democracy, and to institute a system of public education: "I consider the continuance of republican government as absolutely hanging on these two hooks."[3]

NEEDED: AN EDUCATED PEOPLE

For almost fifty years Jefferson worked to develop public education in America, and particularly in Virginia. He considered the Bill for General Education in the Revisal as one of four pillars essential to the structure of a truly democratic government.[4] Throughout his life he argued that only the people could be relied on to preserve freedom and protect a nation from the evils of government, but to do this they had to be informed:

> The people, especially when moderately instructed, are the only safe, because the only honest, depositories of the public rights, and should therefore be introduced into the administration of them in every function to which they are sufficient; they will err sometimes and accidentally, but never designedly and with a systematic and persevering purpose of overthrowing the free principles of government.[5]

On the other hand, every government, Jefferson observed, no matter how high a plane it may start on, degenerates when trusted to the rulers of the people alone.[6]

Jefferson's ceaseless drive to have his state and nation institute a system of public education was based on his pro-

3. To Joseph C. Cabell, Jan. 31, 1814 (Ford, *9*, 452).
4. *Autobiography* (Ford, *1*, 68–69).
5. To A. Coray, Oct. 31, 1823 (LB, *15*, 483). For earlier examples see letter to George Wythe, Aug. 13, 1786 (LB, *5*, 396–97); to James Madison, Dec. 20, 1787 (Boyd, *12*, 442); to W. C. Jarvis, Sept. 28, 1820 (LB, *15*, 278); and elsewhere in this chapter.
6. See *Notes on Virginia*, Query 14 (Ford, *3*, 224, 254).

found belief that the destinies of a nation are determined not by devices but by men. Ultimately the choices of any society, for good or evil, were to be attributed to the force of public opinion, "the safest guide and guardian of public morals and welfare, the arbitress in every age of its destinies to happiness or wretchedness, and the source to which, as either pure or corrupted, the changes of condition in every country on earth may be traced and ascribed."[7] Jefferson's purpose in public education was to give a wholesome direction to this force of ultimate decision. The diffusion of information could thus enable men to preserve their freedom by arraigning all abuses at the bar of public reason.[8]

EDUCATION'S POWER

Jefferson's cautious but invincible optimism about human nature is reflected throughout all his thought on public education. Undeniably his thought on man contained unresolved contradictions. He was convinced that men were divided naturally, by temperament, into two types or parties. Nevertheless, he also believed they were fundamentally educable, and that education was a powerful force to change men permanently. Those educated in republicanism could not possibly become apostates to royalism.[9] Advances in science and discoveries in the arts would lead to greater wisdom in mankind.[10] Education was the means to progress:[11]

> Although I do not, with some enthusiasts, believe that the human condition will ever advance to such a state of perfection as that there shall no longer be pain or

7. Report of the Board of Visitors of the University of Virginia, Oct. 4, 1819 (Cabell, ed., *Early History*, pp. 459–60).
8. First Inaugural Address (LB, *3*, 322).
9. To James Madison, March 15, 1789 (Ford, *5*, 80–83).
10. To Benjamin Waterhouse, March 3, 1818 (Ford, *10*, 103–04).
11. Rockfish Gap Report (Cabell, pp. 435–37); to Joseph C. Cabell, Nov. 1820 (Ford, *10*, 166).

vice in the world, yet I believe it susceptible of much improvement, and most of all, in matters of government and religion; and that the diffusion of knowledge among the people is to be the instrument by which it is to be effected.[12]

He had tremendous faith in the powers of literacy to foster progress and prevent retrogression. Twice he wrote to John Adams that the art of printing alone would prevent the destruction of culture or the reversal of progress toward freedom in Europe.[13] Literacy and freedom of the press would make democracy inevitable: "It would seem impossible that an intelligent people, with the faculty of reading & right of thinking, should continue much longer to slumber under the pupilage of an interested aristocracy of priests & lawyers, persuading them to distrust themselves, & to let them think for them."[14]

LITERACY'S LIMITATIONS

Jefferson has been accused of having a mechanical idea of literacy, of believing that the ability to read would in itself work for good. He is said never to have suspected the ease with which literacy is perverted or that a people of well-perverted literacy might be not only much more ignorant than illiterates, but invincibly unintelligent.[15] In view of several of Jefferson's remarks concerning the effect of a perverted free press upon the minds of the people, this may be somewhat difficult to defend.[16] Jefferson nowhere says

12. To P. S. Dupont de Nemours, April 24, 1816 (Ford, *10*, 25).
13. To John Adams, Sept. 12, 1821 (LB, *15*, 334); to John Adams, Sept. 4, 1823 (LB, *15*, 464–65).
14. To Thomas Seymour, Feb. 11, 1807 (Ford, *9*, 30–31).
15. See Nock, *Jefferson*, pp. 313–14.
16. E.g. letter to John Norvell, June 14, 1807 (Ford, *9*, 71–74); to Walter Jones, Jan. 2, 1814 (Ford, *9*, 446–47).

flatly that literacy will by itself lead to freedom; it must always be accompanied by the right to think and to communicate. Nor does this combination guarantee that the people can defend themselves against all designs upon their rights and interests. The people could be duped "once in an age at least."[17]

Education was a great power, to Jefferson, but not a panacea. There were practical problems caused by corruption which would baffle the best educators, conditions which education could ameliorate only over a discouragingly long period of time, if at all. Ancient Rome, for example, steeped in corruption, vice, and venality, its people demoralized and depraved, might have proved too much for the best intentioned of its greatest Caesars, had they ever wanted to reform it.[18] Jefferson's observations of the scene in Europe caused him while there to make the prediction: "ignorance, superstition, poverty, and oppression of body and mind, in every form, are so firmly settled on the mass of the people, that their redemption from them can never be hoped."[19] His later optimism as to Europe's ultimate liberation recognized that there was first a long, tough row to hoe.[20]

The effect of slavery upon man's ability to govern himself was another problem Jefferson thought might be too great for education. Jefferson never doubted that slavery did have a deleterious effect upon man's ability to govern himself.[21] In whites there was evidence, however, that the damage could be repaired. The problem of the Negro slave was more complicated, because of his own observations of their behavior and the conclusions he drew from the Linnaean

17. To Francis Eppes, April 14, 1792 (Ford, 5, 508).
18. To John Adams, Dec. 10, 1819 (LB, 15, 233–34).
19. To George Wythe, Aug. 13, 1786 (LB, 5, 395–96).
20. To John Adams, Oct. 28, 1813 (Ford, 9, 429).
21. See letter to Edward Bancroft, Jan. 26, 1789 (Ford, 5, 66–68); and *Notes on Virginia*, Query 14 (Ford, 3, 266–67).

principles of biology. According to these principles, members of the human race who had domesticated themselves in Africa could have been so affected by generations of living in that environment that their mental and physical capacities were no longer equal to those of the whites. Jefferson felt reluctantly and halfheartedly that this might be true. He did not want to admit that this was an inequality which education could never make up, but his observations and his scientific beliefs and theories gave him no alternative.[22] Throughout his life he vacillated on the question of the physical and intellectual equality of Negroes and whites, hoping to find conclusive evidence that condition, not nature, made the distinction. The very fact of his vacillation, though, would seem to show that basically he believed the distinction was natural and therefore beyond the powers of education to change.[23]

Finally, Jefferson was aware that science of itself is not always a power favoring the development of a moral society: "As for France and England, with all their pre-eminence in science, the one is a den of robbers, and the other of pirates. And if science produces no better fruits than tyranny, murder, rapine, and destitution of national morality, I would rather wish our country to be ignorant, honest, and estimable, as our neighboring savages are."[24]

IGNORANCE VERSUS FREEDOM

Public gullibility, then, and human rapacity make it quite possible for science and knowledge to produce evil. But an honest and estimable country lacking science and

22. *Notes on Virginia* (Ford, *3*, 246–48). See above, p. 48.

23. See letter to Henri Grégoire, Feb. 25, 1809 (Ford, *9*, 246–47); to Joel Barlow, Oct. 8, 1809 (Ford, *9*, 261–62); to David Barrow, May 1, 1815 (Ford, *9*, 516). Good discussion of Jefferson's anthropology and his inability to make up his mind in Boorstin, *Lost World*, pp. 81–98.

24. To John Adams, Jan. 21, 1812 (Ford, *9*, 333–34).

knowledge is possible only among savages. Whereas Jefferson does not say that literacy leads inevitably to freedom, he does say that in a state of civilization freedom will not exist long without it. Other conditions are also necessary, but literacy is a *sine qua non*. No civilized people can hope to remain both free and ignorant: "For I lay it down as one of the impossibilities of nature that ignorance should maintain itself free against cunning, where any government has once been admitted."[25]

For this reason Jefferson had very little hope that the countries of Spanish America, then fighting for independence from Spain, would achieve any form of democracy. History had furnished no example of an ignorant people maintaining themselves free in a state of civilization. Civil and religious leaders would invariably avail themselves of popular ignorance for their own purposes. More than a generation of education would be necessary to teach the Latin Americans to recognize and cherish their freedoms. Meanwhile these people, unprepared for liberty, subject to ignorance, bigotry, prejudice, jealousy, and superstition, could only use the liberty brought to them by chance to construct a new tyranny. Jefferson saw nothing ahead for Spanish America but military despotism developed by cunning leaders playing off mutual jealousies and hatreds against each other for power. Light might come to the Spanish Americans eventually, but only after a long and slow development.[26] Science, then, is essential to the success of democratic government. Whatever else they may need, people must have education to remain free in a state of civilization. To Jefferson, public education was the people's ultimate weapon.

25. To the Marquis de La Fayette, Nov. 30, 1813 (Ford, 9, 436).

26. To P. S. Dupont de Nemours, April 15, 1811 (Ford, 9, 322); to Baron Von Humboldt, Dec. 6, 1813 (Ford, 9, 430–31); to the Marquis de La Fayette, Nov. 30, 1813 (Ford, 9, 435–36); to the Marquis de La Fayette, Feb. 14, 1815 (Ford, 9, 505); to P. S. Dupont de Nemours, April 24, 1816 (Ford, 10, 25).

A System of General Education

GENERAL AIMS

Theoretically, public education did not differ from private education but was rather the same process adapted to meet two specific needs in the democratic state. First, all men needed enough education to know their own interests and how to safeguard them by choosing representatives of good character to manage the affairs of society. Second, the natural *aristoi,* an elite comprising the finest minds in the nation, provided by the Creator to manage society's affairs, had to be sought out and fully trained for leadership in the professions and government.[27]

Many of Jefferson's contemporaries maintained that education should be cared for by private philanthropy and individual enterprise. Among these were such leaders of Enlightenment thought as Adam Smith and Dugald Stewart, both of whom, incidentally, were quoted by Jefferson's opposition during the debate in the Virginia legislature over his plans.[28] Because of his understanding of the requirements of democratic government, however, Jefferson was adamant on the issue of finances. Unless the state supported a system of public education, lack of means would not only prevent most citizens from being properly qualified for their civil pursuits and duties, but would cause the genius of many members of the natural aristoi to be lost to the use of society. For this reason Jefferson opposed George Washington's generous plan to use part of his own income to set up charity schools for the instruction of the poor.[29] Charity schools were a worthy aim, but they were no system for providing for the needs of a democracy. Those needs could be met surely only if the government provided free ele-

27. To John Adams, Oct. 28, 1813 (Ford, *9,* 425).
28. See Arrowood, *Jefferson and Education,* p. 60.
29. To George Washington, Jan. 4, 1786 (Boyd, *Papers of Jefferson, 9,* 151).

mentary education for all and free advanced education to children with the best minds in the state.

ELEMENTARY EDUCATION

Importance. The elementary or primary level of public education was to Jefferson the most important of all the grades for a democracy. In the midst of his efforts to develop a state university in Virginia, he described his basic hierarchy of values in this wise: secondary schooling, he said,

> may be more conveniently than either of the others left to private enterprise. . . . Were it necessary to give up either the Primaries or the University, I would rather abandon the last, because it is safer to have a whole people respectably enlightened, than a few in a high state of science, and the many in ignorance. This last is the most dangerous state in which a nation can be.[30]

Because it was this important to the safety of society, Jefferson longed for the state to construct a truly effective system of public elementary education. Although he had strong opinions about its ideal form, he nevertheless said that he would be thankful for a system of general instruction in any shape, provided it reached every citizen.[31] That it should reach every citizen was his main target. He was therefore deeply disappointed by the slow and incomplete action of the Virginia legislature on the bills concerning education in the Revisal:

> These bills were not acted on until the . . . year '96. and then only so much of the first as provided for elementary schools. . . . And in the Elementary bill they inserted a provision which completely defeated it, for

---

30. To Joseph C. Cabell, Jan. 13, 1823 (Cabell, pp. 267–68).
31. To Joseph C. Cabell, Jan. 14, 1818 (Ford, *10*, 2).

they left it to the court of each county to determine for itself when this act should be carried into execution, within their county. One provision of the bill was that the expenses of these schools should be borne by the inhabitants of the county, every one in proportion to his general tax-rate. This would throw on wealth the education of the poor; and the justices, being generally of the more wealthy class, were unwilling to incur that burthen, and I believe it was not commenced in a single county.[32]

Question of compulsion. Jefferson was fully aware that the state's providing free, general, elementary education was no guarantee that all the children of the poor would take advantage of it. Their parents might not let them. Yet he was unwilling to make elementary education compulsory lest this violate the parent's natural right in relationship to his child. For this reason Jefferson thought highly of the draft of a new constitution for Spain which contained a provision that no person acquire the rights of citizenship until he could read and write: "This is new, and is the fruitful germ of the improvement of everything good, and the correction of everything imperfect in the present constitution. This will give you an enlightened people, and an energetic public opinion which will control and enchain the aristocratic spirit of government."[33]

The connection between public education and self-government is explicit. Jefferson tried to incorporate a similar provision in his Bill for Establishing Elementary Schools in 1817. In an accompanying comment, Jefferson admitted that society might have neither the right nor the duty to care for children in opposition to the will of their parents, but, he concluded,

32. *Autobiography* (Ford, *1*, 67).
33. To Chevalier Luis de Onis, April 28, 1814 (LB, *14*, 129). See also letter to P. S. Dupont de Nemours, April 24, 1816 (Ford, *10*, 24–25).

What is proposed here is to remove the objection of expense, by offering education gratis, and to strengthen parental excitement by disfranchisement of his child while uneducated. Society certainly has a right to disavow him whom they offer, and are not permitted, to qualify for the duties of a citizen. If we do not force instruction, let us at least strengthen the motives to receive it when offered.[34]

Proposals. Over a period of forty years Jefferson's several proposals for a system of general elementary education show a consistency of approach.[35] Invariably Jefferson wanted the state to have the counties organize wards to set up elementary schools within convenient reach of every child in the state. These schools were to be tax-supported and subject to local supervision. They were to offer to every child, between the ages of ten and twelve, three years of free instruction in reading, writing, and arithmetic. Those who wished to, and could afford it, could stay on as long as they liked. The reading was to be in the fields of history, geography, and morality. The objects of primary education were carefully described. In addition to those aims we have previously considered above in chapter 7, there were the following: "To know his rights; to exercise with order and justice those he retains; to choose with discretion the fiduciary of those he delegates; and to notice their conduct with diligence, with candor, and judgment."

Jefferson summarized aim and content with these words:

To instruct the mass of our citizens in these, the rights, interests, and duties, as men and citizens, being then

34. Joseph C. Cabell to Thomas Jefferson, Dec. 13, 1817 (Cabell, p. 97). Believing this and several other passages to be political dynamite, Cabell removed them from the bill before presenting it to the legislature, and informed Jefferson that he had done so.

35. His two bills, written in 1777–79 and 1817, are analyzed and compared in Honeywell, *Educational Work*, chap. 3. Jefferson also discussed his ideas in *Notes on Virginia*, the *Autobiography*, and numerous letters.

the objects of education in primary schools, whether public or private, in them should be taught reading, writing, and numerical arithmetic, the elements of mensuration, (useful in so many callings,) and the outlines of geography and history.[36]

The state's educational responsibility for *all* children would stop here. Jefferson's plan would have provided the opportunity for this minimum of free education for all citizens, and brought moderate pressure to bear upon them to accept it. This training would qualify the laboring class for citizenship, and serve as the foundation for all further acquirements of the learned.[37]

SECONDARY EDUCATION

Proposals. The variety of Jefferson's proposals for intermediate education would seem to indicate that he had no fixed ideas concerning the purpose of the grammar schools, the extent of their curriculum, their locations, nor even their size. This can be attributed to external factors. Each of his proposals for secondary education seems to have been designed for circumstances obtaining in Virginia at the moment. A typical example is his proposal in 1814 to extend the scope of the intermediate schools far into the field which both earlier (1779) and later (1818) he set apart for the university. At the moment there was no real university within the state. Jefferson, therefore, tried to expand his plans for Albemarle Academy to include areas of instruction which would normally be in higher education. Four years later when the University of Virginia was to become a fact, he planned to set up nearby a preparatory school in which the curriculum was limited almost entirely to subjects proposed for secondary education in 1779.[38]

36. Rockfish Gap Report (Cabell, p. 434).
37. To Peter Carr, Sept. 7, 1814 (LB, *19*, 213).
38. Excellent discussion of the effect of external factors on Jefferson's plans for secondary education in Honeywell, chap. 4.

The constant factors which emerge from Jefferson's plans for public secondary education are these. The state was to be divided into a number of districts, within each of which a "college" (intermediate, secondary, or grammar school) was to be set up. These districts were to be laid out so that there would be one college within a day's ride of every home in the state, and there would be enough students (usually about thirty) within each district to guarantee the support of the school. Supervision of the schools was to be provided by the people of the district it served. Each school was to be supported by the tuition fees paid by the students in attendance. In addition, from among the children of the poor the most promising students discovered in the elementary schools would be sent to the grammar schools at state expense. Thus virtue and talent would not be lost to the service of the state because of lack of ability to pay for education. At the end of their secondary education, the best of the pupils educated at public expense would be sent on to the university; the others would become masters of the public elementary schools. At each grammar school would be two masters to teach the "tools of learning," those disciplines necessary for students to do effective work in higher education.

Purpose. The importance of all this lies in Jefferson's intention to insure that an adequate bridge be set up between public elementary and public higher education. Somehow the opportunity had to be provided for everyone who deserved or who could afford to prepare for higher education.[39] Only the state was competent to guarantee that this would be done.

39. To George Ticknor, Nov. 25, 1817 (Ford, *10*, 95–96); to John Adams, Oct. 28, 1813 (Ford, *9*, 427). Here again, Nock is misleading when he says of Jefferson, "Like his contemporary, the Iron Duke, he was well aware that it was possible for a man's education to be too much for his abilities" (see *Jefferson*, p. 312). Jefferson at no point took the position that a man's edu-

COLLEGIATE EDUCATION

Jefferson's proposals for public higher education in the United States and in Virginia were almost as varied as his proposals for public secondary education, and for the same reason: to take advantage of circumstances existing at the moment. There were four ways in which a state or national university could be established, and Jefferson tried them all. An existing college could be modified and taken over by the state; Jefferson attempted to do this with the College of William and Mary. A European university could be transplanted to American soil; Jefferson actively hoped at one time to bring the faculty and library of the University of Geneva across the Atlantic, and seems to have had similar dreams concerning Edinburgh later. A university could be started from scratch, as he urged Congress to do while he was President. Or an existing secondary school could be made to form the nucleus of an institution of higher education. Jefferson's successful efforts to establish the University of Virginia were actually a combination of the last two approaches: Albemarle Academy became Central College, which in turn, although still entirely in the planning stage, became the nucleus of the projected state university.[40]

Here again, despite variety in details, certain constants appear in all Jefferson's proposals. Throughout his life his objects for public higher education remained similar to those described in the Rockfish Gap Report. In addition to

---

cation should be limited. Any man was entitled to as much education as he desired and could afford. Jefferson did believe, however, that only boys of the finest intellect should continue their education at public expense, and that each person's schooling should include training in all things useful to him.

40. See Honeywell, chap. 5, for a complete discussion of Jefferson's lifelong efforts to have the government commit itself to the establishment of an institution of public higher education.

the aims Jefferson had for any sound higher education, he wanted the tax-supported college or university:

> To form the statesmen, legislators and judges, on whom public prosperity and happiness are so much to depend; To expound the principles and structure of government, the laws which regulate the intercourse of nations, those formed municipally for our own government, and a sound spirit of legislation, which, banishing all arbitrary and unnecessary restraint on individual action, shall leave us free to do whatever does not violate the equal rights of another; To harmonize and promote the interests of agriculture, manufactures, and commerce, and by well informed views of political economy to give a free scope to the public industry.[41]

Certain provisions also remained constant. As in secondary education, the students were to include all those who desired and could afford to attend, as well as the most promising of those students educated at public expense in the intermediate schools, who were to continue in the university free: "Worth and genius would thus have been sought out from every condition of life, and completely prepared by education for defeating the competition of wealth and birth for public trusts."[42]

Curriculum provisions may have varied bewilderingly, but one standard, contemporary utility governed every proposal. The university was to include instruction in *all useful knowledge.* It was to be: "a single University embracing every science deemed useful in the present state of the world,"[43] "an University in which all the branches of science deemed useful at this day, shall be taught in their highest degree."[44] This aim was too big to be left safely to

41. Aug. 1, 1818 (Cabell, pp. 434–35).
42. To John Adams, Oct. 28, 1813 (Ford, *9*, 427).
43. To George Ticknor, May ?, 1817 (Ford, *10*, 81).
44. To George Ticknor, Nov. 27, 1817 (Ford, *10*, 95–96).

"private enterprise, which manages so much better all the concerns to which it is equal; but a public institution can alone supply those sciences which, though rarely called for, are yet necessary to complete the circle, all the parts of which contribute to the improvement of the country, and some of them to its preservation."[45]

PROFESSIONAL AND VOCATIONAL EDUCATION

A system of education in any state would not be complete without adequate provision for training in the several professions. This would normally be included in the scope of the university, but being distinct in the thought of Jefferson from liberal arts and general instruction in science, it forms for our purposes a fourth level of education. Since the purpose of a school of law or of medicine was the same to Jefferson as it is to us, most of the provisions he made at this level need no discussion here.[46]

One provision does call for attention, however: the school of technical philosophy, intended by Jefferson to teach laborers and tradesmen as much science as necessary to do their work with intelligence:

The school of technical philosophy will differ essentially in its functions from the other professional schools. The others are instituted to ramify and dilate the particular sciences taught in the schools of the second grade on a general scale only. The technical school is to abridge those which were taught there too much *in extenso* for the limited wants of the practical man. These artificers must be grouped together, according to the particular branch of science in which they need elementary and practical instruction; and a special lecture or lectures should be prepared for each group. And these lectures should be given in the evening, so

45. Sixth Annual Message to Congress, Dec. 2, 1806 (Ford, *8*, 494).
46. To Peter Carr, Sept. 7, 1814 (LB, *19*, 216–19).

as not to interrupt the labors of the day. The school, particularly, should be maintained wholly at the public expense, on the same principles with that of the ward schools.[47]

In other words, Jefferson here envisions a project in adult education: a high school, and a night school at that. In this, Jefferson was a prophet of one of the great developments in American public education. Moreover, the need for all men to have access to whatever technical information they could use was also one of his favorite arguments for founding local public libraries.[48] Technical training was essential to the development of the nation and therefore honorable in any system of public education.

Nor did Jefferson believe that such training was proper only for laborers and tradesmen. His agrarian ideal finds expression in his cherished hope that the science of agriculture might become the crown of all the other sciences for young men completing their education, and that "in every College and University, a professorship of agriculture, and the class of its students, might be honored as the first."[49] Jefferson believed that because of a perversion of social values stemming back to the Renaissance, agriculture was languishing under contempt and oppression. By restoring it to the place of honor in education, he hoped to encourage fully educated men to return to farming, invigorate this calling, and make it first in respect, as it had always been first in utility.

Education, Corruption, and Reform

In many respects Jefferson's plans for public education have been completely outstripped by actual developments in the intervening years. It would therefore be well to keep

47. Ibid., p. 219.
48. To John Wyche, May 19, 1809 (LB, _12_, 282).
49. To David Williams, Nov. 14, 1803 (LB, _10_, 428–30).

in mind, when evaluating his desires, that in his own day this statesman was trying to use public education to effect major social reforms. America needed the system he envisioned, as he viewed the scene, because available education was not only insufficient to supply the needs of democracy, but in various specific ways was doing the cause of self-government positive harm.

EUROPE

Jefferson worried most about the corruption of political principles to which American youth might be subject in education. Not the least of the dangers of studying in Europe was a loss of understanding of the principles of self-government. He blamed the antirepublican sentiments of many fellow Americans upon foreign education.[50] Nor was the danger limited to the other side of the Atlantic. Its presence in other American states aroused his objections to sending the youth of Virginia elsewhere to be educated:

> I am . . . alarmed to see, in the other states, the general political dispositions of those to whom is confided the education of the rising generation. . . . I have great confidence in the common sense of mankind in general: but it requires a great deal to get the better of notions which our tutors have instilled into our minds while incapable of questioning them, & to rise superior to antipathies strongly rooted.[51]

THE NORTHERN STATES

Just as Jefferson held that European discipline could not supply the peculiar wants of Americans, so he also felt that for Virginians a Southern education was preferable to any available in the North.[52] He felt that sending Virginians

50. To James Sullivan, Feb. 9, 1797 (Ford, 7, 117-18).
51. To Jeremiah Moore, Aug. 14, 1800 (Ford, 7, 455).
52. Cabell, p. xix; to Thomas Cooper, Aug. 14, 1820 (LB, *15*, 264).

to other regions was a financial burden upon the state, and hoped to arrest "the heavy tribute we are annually paying to other States and countries for the article of education."[53] A worse burden was the loss of patriotic and democratic sentiment, "the tax of toryism, fanaticism and indifferentism to their own State, which we now send our youth to bring from those of New England."[54] The cure for this educational corruption was the establishment of the University of Virginia. That done, Jefferson rejoiced: "That institution is now qualified to raise its youth to an order of science unequalled in any other State; and this superiority will be the greater from the free range of mind encouraged there, and the restraint imposed at other seminaries by the shackles of a domineering hierarchy, and a bigoted adhesion to ancient habits."[55]

TEXTS AND ORTHODOXY

Yet the serpent of corruption might even creep into the Garden of Eden. The minds of American students could be corrupted either by textbooks or teachers even in the University of Virginia. In a letter devoted to a detailed discussion of what should be read in ancient and modern history, Jefferson warned that to read Hume is to endanger one's natural republican sentiments. He argued that the central thesis of Hume's three-volume history of England was that it was the people who encroached on the rights of the sovereign, not the sovereign who usurped the rights of the people. In creating Tories, Hume's work was diabolical:

> So bewitching was his style and manner, that his readers were unwilling to doubt anything, swallowed everything, and all England became Tories by the magic of

53. Report of the Board of Visitors, Oct. 3, 1820 (Cabell, p. 464).
54. To Charles Yancy, Jan. 6, 1816 (Ford, *10*, 4).
55. "Thoughts on Lotteries," Feb. 1826 (Ford, *10*, 370–71).

his art. His pen revolutionized the public sentiment of that country more completely than the standing armies could ever have done, which were so much dreaded and deprecated by the patriots of that day. . . . If first read, Hume makes an English Tory, from whence it is an easy step to American Toryism.[56]

When he wrote the above passage Jefferson had already proposed that the student's reading in the field of government be rather rigidly prescribed. He argued in this manner:

In most public seminaries, textbooks are prescribed to each of the several schools, as the *norma docendi* in that school; and this is generally done by authority of the trustees. I should not propose this generally in our University, because, I believe none of us are so much at the heights of science in the several branches to undertake this; and therefore that it will be better left to the professors, until occasion of interference shall be given. But there is one branch in which we are the best judges, in which heresies may be taught, of so interesting a character to our own State, and to the United States, as to make it a duty in us to lay down the principles which shall be taught. It is that of government. Mr. Gilmer being withdrawn [as Law Professor], we know not who his successor may be. He may be a Richmond lawyer, or one of that school of quondam federalism, now consolidation. It is our duty to guard against the dissemination of such principles among our youth, and the diffusion of that poison, by a previous prescription of the texts to be followed in their discourses. I therefore inclose you a resolution which I think of proposing.[57]

56. To ———, Oct. 25, 1825 (LB, *16*, 124–28).
57. To Joseph C. Cabell, Feb. 3, 1825 (Cabell, p. 339).

The resolution which Jefferson sent to Cabell and Madison evidently proposed that a textbook for the School of Law be composed of Algernon Sidney's and John Locke's works on government, the Declaration of Independence, the Constitution, the Federalist Papers, the Virginia and Kentucky Resolutions, and Madison's Report on the Virginia Resolutions.[58] It was intended to be an effective safeguard against heretical intrusions into the field of politics.[59] All this was to take place in the university of which Jefferson had insisted, "This institution of my native state, the Hobby of my old age, will be based on the illimitable freedom of the human mind, to explore and to expose every subject susceptible of it's contemplation."[60] For "here we are not afraid to follow truth wherever it may lead, nor to tolerate error as long as reason is left free to combat it."[61]

In reply, Madison expressed approval of Jefferson's intention but doubted the efficacy of the method: "It is certainly very material that the true doctrines of liberty, as exemplified in our Political System, should be inculcated on those who are to sustain and may administer it. It is, at the same time, not easy to find standard books that will be both guides & guards for this purpose."[62] He proceeded to point out that every work listed by Jefferson for this purpose was subject to misconstruction of meaning, and that some of them were partisan enough not to be acceptable even to good republicans. Madison then put his finger on the heart of the problem: "In framing a political creed, a like difficulty occurs as in the case of religion. . . . If the Articles be in very general terms, they do not answer the purpose; if in very particular terms, they divide & exclude

58. James Madison to Thomas Jefferson, Feb. 8, 1825, in Gaillard Hunt, ed., *Writings of James Madison, 9* (New York, 1900–10), 218–21.

59. See Koch, *Jefferson and Madison,* pp. 275–78.

60. To Destutt de Tracy, Dec. 26, 1820 (Ford, *10,* 174).

61. To William Roscoe, Dec. 27, 1820 (LB, *15,* 302–03). See also Nock, pp. 318–19.

62. Hunt, *Writings of Madison, 9,* 218.

where meant to unite & fortify." Madison's solution was to take a different tack: "The best that can be done in our case seems to be, to avoid the two extremes, by referring to selected Standards without requiring an unqualified conformity to them, which indeed might not in every instance be possible. The selection would give them authority with the Students, and might control or counteract deviations of the Professor."

"AN ABLE & ORTHODOX PROFESSOR"

However, Madison's final remark was that "After all, the most effectual safeguard against heretical intrusions into the School of Politics, will be an Able & Orthodox Professor, whose course of instruction will be an example to his successors, and may carry with it a sanction from the visitors."[63]

That Jefferson came around to Madison's point of view on this matter seems evident from a letter he wrote subsequently on the same problem:

> In the selection of our Law Professor, we must be rigorously attentive to his political principles. You will recollect that before the revolution, Coke Littleton was the universal elementary book of law students, and a sounder whig never wrote, nor of profounder learning in the orthodox doctrines of the British constitution, or in what were called English liberties. You remember also that our lawyers were then all whigs. But when his blackletter text, and uncouth but cunning learning got out of fashion, and the honeyed Mansfieldism of Blackstone became the student's hornbook, from that moment, that profession (the nursery of our Congress) began to slide into Toryism, and nearly all the young brood of lawyers are now of that hue. They

63. Ibid., p. 219.

suppose themselves, indeed, to be Whigs, because they no longer know what Whigism or republicanism means. It is in our seminary that that vestal flame is to be kept alive; it is thence it is to spread anew over our own and the sister States. If we are true and vigilant in our trust, within a dozen or twenty years a majority of our own legislature will be from one school, and many disciples will have carried its doctrines home with them to their several States, and will have leavened thus the whole mass.[64]

EDUCATION FOR FREEDOM?

What had happened is easy to see. The Sage of Monticello had been caught between the horns of a dilemma which occurs repeatedly in education for freedom. The purpose of public education was to safeguard and foster democracy by bringing about the commitment of American citizens and political leaders to the principles of self-government. Responding to that purpose, Jefferson, with his flair for bold and often dogmatic action, had proposed the inculcation of a creed. Commitment to principle, however, as Madison pointed out, must be distinguished from unqualified, blind acceptance of a system of formulated propositions. Jefferson recognized that his device was destructive to his end, and readily changed his approach.

DEVICE VERSUS PURPOSE

He had not dropped his great purpose, however. Education was a power. It could make or break man's ability to be free. As Jefferson saw the matter, this power of education made it the concern of the whole of a democratic society. Potentially it was the cradle of great social reform.

64. To James Madison, Feb. 17, 1826 (Ford, *10*, 376).

It could teach men to know their rights. It could enable men to recognize threats to their freedom. It could prepare worth and genius to defeat the competition of wealth and birth for public trusts. Finally, it was a means to great material progress.[65]

Yet Jefferson's devices might even here be destructive to his over-all purpose. For instance, if education as conceived by Jefferson was a weapon for social reform, we must recognize that it could also be one for rigid conservatism. The recurrent emphasis upon giving each person useful knowledge can be another way of insisting that he be trained and adjusted to his actual role in society, and thus it could easily become a means of preserving social inequalities. To take just one example, Jefferson's concept of education for women is open to this criticism. Women were to be given enough of man's education to take over their husband's duties in educating their sons if necessary, but they were not to assume the functions of men any further. Their womanhood determined their vocations. It is doubtful whether Jefferson ever saw that his ideas on education contained this danger.

65. To Joseph C. Cabell, Nov. 28, 1820 (Ford, *10*, 166).

CHAPTER 10

*P*ublic Education and Religious Instruction

Aims

Jefferson's thought concerning religion in education can be portrayed by the following diagram of an educational ladder.

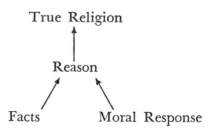

To Jefferson this ladder and the curriculum which gave it substance were suitable to all proper education, including public education in a democracy, because in his mind the aim of public education, as that of private education, extended into the field of social and political relationships.

Like private instruction, general instruction had the purpose of producing moral, healthy, capable adults. It also had two auxiliary purposes essential to democratic society: instructing all men in their rights, interests, and duties as citizens, and training the gifted or talented for leadership or management of society's affairs.[1]

To Jefferson the purpose of religion in public education was the same as in private education: to make men moral. There were also two auxiliary purposes of specific social application. The first was to enable all men, both the masses and the gifted elite, to exercise their rights with order and justice, and to cherish those of others. The second concerned those destined for posts of leadership, "the statesmen, legislators and judges, on whom public prosperity and individual happiness are so much to depend."[2] They were to learn the precepts of virtue and order, and to form habits of reflection and correct action; this would render them public examples of virtue in their relationships with individuals and with other governments. Jefferson felt this to be essential to the health of the country: "I have ever cherished the same spirit with all nations, from a consciousness that peace, prosperity, liberty, and morals have an intimate connection."[3]

Jefferson's efforts to define and implement the role of religion in public education, however, had another motivation as well, springing from his concept of progress. Progress was not inevitable, but depended upon the intelligent, free, moral actions of men. Public opinion was ultimately the guide and guardian of public morals and welfare, and the arbitress in every age of the destinies of society.[4] The bulwarks of progress, then, were a democratic society, science,

1. Bill for the More General Diffusion of Knowledge (Boyd, *Papers of Jefferson*, 2, 526–27).
2. Rockfish Gap Report (Cabell, *Early History*, pp. 434–35).
3. To George Logan, Oct. 3, 1813 (Ford, *Writings of Jefferson*, 9, 421).
4. Report of Board of Visitors, Oct. 4, 1819 (Cabell, p. 460).

and a sound education to give public opinion a wholesome direction.[5]

According to Jefferson, progress was possible in all fields, including religion. He disagreed with those who believed, as he saw it, "that government, religion, morality & every other science were in the highest perfection in the ages of darkest ignorance, and that nothing can ever be devised more perfect than what was established by our forefathers."[6] Wherever freedom of the mind had been allowed to any appreciable degree, progress in religion had already taken place in the form of a revival of simple, rational, moral, primitive Christianity, the doctrine he held to have been taught by Jesus and believed by the early church.[7]

What had happened simply because freedom had been allowed could be made to flourish under the right conditions. But these conditions involved an end to the thousands of conflicting and unprovable religious mysteries and dogmas which drove men mad, made them immoral, and turned the world into bedlam. No one man could bring that about: "To undertake to bring them all right would be like undertaking single-handed, to fell the forests of America."[8] The task was not impossible, however. There was a way in which it could be done. Jefferson believed the human condition "to be susceptible of much improvement, and most of all, in matters of government and religion; and that the diffusion of knowledge is to be the instrument by which it is to be effected."[9]

Jefferson's private correspondence shows that he hoped public education would bring about two conditions he longed to see in the field of religion: first, "a quiet eutha-

5. Ekirch, *Idea of Progress*, p. 32.

6. To Elbridge Gerry, Jan. 26, 1799 (Ford, 7, 328–29).

7. To John Adams, Aug. 22, 1813 (Ford, 9, 409–14); to James Smith, Dec. 8, 1822 (LB, *15*, 408–09).

8. To Charles Clay, Jan. 29, 1815 (LB, *14*, 232). See also letter to Mathew Carey, Nov. 11, 1816 (Ford, *10*, 67–68).

9. To P. S. Dupont de Nemours, April 24, 1816 (Ford, *10*, 25).

nasia of the heresies of bigotry and fanaticism which have
so long triumphed over human reason and so generally and
deeply afflicted mankind,"[10] and second, the flourishing of
a general religion of peace, reason, and morality.[11] He
prophesied: "The genuine and simple religion of Jesus
will one day be restored: such as it was preached and prac-
tised by himself. Very soon after his death, it became muffled up in mysteries, and has been ever since kept in con-
cealment from the vulgar eye. To penetrate and dissipate
these clouds of darkness, the general mind must be strengthened by education."[12]

Curriculum

RELIGION AND THE PURPOSE
OF PUBLIC EDUCATION

Because these were Jefferson's aims, there is no significant
difference between his curriculum proposals concerning
religion to the many young people he advised privately, and
the provisions he suggested in the field of public education.
In both cases the aims would be aided by the teaching of
true religion or morality and thwarted by instruction in
dogmas or religio-metaphysical abstractions. The ability of
the latter to wreck the mind would turn the common people, the masses, the ordinary citizens, into dupes or fools
incapable of understanding or cherishing their own rights
or those of others. To Jefferson one of the enduring examples of this kind of corruption was that of New England's
residents, who were incapable of advancing to liberty be-

10. To William Short, Oct. 31, 1819 (Ford, *10*, 144).

11. To Thomas Cooper, Nov. 2, 1822 (Ford, *10*, 243).

12. To Adrian Van der Kemp, 1820 (quoted in Padover, *Jefferson on Democracy*, p. 118). See also letter to Elbridge Gerry, Jan. 26, 1799 (Ford, *7*,
328–29); to Samuel Kercheval, Jan. 19, 1810 (LB, *12*, 345–46); to Benjamin
Waterhouse, March 3, 1818 (Ford, *10*, 103–04).

cause their clergy saw to it that no mind developed there beyond mediocrity.[13]

If dogmatic religion made the common people dupes, it made their leaders tyrants. As Jefferson saw it, those among the elite whose minds had been corrupted by creeds would no longer cherish the rights of all nor set examples of virtue and justice in their official actions concerning constituents or other nations. Instead they would attempt by perversion of the law or seduction of public opinion to compel all men to accept their particular creed.[14] Religious enthusiasm in the popular assembly could lead not only to immoral acts of legal oppression but also to leaders inflaming the passions of the masses and turning them into mobs in order to destroy the opposition of men who still retained rationality, morality, and concern for the rights of others.[15]

PUBLIC EDUCATION AND
RELIGIOUS FREEDOM

Jefferson's personal influence on those who requested his guidance was enough to encourage them to apply their attention to morality and ignore dogmatic religion. He could only deplore the case of young men being miseducated in private. In public education, however, the principle of the separation of church and state (embodied in the Virginia Statute for Religious Freedom and the First Amendment to the Constitution) could be applied. Those doctrines which could ruin the mind were not the beliefs all men held in common but the conflicting dogmas and assertions of

13. To Pierpont Edwards, July 21, 1801 (Ford, *8,* 75); to Horatio Gates Spafford, Jan. 10, 1816 (Ford, *10,* 13). See also *Notes on Virginia* (Ford, *3,* 265).

14. To Edward Dowse, April 19, 1803 (LB, *10,* 378). See also William E. Dodd, *Statesmen of the Old South* (New York, 1929), pp. 20–21.

15. To Samuel Kercheval, Jan. 19, 1810 (LB, *12,* 345–46); to John Adams, Aug. 22, 1813 (Ford, *9,* 417); to Pierpont Edwards, July 21, 1801 (Ford, *8,* 74–75); to Levi Lincoln, Aug. 26, 1801 (Ford, *8,* 83–85).

particular sects. Public education was to be supported (wholly at the primary level, and at least in part at all others) by taxes levied upon all the people. To teach sectarian doctrines and dogmas within state-supported schools, as Jefferson saw it, was inevitably "to compel a man to furnish contributions of money for the propagation of opinions which he disbelieves and abhors."[16] It was an intrusion of public authority into the realm of religious freedom.[17]

On this basis Jefferson felt that those aspects of religion whose effects could only be pernicious might properly be excluded from democratic public education. In no way did he see this move as an attack upon religion. Instead, it was a means of guaranteeing religious freedom. It provided simply that no sect or group of sects could get any advantage over others through control of, or establishment within, public education. Jefferson expected that the sects would recognize the fact that their own interests were involved and cooperate willingly in enforcing this limitation of what could be taught in public education: "In conformity with the principles of our Constitution, which places all sects of religion on an equal footing, with the jealousies of the different sects in guarding that equality from encroachment and surprise, and with the sentiments of the Legislature in favor of freedom of religion, manifested on former occasions, we have proposed no professor of divinity."[18]

The practical educational consequences would be salutary. Eliminated from the field of public education would be exactly the doctrines and beliefs upon which no one could agree anyway. Jefferson's provision for the elementary schools put the matter in just those terms. "The said teachers shall, in all things relating to the education and govern-

16. Bill for Establishing Religious Freedom (Boyd, 2, 545).
17. Rockfish Gap Report (Cabell, pp. 441–42); Report of Board of Visitors, Oct. 7, 1822 (Cabell, pp. 473–75); to Thomas Cooper, Nov. 2, 1822 (Ford, *10*, 243).
18. Rockfish Gap Report (Cabell, p. 441).

ment of their pupils, be under the direction and control of the Visitors; but no religious reading, instruction, or exercise, shall be prescribed or practiced inconsistent with the tenets of any religious sect or denomination."[19]

To Jefferson the elimination of whatever was inconsistent with the tenets of any particular sect did not mean that religion itself was to be outlawed in public education, any more than the interdiction of the government from meddling with religious institutions, doctrines, disciplines, or exercises meant to Jefferson that the government was without religion.[20] This he denied.[21] Rather, the purpose of this provision was to guarantee and encourage religious freedom. This meant that those areas of religion upon which all sects agreed were certainly to be included within the framework of public education.

Jefferson never doubted that these areas existed. Indeed, he claimed to confine his religious reading to them alone.[22] The most important of these was morality. "The moral branch of religion which is the same in all religions . . . instructs us how to live well and worthily in society."[23] All religions agreed on the precepts of morality, which could be summed up in a few words: "Be just and good—Fear God and love thy neighbor."[24] This was common ground fit for use at all levels of public education. A second area in which Jefferson felt that all denominations recognized common interest and agreement was that of classical

19. Bill for Establishing Elementary Schools (Honeywell, *Educational Work*, p. 235). This and other clauses concerning religion were omitted by Joseph Cabell before he presented Jefferson's bill to the Virginia legislature. See letter from Joseph C. Cabell, Dec. 13, 1817 (Cabell, p. 97).

20. To DeWitt Clinton, May 24, 1807 (Ford, *9*, 62–64). Cf. letter to Samuel Miller, Jan. 23, 1808 (Ford, *9*, 174).

21. To Thomas Cooper, Nov. 2, 1822 (Ford, *10*, 243).

22. To Thomas Leiper, Jan. 21, 1809 (Ford, *9*, 238). See also letter to John Adams, Aug. 22, 1813 (Ford, *9*, 418).

23. To Thomas Leiper, Jan. 21, 1809 (Ford, *9*, 232).

24. To George Logan, Nov. 12, 1816 (Ford, *10*, 68); to John Adams, Jan. 11, 1817 (Ford, *10*, 73).

tongues: "the Hebrew, Greek, and Latin languages, the depositories of the originals, and of the earliest and most respected authorities of the faith of every sect."[25] Finally, Jefferson held that all religions concurred in certain arguments plain to every man of reason, and in their moral and ethical implications. These were "proofs of the being of a God, the creator, preserver, and supreme ruler of the universe, the author of all the relations of morality, and of the laws and obligations these infer."[26] Morality, languages, reasoned conclusions from the evidence of the senses, these aspects of religion were common ground for all persuasions. Here was nothing inconsistent with the tenets of any religious sect or denomination. These were essential in any scheme of public education which was aimed at producing the moral man and fostering religious freedom.

SPECIFIC CURRICULUM PROPOSALS

All of Jefferson's proposals for public—i.e. tax-supported —education are intended to allow, and indeed to provide for, instruction in these aspects of religion. None of his proposals was intended to go one step further and admit instruction in doctrines he considered to be sectarian. These were educationally pernicious; they could ruin the minds and morals of the students. They were socially divisive and led to persecution and oppression. They could not be included in tax-supported instruction without violating the principle of religious freedom by giving some sects advantages over others and compelling taxpayers to furnish contributions of money for the propagation of religious opinion. They had no place in public education.

There is confusion about this because certain of his concrete proposals have been mistakenly interpreted to indicate a willingness on his part to have instruction in areas of re-

25. Report of Board of Visitors, Oct. 7, 1822 (Cabell, pp. 473–74).
26. Rockfish Gap Report (Cabell, p. 441).

ligion other than "the moral branch on which all sects
agree" given in tax-supported institutions of higher education. Others have been misinterpreted to show that he
would have preferred to eliminate all religion from public
education. Chief among these are the proposed and actual
revisions made in the curriculum of William and Mary
College in 1779, the proposal concerning a theological
school in the letter to Peter Carr of 1814, the Rockfish Gap
Report's provisions for religious worship and instruction
at the University of Virginia, and the famous "Schools on
the Confines" proposal for the university in 1822. It seems
advisable at this point to take them up in chronological
order, and analyze each one in detail.

REVISION AT THE COLLEGE
OF WILLIAM AND MARY

Jefferson's proposal to change the College of William and
Mary was part of his attempt to provide a complete system
of public education for Virginia in 1779.[27] At the time the
college had six professorships, including one for moral philosophy, one for the instruction of Indians in elementary
subjects and the principles of Christianity, and two of "divinity."[28] The last two Jefferson called: "one school of sacred theology, with two professorships therein, to wit, one
for teaching the Hebrew tongue and expounding the holy
scriptures; and the other for explaining the commonplaces
of divinity, and the controversies with heretics."[29] On the

27. A Bill for Amending the Constitution of William and Mary, and
Substituting More Certain Revenues for Its Support (Boyd, 2, 535–43). Only
the provisions concerning religion shall concern us here. Descriptions of
the complete revision are in Bowers, *Young Jefferson*, pp. 185–87; Chinard,
Jefferson, pp. 98–100; Kimball, *Jefferson: War and Peace*, pp. 15–16; and
Malone, *Jefferson*, *1*, 284–85.

28. So-called in *Notes on Virginia* (Ford, *3*, 255). In the *Autobiography*
Jefferson called them: "the two professorships of Divinity & Oriental languages" (Ford, *1*, 69–70).

29. Boyd, 2, 538.

basis of this description it is probably safe to assume that when Jefferson used the word divinity he was referring to what we would call biblical studies, theology, and apologetics.

Jefferson hoped to transform this college from "an establishment purely of the Church of England"[30] into a state-supported university. In his bill he proposed to abolish the two professorships of divinity, preserve the professorship of moral philosophy (and include under it instruction in the law of nature and nations), and substitute for the professorship for the Indians a "missionary" whose chief duties would be research into all phases of Indian culture. Provision was also made for the study of ecclesiastical history under a professorship of history.

The bill was never passed.[31] However, in 1779, shortly after Jefferson was elected a Visitor of William and Mary, he used his position to bring about some of the changes he had proposed. The professorships of divinity were abolished and others substituted; no provision was made for instruction of ecclesiastical history; and the professorship to the Indians evidently remained unchanged, although Jefferson did not lose hope.[32] He was pleased with the results of the changes, as far as they went.[33] In 1800 he attempted to complete the transformation but got nowhere and finally turned his efforts elsewhere.

Jefferson felt the legislature would be justified in making the changes he proposed, because to him the college had always been a public institution: "Being founded and endowed with the lands and revenues of the public, and intended for their sole use and improvement, and no wise in nature of a private grant, the same is of right subject to

30. *Autobiography* (Ford, *1*, 67).

31. Boyd, 2, 543 n.

32. See *Notes on Virginia*, Query 15 (Ford, *3*, 256); *Autobiography* (Ford, *1*, 70).

33. To Samuel Henley, Oct. 14, 1785 (Boyd, *8*, 635).

the public direction and may by them be altered and
amended, until such form be devised as will render the
institution publicly advantageous, in proportion as it is
publicly expensive." To render proper public service the
college as a whole had to be improved so that "those who
are to be the future guardians of the rights and liberties of
their country may be endowed with science and virtue, to
watch and preserve the sacred deposit."[34]

Jefferson's motivation in suppressing the professorships
of divinity cannot be explained merely as a desire to eliminate sectarian instruction from public higher education. It
must be seen, rather, as a recognition of a need to clear the
way for the college's proper expansion as a public institution into all of the sciences useful to the population and
leadership of the state. The changes actually made were a
step in this direction. That this did not mean to Jefferson
that the state must have nothing whatever to do with religion can be seen in his comments concerning his hopes for
the Indian school:

> The purposes of the . . . institution would be better
> answered by maintaining a perpetual mission among
> the Indian tribes, the object of which, besides instruct-
> ing them in the principles of Christianity, as the found-
> er requires, should be to collect their traditions, laws,
> customs, languages, and other circumstances which
> might lead to a discovery of their relation with one an-
> other, or descent from other nations. When these ob-
> jects are accomplished with one tribe, the missionary
> might pass on to another.[35]

Religion was not to be excluded. The principle of separation is simply not raised. It seems obvious, however, that
to Jefferson the possibility of using such a missionary for

34. Bill for Amending Constitution of William and Mary (Boyd, 2,
538–39).
35. *Notes on Virginia*, Query 15 (Ford, 3, 256).

research was paramount. The educational requirements of the state governed all of his changes, proposed or accomplished, at William and Mary.

THE 1814 "LETTER TO PETER CARR"

As we have seen, Jefferson's efforts during and after the Revolutionary War to introduce a comprehensive system of public education into his native state came to very little. Never satisfied with these results, he returned to the problem (which, indeed, he had never dropped) after he had retired from the Presidency. He became a member of the Board of Visitors of Albemarle Academy, a private secondary school then in the planning stage at Charlottesville. At the request of the Visitors, Jefferson drew up a plan for education in the form of a letter addressed to Peter Carr.[36] His discussion was not limited to immediate objectives for Albemarle Academy, however, but included a survey of the total educational needs of the state of Virginia. As a result, this letter has proved to be one of the chief causes of difference of opinion concerning Jefferson's thought on religion in public education.

In the opening chapter we discussed this difference of opinion. It was pointed out that on the basis of this letter J. M. O'Neill argued that Jefferson advocated the use of public funds in Virginia for a school of theology, a department of "Theology and Ecclesiastical History" for the training of clergymen.[37] To this contention R. F. Butts replied that Jefferson had advocated setting up a professional school of theology only in connection with a private academy, and that he dropped this part of the plan when he turned to the promotion of a publicly supported state university. Butts believed the use of private funds alone made the setting up of a theological seminary permissible to Jefferson.[38]

36. To Peter Carr, Sept. 7, 1814 (LB, *19*, 211–21).
37. See *Religion and Education*, pp. 76–77, 205–06, 215.
38. See *American Tradition*, pp. 112–23.

Which of these two gentlemen was right? Actually, neither, as we shall see. Jefferson did include in this document provision for a school of "Theology and Ecclesiastical History," to which he intended "ecclesiastics" to go after they had completed their liberal education. The suggestion was deliberate; he mentioned the school twice, once in the body of his discussion and once in a tabular summary of his plan. It is also unique; it appears only in this document. There is no evidence that Jefferson ever made a similar suggestion at any other time in his life.

This letter gives no support, however, to the contention either that Jefferson advocated the use of public funds for teaching theology *or* that he felt a theological school should be financed by private sources alone. The letter nowhere discusses the financing of any school mentioned except the school of technical philosophy and the ward or elementary schools. One sentence covers them both, and in so doing makes Jefferson's intentions for financing the others completely ambiguous: "The school [of technical philosophy], particularly, should be maintained wholly at the public expense on the same principles with that of the ward schools."[39]

The ambiguity is caused by the purpose of this particular one of Jefferson's educational proposals. It is not intended to be a blueprint, a working drawing in which all details have been ironed out and upon the basis of which construction may be begun. Jefferson called it "a survey of the general field of science." It is a vision, a dream of a complete and integrated system of education, presented to the trustees of Albemarle Academy, a group of men in a position to try to bring only a portion of that dream into actuality: "In the first place, we must ascertain with precision the object of our institution, by taking a survey of the general field of science, and marking out the portion we mean to occupy at

39. LB, *19*, 219.

first, and the ultimate extension of our views beyond that, should we be enabled to render it, in the end, as comprehensive as we would wish."[40] The survey envisions education on three integrated levels: elementary, general, and professional. The theological school is placed in the last category.

Having completed the survey and summed it up briefly in a tabular statement, Jefferson turns to practical matters: "On this survey of science, then, I recur to the question, what portion of it we mark out for the occupation of our institution? With the first grade of education we shall have nothing to do. The sciences of the second grade are our first object."[41] Dreaming is over and real planning is begun, as Jefferson groups the subjects of the second grade under four professorships. The third grade of education is not mentioned again. The suggestion concerning the school of theology is only a suggestion, put forth without discussion of what might be involved in the way of philosophy, principle, or practice. It is not a proposal for action.

Jefferson sent a copy of this letter, leaving wide margins, to Thomas Cooper, requesting the latter's comments and suggestions.[42] Cooper replied advising Jefferson to omit theology, because there was no available criterion for the various conflicting systems.[43] Jefferson answered:

> I agree . . . that a professorship of Theology has no place in our institution. But we cannot always do what is absolutely best. Those with whom we act, entertaining different views, have the power and right of carrying them into practice. Truth advances and error recedes step by step only; and to do our fellow men the most good in our power, we must lead where we can,

40. Ibid., p. 213.
41. Ibid., p. 220.
42. To Thomas Cooper, Sept. 10, 1814 (LB, *14*, 179–80).
43. From Thomas Cooper, Sept. 22, 1814 (Jefferson Papers, Library of Congress, CCII; cited in Malone, *Public Life of Thomas Cooper*, New Haven, 1926, p. 227).

follow where we cannot, and still go with them, watching always the favorable moment for helping them to another step. Perhaps I should concur with you also in excluding the *theory* (not the *practice*) of medicine. This is the charlatanerie of the body, as the other is of the mind.

In other words, Jefferson explained the inclusion of a school of theology as an attempt to gain support of many who disputed his low opinion of its educational value. Cooper's letter had brought him back to himself by reminding him that he had compromised his educational standards. In subsequent proposals for higher education Jefferson omitted theology. It was not science but fraud, a subject which cannot be justified educationally, which cannot be demonstrated to be a useful science, and which therefore has no place in any valid scheme of education. Again, Jefferson never raised the question of the separation of church and state.[44]

PROVISIONS FOR THE UNIVERSITY OF VIRGINIA

The Rockfish Gap Report. Growing ever more favorable to the idea of establishing a state university, the Virginia legislature authorized a meeting of twenty-four commissioners, appointed by the Governor and his Council, from all over the state to fix the site for the proposed institution and settle other matters to be included in a working plan. The commissioners met at Rockfish Gap on August 1, 1818. Jefferson was one of them, and assumed leadership in the deliberations. The site of Albemarle Academy (which had since been transformed into Central College but was still only the dream of its board of trustees) and Jefferson's rules

---

44. To Thomas Cooper, Oct. 7, 1814 (LB, *14*, 220–21). Italics Jefferson's. Incidentally, in this letter he disagreed with Cooper about botany and anatomy; Jefferson held that they *were* useful sciences.

and plans were adopted, and a report was drawn substantially as he had written it.[45]

In the Rockfish Gap Report religion is mentioned twice,
once with respect to worship and once with respect to cur-
ricular provisions for instruction in the field. The suggestion concerning religious worship is so brief and lacking
in commentary that it is almost impossible to evaluate. It
appears in the section on architecture for the university:
"It is supposed probable that a building of somewhat more
size in the middle of the grounds may be called for in time,
in which may be rooms for religious worship, under such
impartial regulations as the Visitors shall prescribe, for
public examinations, for a library, for the schools of music,
drawing, and other associated purposes."[46] It is difficult on
the basis of this brief reference to a tentative idea to determine what Jefferson and the other commissioners at Rockfish Gap had in mind concerning specific provisions for
religious worship at the University of Virginia. It is obvious,
nevertheless, that religious worship was not automatically
to be ruled off the campus. Under impartial regulations
prescribed by the Board of Visitors it could be held. This
was in accord with Jefferson's consistent practice of including whatever aspects of religion all people agree on in any
educational curriculum.

The statement concerning religion in the curriculum of
the University is fuller and lends itself more easily to interpretation: "In conformity with the principles of our Constitution, which places all sects of religion on an equal footing, with the jealousies of the different sects guarding that
equality from encroachment and surprise, and with the sentiments of the Legislature in favor of freedom of religion,
manifested on former occasions, we have proposed no professor of divinity . . ."[47]—that is, the teaching of such sub-

45. See Schachner, *Jefferson*, 2, 957–58.
46. Rockfish Gap Report (Cabell, p. 434).
47. Ibid., p. 441.

jects as theology, apologetics, and scripture is held to be inevitably sectarian;[48] to have them taught in a tax-supported university would be a violation of the Constitution, which neither the sects nor the legislature would desire.

This does not mean that all religion is to be ruled out of the curriculum, however. The sentence continues:

> and the rather as the proofs of the being of a God, the creator, preserver, and supreme ruler of the universe, the author of all the relations of morality, and of the laws and obligations these infer, will be within the province of the professor of ethics; to which adding the development of these moral obligations, of those in which all sects agree, with a knowledge of the languages, Hebrew, Greek, and Latin, a basis will be formed common to all the sects.

That branch of religion in which all sects supposedly agree (morality, the proofs of the existence of God, and the tools for research into the scriptures) is permissible in the curriculum. The teaching of this branch is, to Jefferson, not an encroachment upon the equality of the sects; it is not a violation of religious freedom or of the principle of separation of church and state.

"Proceeding thus far without offense to the Constitution, we have thought it proper at this point to leave every sect to provide, as they think fittest, the means of further instruction, in their own particular tenets."[49] Instruction in those doctrines in which the sects differ must be provided by the sects themselves. Of all religion, the common core alone can be taught without offense to the Constitution. Of course, although it is not mentioned in the report, this legally permissible "common core" consists of just those areas in religion which Jefferson believed alone had a right to be in any worthwhile education, and the constitutionally

48. See above, p. 211.
49. Cabell, p. 442.

offensive, sectarian tenets were just those religious areas which, Jefferson privately believed, endangered the human reason.

Theological schools on the confines. These curriculum provisions were evidently subject to hostile criticism (which was probably also motivated by certain personnel arrangements which shall be discussed shortly). In 1822 the annual report of the University's Board of Visitors included the "Schools on the Confines" proposal as a response.[50] Beginning with a somewhat condensed and modified version of the paragraph on religious instruction in the Rockfish Gap Report, the proposal proceeds to state the importance of religion in education and in society:

> It was not, however, to be understood that instruction in religious opinions and duties was meant to be precluded by the authorities as indifferent to the interests of society; on the contrary, the relations which exist between man and his Maker, and the duties resulting from those relations, are the most interesting and important to every human being, and the most incumbent on his study and investigation. The want of instruction in the various creeds of religious faith existing among our citizens presents, therefore, a chasm in a general institution of the useful sciences.

In other words, education without religion is seriously incomplete. Unfortunately, the problem of providing for instruction in religion in public education is complicated by the problem of religious freedom: "it was thought that this want, and the entrustment to each society of instruction in its own doctrines, were evils of less danger than a permission to the public authorities to dictate modes or principles of religious instruction, or than opportunities furnished them

50. Report of Board of Visitors, Oct. 7, 1822 (Cabell, pp. 473–75).

of giving countenance or ascendency of any one sect over another."

After this preamble, the central proposal is broached.

> A remedy, however, has been suggested, of promising aspect, which, while it excludes the public authorities from the domain of religious freedom, would give to the sectarian schools of divinity the full benefit of the public provisions made for instruction in the other branches of science. These branches are equally necessary to the divine as to the other professional or civil characters, to enable them to fulfill the duties of their calling with understanding and usefulness. It has, therefore, been in contemplation, and suggested by some pious individuals, who perceive the advantages of associating other studies with those of religion, to establish their religious schools on the confines of the University, so as to give to their students ready and convenient access and attendance on the scientific lectures of the University; and to maintain, by that means, those destined for the religious professions on as high a standing of science, and of personal weight and respectability, as may be obtained by others from the benefits of the University.

The plan briefly stated is this: Since the university offers its students no instruction in denominational religion, let divinity students take courses in science at the university.

The next sentence points out that this proposal might affect favorably the university student's opportunity to worship:

> Such establishments [the divinity schools] would offer the further and great advantage of enabling the students of the University to attend religious exercises with the professor of their particular sect, either in the

rooms of the building still to be erected, and destined to that purpose under impartial regulations, as proposed in the same report of the Commissioners [The Rockfish Gap Report], or in the lecturing room of such professor.

Nothing further is said about that, however. The proposal focuses again on the divinity students admitted to the campus. They would be welcome:

> To such propositions the Visitors are prepared to lend a willing ear, and would think it their duty to give every encouragement, by assuring to those who might choose such a location for their schools that the regulations of the University should be so modified and accommodated as to give every facility of access and attendance to their students, with such regulated use also as may be permitted to the other students, of the library which may be hereafter acquired, either by public or private munificence, but always understanding that these schools shall be independent of the University and each other.

The proposal concludes with a statement that this would be a constitutionally acceptable way of making up the defect in the university's curriculum:

> Such an arrangement would complete the circle of useful sciences embraced by this institution, and would fill the chasm now existing on principles which would leave inviolate the constitutional freedom of religion, the most unalienable and sacred of all human rights, over which the people and authorities of this State, individually and publicly, have ever manifested the most watchful jealousy; and could this jealousy now be alarmed, in the opinion of the Legislature, by what is here suggested, the idea will be relinquished on any

surmise of disapprobation which they might think proper to express.

There is a mysterious anonymity about this proposal: the "pious individuals" who suggested it are never named. In one letter Joseph C. Cabell gives the impression that the plan is Jefferson's own (although the wording may also be interpreted to mean that in a meeting of the Board of Visitors Jefferson had initiated discussion of something previously suggested to him).[51] Another intriguing aspect of the proposal is that if its intention is to "complete the circle of useful sciences embraced by this institution," its structure actually does no such thing. Its essence, as we have seen, is this: Since the University of Virginia offers no instruction in sectarian doctrines, let divinity students registered at other schools take courses in science at the university. No change whatever is proposed for the curriculum of the university students. Although they might attend worship at the adjacent seminaries, nothing is said about them taking courses there. For them "instruction in religious opinions and duties" is still omitted. The "chasm in a general institution of the useful sciences" remains.

One wonders whether Jefferson really believed such a chasm existed, despite the discussion of it in this proposal. His concept of a complete education included thorough training in morality and rationalistic theism, both of which were already provided in the curriculum offerings of the professor of ethics. There is no evidence that Jefferson ever considered the study of "sectarian" doctrines essential to complete education, and plenty of evidence that he considered that branch of religion a fraud and a menace to the student's sanity. To Jefferson the real chasm probably lay in the education of most "ecclesiastics." Their learning was "monkish," divisive, deranging, rather than scientific, mor-

51. From Joseph C. Cabell, Feb. 3, 1823 (Cabell, p. 273).

al, and rational, because their training in supernatural and immaterialist doctrines neglected natural, material, tested knowledge. The "Schools on the Confines" plan was suited for filling this chasm, not the lack of instruction in religion for the university student. The avowed purpose was to enable the clergy "to fulfill the duties of their calling with understanding and usefulness," and "to maintain . . . those destined for the religious professions on as high a standing of science, and of personal weight and respectability, as may be obtained by others from the benefits of the University." This undoubtedly reveals Jefferson's basic motives. By this means he hoped to counteract the deplorable, narrow-minded sectarianism that he believed to be typical of the denominational clergy.

His sights may have been higher, even higher than he realized. As we have seen, Jefferson prophesied the spread of primitive Christianity throughout the United States, and felt that in this expansion education was to play an important role. The "Schools on the Confines" plan may well have reflected Jefferson's yearning to see his prophecy come to pass. The letter in which he informed Thomas Cooper of the plan may be significant.[52] Its opening paragraph discusses the religious state of the nation: "The atmosphere of our country is unquestionably charged with a threatening cloud of fanaticism, lighter in some parts, denser in others, but too heavy in all." Jefferson's discussion of various sections of the United States makes it obvious that he believed the density of the cloud to be in direct ratio to the amount of control exercised locally by the Calvinists. In Charlottesville, where they are only one of four equally powerful sects, all is harmony. "It is not so in the districts where Presbyterianism prevails undividedly. Their ambition and tyranny would tolerate no rival if they had power. Systematical in grasping at an ascendancy over all other

52. To Thomas Cooper, Nov. 2, 1822 (Ford, *10*, 242–45).

sects, they aim, like the Jesuits, at engrossing the education
of the country, are hostile to every institution which they
do not direct, and jealous at seeing others begin to attend
at all to that object." Jefferson suggests two remedies for
this fever of fanaticism: general education and the progress
of Unitarianism.

Immediately after his opening he informs Cooper about
the proposal to establish sectarian schools on the confines
of the university. Having given a condensed version of the
official presentation of the plan by the Board of Visitors,
Jefferson concludes by adding two personal comments: "I
think the invitation will be accepted, by some sects from
candid intentions, and by others from jealousy and rivalship. And by bringing the sects together, and mixing them
with the mass of other students, we shall soften their asperities, liberalize and neutralize their prejudices, and make the
general religion a religion of peace, reason and morality."
Jefferson really hoped this plan to establish divinity schools
on the confines of the University of Virginia would help to
bring about that quiet euthanasia of sectarianism he so
greatly longed to see. He felt that the divinity students on
the campus of the university, studying rational and materialistic science, mixing with students who were daily encouraged to strengthen the moral sense through practice,
hearing the proofs of the existence of God and the utilitarian arguments for morality, were bound to make intellectual and religious progress. They could not help but have
their sectarian blindfolds removed and their eyes opened
to the incontrovertible fact that the only branch of religion
having importance was that in which all sects agree, the
branch of morality and simple theism. Once they had seen
this under conditions encouraging free thought, they could
not help but accept it and at the end of their studies go
forth to preach. The euthanasia of sectarianism and the development of a general religion that was "a religion of
peace, reason, and morality" would be well on its way.

PROPOSALS EVALUATED

All of the religion curriculum proposals advocated by Jefferson in the field of public education, then, were shaped to attain his main goal, the development of moral individuals who would form the moral society. Sectarian tenets (either useless or destructive to this end, in any case) were inadmissible because in a tax-supported educational system they would upset the equal footing of all sects. Yet he felt that his own "non-sectarian" position was admissible because it supported the equality of the sects. At the same time it was essential to any education calculated to achieve the moral end. Theology was therefore omitted from the curriculum, or if it was brought near as a subject of study, its deleterious effects were counteracted by a set of circumstances strongly favoring a general religion of peace, reason, and morality. There is no basic difference between these proposals and the curriculum guidance he gave privately to students who put themselves under his tutelage.

The legitimacy of these proposals depends upon the truth of one of Jefferson's enduring convictions: that his religious position was indeed nonsectarian. There is no reason to question the genuineness of that conviction. He did not believe he was sectarian. He probably never realized the depth of truth in his own remark, "I am of a sect by myself, as far as I know."[53] He believed himself to be a neutral, rational advocate of only those principles on which all religions agree. Yet sectarian he was. And in his efforts to form a curriculum in religion limited entirely to what he believed to be the common core of all beliefs, at William and Mary, at the University of Virginia, and in elementary public education, he was undoubtedly yielding to a powerful, unconscious drive to bring everyone over to his own religious point of view. He believed that the sectarians were

53. To Ezra Stiles, June 25, 1819 (LB, *15*, 203–04).

wrong and that he was right. As a result, without realizing
it, he did exactly what he had condemned as sinful and
tyrannical: he tried to compel others to furnish contributions of money for the propagation of opinions which they
disbelieved and abhorred.[54]

In other words, although he believed his own words completely, it was not quite true that "this institution . . . will
be based on the illimitable freedom of the human mind, to
explore and expose every subject susceptible of its contemplation."[55] Nor was it precisely accurate to say, "Here we
are not afraid to follow truth wherever it may lead, nor to
tolerate error so long as reason is left free to combat it."[56]
Certain subjects were not to be offered. Their exploration
was to be discouraged. And certain other studies by contrast were to be cloaked with educational respectability and
given the strength that comes from being pronounced constitutionally acceptable.

54. Bill for Establishing Religious Freedom (Boyd, 2, 545).
55. To Destutt de Tracy, Dec. 26, 1820 (in *Jefferson et les idéologues*, ed.
Gilbert Chinard, Baltimore, 1925, p. 203).
56. To William Roscoe, Dec. 27, 1820 (LB, *15*, 203).

CHAPTER 11

Public Education and the Clergy

Visitors

Jefferson's concept of effective means for fostering religious freedom also affected his understanding of the proper qualifications for teachers and administrators in public education. It will be recalled that all Jefferson's constitution drafts for Virginia in 1776–79 had clauses excluding ministers of the gospel from legislative office, but that years later Jefferson said that he changed his mind.[1] He argued that as long as the clergy did not strive to get for themselves any special civil privilege, they should not be deprived of any civil rights.[2] His fears of the intrigues and designs of the "priesthood," however, were evidently not permanently allayed, for he included an attempt to declare them ineligible for a particular civil office in his Bill for Establishing a System of Public Education of 1817.[3]

1. See above, pp. 136–38.
2. To Jeremiah Moore, Aug. 14, 1800 (Ford, *Writings of Jefferson*, 7, 454–55).
3. See Cabell, *Early History*, pp. 413–27.

The attempt never reached the Virginia legislature; Joseph Cabell deleted the provision before submitting the bill to the chairman of the Committee on Schools and Colleges.[4] Cabell explained, "Judge Roane and others advised me to to leave out the clauses respecting religion; if proper in themselves they were supposed of a nature to excite prejudices, as coming from you; and they were not considered essential."[5] Cabell was sensitive and acute. Here, placed in italics, are the words he omitted:

> At the first session of the Superior Court in every county . . . the Judge thereof shall appoint three discreet and well informed persons, residents of the county and *not being ministers of the gospel of any denomination* to serve as Visitors of the primary schools . . . *Ministers of the gospel are excluded to avoid jealousy from the other sects, were the public education committed to a particular one; and with the more reason than in the case of their exclusion from the legislative and executive functions.*[6]

Jefferson did not protest the omission. He had already given Cabell full permission to make any changes he thought wise. His desire was to see a public-school bill passed in any form whatever, since he had confidence that posterity would have the wisdom and the ability to make necessary changes and improvements.[7] But he persisted in his belief that the clergy should not become members of the boards of visitors of the local public schools. He gave this reason for his hope to see wards as the basic unit of government rather than counties: their effect upon the choice of school visitors would be salutary. "I think ward

4. From Joseph C. Cabell, Dec. 29, 1817 (Cabell, pp. 89–98).

5. Ibid., p. 91. Cabell also deleted the clause and comment requiring literacy for full citizenship (ibid., p. 97).

6. Ibid., pp. 96, 413.

7. To Joseph C. Cabell, Sept. 9, 1817 (Cabell, pp. 79–80), and Jan. 14, 1818 (Cabell, p. 106); and elsewhere.

elections better for . . . that it will keep elementary education out of the hands of fanaticising preachers, who, in
county elections, would be universally chosen, and the pre-
dominant sect of the county would possess itself of all its
schools."[8] Jefferson's records show no such provision for
making the clergy ineligible for the board of visitors of any
public college or university. Since the problem never came
up, so far as we know, his thought on this matter can only
be conjectured.

Faculty

THE INFLUENCE OF WILLIAM AND MARY

Jefferson's attitude concerning clergy as teachers in higher education may possibly have been influenced by his own
college experience at William and Mary. When he entered
in 1760, all but one of the faculty were members of the
cloth. The president of the college was a habitual tippler.
Two of the faculty had led the students in a town-and-gown
riot. A six-year controversy between the faculty and the
local political authorities was in process. Characterized by
scandal and confusion, the clergy gave a uniformly low
impression in learning and morals. William Small, the one
layman on the faculty, was by contrast a brilliant scholar
of sterling character, who was credited by Jefferson with
doing the most to fix the young student's destinies in later
life.[9] Small introduced Jefferson to his friends, George
Wythe and Governor Fauquier. The four formed a circle
which Jefferson was later to look back on as the group providing the most intellectual stimulus and pleasure in his
memory. Consisting exclusively of laymen, its contrast to
the clergy on the faculty was striking. The seeds of Jefferson's anticlericalism may well have been sown at this time.

8. To Joseph C. Cabell, Nov. 28, 1820 (Ford, *10*, 68).
9. See Chinard, *Jefferson*, pp. 11–13; Malone, *Jefferson*, *1*, 50–55; Padover, *Jefferson*, p. 14.

Seldom did Jefferson recommend a clergyman as teacher. In his periodic advice to young men and their parents concerning education, his repeated recommendation of William and Mary in preference to schools in Europe was a recommendation of the laymen, not the clergy, on the faculty. His standards were high, but as long as men like Wythe, Bellini, and McLurg were teaching at William and Mary he recommended it as the finest school in the world for young Americans planning to study law, languages, and medicine.

When the time came to appoint teachers for Central College and the University of Virginia, he insisted that only the best would do.[10] To Jefferson's mind, the necessary qualifications in a professor seem to have been eminence in his own field of scholarship, broad culture, teaching ability, integrity, and amiability. He also desired for the University of Virginia a sympathetic understanding of republican principles.[11] No record exists that Jefferson or the Board of Visitors ever inquired into or discussed the religious beliefs of prospective candidates for the faculty or of those who were finally hired.[12] Only the question of whether a man was a minister or not ever became an issue in the matter of his qualifications to hold a teaching post at the university.

SAMUEL KNOX

In respect to this issue, Jefferson was not entirely consistent. A clergyman was offered the first appointment to the faculty of Central College. The Board of Visitors in July

10. The procuring of the faculty for the University of Virginia is discussed in detail in Herbert B. Adams, *Thomas Jefferson and the University of Virginia* (Washington, D.C., 1888), chap. 8, and in Honeywell, chap. 7. Brief descriptions are in Arrowood, *Jefferson and Education*, pp. 46–48; Chinard, *Jefferson*, pp. 510–11; and Padover, *Jefferson*, pp. 172–73.

11. See Honeywell, *Educational Work*, pp. 86–89; Koch, *Jefferson and Madison*, p. 265.

12. See Honeywell, pp. 92–93.

1817 agreed to make application to the Reverend Samuel Knox, a Presbyterian minister and President of Baltimore College, "to accept the Professorship of Languages, Belles Lettres, Rhetoric, History, and Geography."[13] Doctor Knox did not agree with Jefferson's religious views; he had published a sermon condemning the opinions of Joseph Priestley. On the other hand, he had supported Jefferson for the Presidency, vindicated Jefferson's religious conduct and principles,[14] and written a treatise on education which may have influenced Jefferson's plans for a university.

Evidently the news of the appointment did not reach Knox. In September Jefferson reported to Cabell, "Dr. Knox has retired from business and I have written to Cooper."[15] A month later the Board of Visitors rescinded the appointment "on information that the Rev. Mr. Knox, formerly thought of for a professor of languages, is withdrawn from business."[16] The information must have been false. More than a year later Knox learned of the nomination and wrote to Jefferson asking for a post, but nothing came of it.[17]

THE THOMAS COOPER CONTROVERSY

The Controversy's history. Following the rescinding of the appointment of Dr. Samuel Knox as first professor of the faculty of Central College, the Board of Visitors elected Dr. Thomas Cooper as professor of chemistry and law, and thereby precipitated a *cause célèbre*.[18] Public opposition to

13. Minutes of the Visitors of Central College, July 28, 1817 (Cabell, p. 396).

14. In *A Vindication of the Religion of Mr. Jefferson, and a Statement of His Services in the Cause of Religious Liberty,* Baltimore, 1800.

15. To Joseph C. Cabell, Sept. 10, 1817 (Cabell, p. 81).

16. Minutes of the Visitors of Central College, Oct. 7, 1817 (Cabell, p. 397).

17. See Honeywell, p. 89.

18. See Minutes of the Visitors of Central College, Oct. 7, 1817 (Cabell, pp. 396–99). Good discussions of this affair can be found in Malone, *Thomas Cooper,* pp. 234–46; Herbert B. Adams, pp. 106–09; Honeywell, pp. 89–92.

this appointment was evidently present right from the start, but as long as Dr. Cooper was being engaged for the faculty of Central College, a private institution, the criticism was fairly mild. When that college became the nucleus of the University of Virginia, however, and the university's Board of Visitors confirmed Cooper's previous nomination, public criticism grew widespread and acrimonious. The charges were that Cooper drank too much, had a bad temper, and that the liberality of his religious views made him an improper instructor of youth. No attack was made upon his academic or scholastic attainments, which were evidently considerable.

The charge of intemperance turned out to be a dead issue at best. He probably did have a bad temper; although genial with intimate friends, Cooper's ability in public to give an irritating impression of truculence, omniscience, and contempt for others' opinions made him thoroughly unpopular. These problems would probably not have been insoluble, however, were it not for Cooper's heterodox religious views. On the basis of these an attack was mounted, chiefly by the Presbyterian clergy, against the appointment of Cooper to the University of Virginia. Ultimately he had to resign. To Jefferson this was a plain case of the church persecuting a man for his religious views, and there was no other explanation.[19] From one point of view it was that, to be sure, but the case had other facets which Jefferson did not see but which should be explored.

Rice's criticism. The main attack on Cooper's appointment was instigated by Dr. John Rice, a Presbyterian clergyman and editor of the *Virginia Evangelical and Literary Magazine*. Rice had previously taken an energetic part in creating a popular sentiment favorable to the passage of

19. Some of Jefferson's biographers assume that this is the whole story. See Koch, *Jefferson and Madison*, p. 264; Nock, pp. 317–18; Padover, *Jefferson*, p. 173. But cf. discussions in Malone, Herbert Adams, and Honeywell mentioned in note above.

Jefferson's university bill. Now he wrote a vigorous but temperate article condemning Cooper's employment as a teacher of youth.[20] Rice's criticism was based on an analysis he had made of Cooper's own writings, particularly the comments on Priestley's *Memoirs*, among which can be found Cooper's remark, "The time seems to have arrived, when the separate existence of the human soul, the freedom of the will, and the eternal duration of future punishment, like the doctrines of the Trinity and transubstantiation, may no longer be entitled to public discussion."[21] This statement could antagonize nearly all denominations.

Rice's main objection was that the direction of the youth of the state should not be committed to a man who obtruded such views on the public and who himself lacked some of the most important requisites in the character of a philosopher. He summed up Cooper's temperament with these words: "Dr. Cooper appears in his book, rash, dogmatical and peremptory. The intrepidity of his conclusions is really appalling; his hardihood is fearful. At the same time his prejudices appear to us violent; and all his liberality is reserved for his own party." Rice did not refer to Cooper's particularly abusive remarks about Calvinistic theology. He argued that placing such a man in a prominent position in the university would alienate many who wanted to support the institution, which would become a "mere party affair countenanced and supported by a particular class of persons."[22]

20. See Philip A. Bruce, *History of the University of Virginia, 1819–1919*, *1* (New York, 1920), 204; Malone, *Cooper*, p. 240. See also letter from J. C. Cabell, Dec. 4, 1819 (Cabell, pp. 157, 234–35).

21. Priestley's *Memoirs*, *1*, 335. Quoted in *Virginia Evangelical and Literary Magazine*, *3* (1820), 49, 63–74. Quoted in turn in Malone, *Cooper*, p. 240. Malone's discussion of the Cooper controversy, pp. 234–46, is excellent and most detailed. A briefer account is in Honeywell, pp. 89–92. Cabell, pp. 233–36 n., should not be ignored. Others tend to be too brief to be of value.

22. *Virginia Evangelical and Literary Magazine*, *3*, 72; quoted in Malone, *Cooper*, p. 241.

Cabell's interpretation. There is no indication that Jefferson ever understood Rice and his supporters in this issue, or that Jefferson ever realized that the objections raised might not be mere Presbyterian obscurantism and factionalism—this despite the fact that Joseph Cabell, whom Jefferson certainly trusted, tried repeatedly to explain what was going on. Cabell's role vis-à-vis Jefferson in the Cooper affair is best described as loyal opposition. For years he had worked hard and loyally as Jefferson's liaison with the legislature. He presented bills, explained them tirelessly to other legislators, and fought earnestly for acceptance and support of Jefferson's educational ideas. In the establishment of the University of Virginia, Cabell's efforts were probably second in value only to Jefferson's.[23]

After the legislature had approved the choice of Charlottesville for the site of the university and the adoption of Central College as its nucleus, Cabell wrote Jefferson a letter listing and commenting on the names of those who had supported the university bill. Concerning one of a number of articles published in journals around the state, Cabell reported, "Mr. Rice, a Presbyterian clergyman of this place, wrote the essay signed 'Crito.' He discovered remarkable enthusiasm for the measure, and . . . his liberal conduct . . . satisfied me that the sect of Presbyterians did not (as I had expected) exert their influence against Central College [as a site and nucleus for the University of Virginia]."[24] Cabell took this seriously. He also thought that unnecessary obstacles should not be placed in the way of this support, and frankly felt that Cooper was just such an obstacle. He acquiesced in the reconfirmation of Cooper's appointment only after having aired his protests fully.[25]

23. See Herbert B. Adams, pp. 53–54, 97.
24. From Joseph C. Cabell, Dec. 4, 1819 (Cabell, p. 157).
25. See Honeywell, p. 91.

Jefferson's reaction. Cabell's efforts to interpret to Jefferson the feelings of the people whom Rice represented were to continue for some time after Cooper's resignation had been forced by Cooper himself. Jefferson's private correspondence subsequently reflected perhaps the most bitterly anticlerical period in his life.[26] Repeatedly he made accusations such as the following:

> The Presbyterian *clergy* alone (not their followers) remain bitterly federal and malcontent with their government. They are violent, ambitious of power, and intolerant in politics as in religion and want nothing but license from the laws to kindle again the fires of their leader John Knox, and to give us a 2d blast from his trumpet. Having a little more monkish learning than the clergy of other sects, they are jealous of the general diffusion of science, and therefore hostile to our Seminary lest it should qualify their antagonists of other sects to meet them in equal combat. Not daring to attack the institution with the avowal of their real motives, they peck at you, at me, and every feather they can spy out.[27]

During the next several years Jefferson continued to charge Presbyterian clergy with having foul religious opinions, with wishing to have them established by law, with wanting to monopolize education, and generally with maintaining a factious, ambitious spirit, against which friends of freedom and progress had better be on guard. For example, there was this tirade:

26. N. F. Cabell's editorial comment is a model of understatement: "But having been thus traversed in a favorite measure, seems to have somewhat disturbed the usual philosophic serenity of the venerable rector" (Cabell, p. 234 n.).

27. To Thomas Cooper, March 13, 1820 (MS, University of Virginia; cited in Koch and Peden, *Life and Writings*, p. 697).

The Presbyterian clergy are the loudest, the most intolerant of all sects, the most tyrannical and ambitious;
ready at the word of the lawgiver, if such a word could
be now obtained, to put the torch to the pile, and to
rekindle in this virgin hemisphere, the flames in which
their oracle Calvin consumed the poor Servetus, because he could not find in his Euclid the proposition
which has demonstrated that three are one and one is
three, nor subscribe to that of Calvin, that magistrates
have a right to exterminate all heretics to Calvinistic
Creed. They pant to reëstablish, *by law,* that holy inquisition, which they can now only infuse into *public
opinion.* We have most unwisely committed to the
hierophants of our particular superstition, the direction of public opinion, that Lord of the universe. We
have given them stated and privileged days to collect
and catechise us, opportunities of delivering their ora-
cles to the people in mass, and of molding their minds
as wax in the hollow of their hands. But in despite of
their fulminations against endeavors to enlighten the
general mind, to improve the reason of the people, and
to encourage them in the use of it, the liberality of this
State will support this institution [the University of
Virginia] and give fair play to the cultivation of reason.[28]

Similar but briefer eruptions of the same accusations presented singly or in groups occurred periodically in later
letters.[29] Fortunately for the progress of the university, the
full extent of these charges was not openly known until
publication of his letters some years after his death. On the

28. To William Short, April 13, 1820 (LB, *15*, 246–47).
29. E.g. letter to Robert Taylor, May 16, 1820 (LB, *15*, 254); to Thomas
Cooper, Aug. 14, 1820 (LB, *15*, 265–69); to Jared Sparks, Nov. 4, 1820 (LB,
15, 288); to Timothy Pickering, Feb. 27, 1821 (LB, *15*, 323); to Benjamin Waterhouse, June 26, 1822 (LB, *15*, 383–84); to John Adams, April 11, 1823 (LB,
15, 426); to Thomas Cooper, Dec. 11, 1823 (Ford, *10*, 285–86).

other hand, where he stood had certainly never been a secret. He was furious at the frustration of losing Cooper,
but these diatribes are simply emotionally intensified ex-
pressions of attitudes he had customarily maintained during
his whole life.

Presbyterian fears. Because of this, Jefferson was accused
as well as accuser. Doubtless he was sensitive personally to
the charges made against him, but no evidence shows that
he was aware of their full implications. He never indicated
awareness of the possibility that his own behavior might
have given the opposition just cause to come into being.
Yet this was precisely what Cabell attempted periodically
to explain. In his letters Cabell repeatedly tried to get Jefferson to take the fears of the Presbyterians seriously:
"They believe . . . that the Socinians are to be installed at
the University for the purpose of overthrowing the pre-
vailing religious opinions of the country."[30] "In reflecting
on the causes of the opposition to the University I cannot
but ascribe a great deal of it to the clergy. . . . It is represented that they are to be *excluded* from the University.
. . . I should suppose that religious opinions should form
no test whatever. I should think it improper to exclude
religious men, and open the door to such as Doctor Cooper.
. . . The clergy have succeeded in spreading the belief of
their intended exclusion, and, in my opinion it is the source
of much of our trouble."[31]
After calling on John Rice and discussing the matter
with him, Cabell reported this to Jefferson:

> They have heard that you have said they may well be
> afraid of the progress of Unitarianism to the South. . . .
> Mr. Rice assured me that he was a warm friend of the
> University; and that, as a matter of policy, he hoped

30. From Joseph C. Cabell, Aug. 5, 1821 (Cabell, pp. 215–16).
31. From Joseph C. Cabell, Jan. 7, 1822 (Cabell, p. 230).

the Visitors would in the early stages of its existence remove the fears of the religious orders. He avowed that the Presbyterians sought no peculiar advantages and that they and the other sects would be well satisfied by the appointment of an Episcopalian. I stated that I knew not what would be the determination of the Board; but I was sure no desire existed anywhere to give any preference to Unitarians; and for my own part, I should not vote against any one on account of his being a professor of religion or free-thinker.[32]

In all of this Cabell was trying to tell Jefferson that the Presbyterians actually saw a threat to their freedom of belief in the way the new university was being managed. Events such as the appointment of Cooper and the remarks attributed to Jefferson that the university was to be a center of Unitarian influence gave substance to fears which had to be taken seriously by the university's Board of Visitors.

Cabell's efforts were not entirely in vain. The "Schools on the Confines" proposal, in the next annual report of the Board of Visitors to the legislature, was doubtless an attempt to allay these fears and placate the opposition. Cabell felt that it succeeded. In a letter which apparently attributes the plan to Jefferson, Cabell wrote, "I think also that your suggestion respecting the religious sects has had great influence. It is the Franklin that has drawn the lightning from the cloud of opposition."[33] The question may be raised whether this Franklin would have drawn as much lightning if the opposition had seen the gratuitous remarks accompanying the copy of the plan Jefferson sent to Thomas Cooper.[34]

32. From Joseph C. Cabell, Jan. 14, 1822 (Cabell, pp. 233–37).

33. From Joseph C. Cabell, Feb. 3, 1823 (Cabell, p. 273).

34. To Thomas Cooper, Nov. 2, 1822 (Ford, *10*, 242–43). See above, pp. 223–24.

Evaluation. Jefferson's role in this controversy was, therefore, as subject to censure as the activities of his opponents.
To begin with, he did not always keep his tongue or pen
under control. His correspondence was studded with remarks which, if repeated, might well have caused worry to
those who differed from him in his religious opinions. In
addition, he seemed capable of making equally indiscreet
remarks in conversation.[35]

Next, he resembled his opponents in a way that would
have surprised him. The controversy on both sides had
"statesmen who are . . . familiar with matters coming within
their own sphere . . . [but] at times entirely mistake the
motives and purposes of those who in other departments
are laboring for the public good." Jefferson never seemed
to grasp the idea that those who criticized some of his
moves as Rector of the University may have had a legitimate say in the matter:

> The University was . . . to be erected, endowed, and
> sustained at the public expense. Of the Virginia public,
> the Presbyterians . . . constituted a large and respect-
> able part. . . . So far as appears from any overt act, they
> desired to participate in, not to monopolize the advan-
> tages of the institution to the establishment of which
> they had contributed their due quota, and it was both
> natural and proper that they should enquire and judge
> of the characters and sentiments of those who were to
> be the future instructors of their sons.[36]

This type of participation was no more than Jefferson had
reserved for himself. In this respect, the difference between
him and the Presbyterians was not principle but opinion
concerning which standard was proper to measure the fit-
ness of a person to teach the youth of Virginia.

35. See Padover, *Jefferson,* p. 172.
36. Cabell, pp. 233–35 n.

Furthermore, legitimate doubts can be raised concerning the worth of Cooper's contribution to the university. His manner of stimulating controversy did not always benefit the cause of toleration and social harmony. There may have been substance to Rice's fear that placing such a man in a prominent position in the university would alienate many who wanted to support it, and make it a mere party affair, countenanced and supported only by a particular class of persons. Cooper caused the Presbyterians to believe that he deliberately went out of his way to insult them. Although insisting throughout his life upon freedom of discussion, he did venture to say that certain subjects, such as traditional Christian beliefs, were no longer entitled to it.[37] The question may well be raised of how this would promote that illimitable freedom of the human mind on which Jefferson insisted the university was to be based. It may also be asked whether this appointment really was in the interests of true religious freedom in the state of Virginia.

SUBSEQUENT POLICY

To what extent this controversy affected Jefferson's standards of qualifications for faculty is hard to say. Certainly, in the period following, Jefferson seems to have been opposed to the employment of ministers of any denomination on the faculty of the university. Before Francis W. Gilmer made his trip to England to recruit suitable professors, Jefferson made it clear to him that no minister was to be engaged.[38] This may have been a symptom of that unusually bitter anticlericalism revealed in his correspondence of this period. If, on the other hand, it was policy based on principle, a letter to Benjamin Waterhouse in 1825 contains some puzzling passages. In it Jefferson writes:

37. See Malone, *Cooper,* pp. 240–41. See also pp. 355, 387 ff.
38. See Bruce, *1,* 195.

Your favor of Dec. 24 is received. The Professors of
our University, 8 in number are all engaged. . . . There
remains therefore no place in which we can avail ourselves of the rev'd mr. Bertrum as a teacher. I wish we
could do it as a Preacher. I am anxious to see the doctrine of one god commenced in our state. . . . I must . . .
be contented to be an Unitarian by myself, although
I know there are many around me who would become
so, if once they could hear the questions fairly stated.[39]

Coming as it does after the instructions to Gilmer not
to consider ministers for positions on the faculty, this implies that in the case of a Unitarian Jefferson would make
an exception to the rule. In view of the Cooper controversy
and of Cabell's efforts to explain the fears of those who opposed Jefferson, this passage is at best a major indiscretion.
When all the evidence is evaluated, Jefferson's opposition
to ministers on the faculty of the university seems to have
been opposition to those "fanaticising preachers" who disagreed with him. The appointment of Samuel Knox, and
Jefferson's remarks concerning the candidacy of Mr. Bertrum (if the latter are to be taken seriously), indicate that
Jefferson did not hold rigidly to the policy of excluding
ministers from the faculty of his college.

In the field of ethics and moral philosophy this practice
of not engaging a member of the clergy as professor produced an academic innovation. Yet although open to others
besides members of the cloth, the professorship was not
open to just anyone. The Board of Visitors did consider it
expedient that this chair, like that of law, must be filled by
an American citizen.[40] No great difficulty was experienced
in finding an American professor of ethics.[41] It is well to
remember, however, that Jefferson thought it a waste of

39. To Benjamin Waterhouse, Jan. 8, 1825 (Ford, *10*, 335–36).
40. See Minutes of the Board of Visitors, April 7, 1824 (LB, *19*, 433).
41. See Honeywell, p. 96; Herbert B. Adams, p. 119.

time for the student to attend lectures in moral philosophy.[42] Similarly, his standards were not as high for a professor in this field as in others. He felt that no great special-
ized preparation was required for the teaching of moral
philosophy: "it is a branch of science of little difficulty to
any ingenious man. Locke, Stewart, Brown, Tracy, for the
general science of the mind furnish materials abundant,
and that of Ethics is still more trite. I should think any
person with a general education rendering them otherwise
worthy of a place among his scientific brethren might soon
qualify himself."[43] Clearly this was a departure from Jefferson's standard for every other professor, who had to have
a complete mastery of the science he was to teach. It was
in accord, however, with his belief in the moral sense and
in what too much over-subtle reasoning might do to it.
Some reading in empiricist, common sense, and materialist
philosophy was sufficient abstract study in this subject for
both student and teacher.

JEFFERSON'S ASSUMPTIONS

When considering Jefferson's concept of the place of
ordained ministers as supervisors and teachers in public
education, we would do well to consider certain of his inve-
terate habits of thought of which he may not have been
aware. One is his recurrent assumption that irrationality
ruins the mind. To Jefferson, this meant that an individual's irrationality in any particular area of thought would
inevitably wreck his mind in all others. Religious irrationality, for instance, could be expected to destroy a person's
political principles. This was reinforced by another assumption, that all men are naturally divided into two

42. To Peter Carr, Aug. 10, 1787 (LB, 6, 255–61); to Thomas Cooper, Aug.
14, 1820 (LB, 15, 264–65).
43. To James Madison, Nov. 30, 1824 (Madison Papers, Library of Congress, as quoted in Koch, *Jefferson and Madison,* p. 274).

types: those who fear the people and insist on ruling them, and those who trust them sufficiently to allow them to rule themselves. Religious, philosophical, and political reasonableness all went together for Jefferson. To him this meant that Trinitarians were Federalists, Tories, enemies to freedom and above all to freedom of belief; they could not be depended upon to abide by majority rule or to safeguard minority rights. Materialists, on the other hand, were strong, moral, reasonable fellows, good Republicans by temperament. If it had been true, then Jefferson had ample reason to try to keep the Trinitarian clergy out of public education. Advocates of religious doctrines which had to be propagated by force, fraud, or madness would never permit their students to adhere to free and reasonable political principles.

However, the assumption should have been highly questionable, even to Jefferson. He knew of too many exceptions to allow the rule to stand. He praised Pendleton and Nicholas, who had fought the disestablishment of the Anglican Church in Virginia to the last ditch and then accepted the will of the people as their own.[44] Samuel Knox was a thoroughly orthodox Presbyterian who had supported Jefferson for the Presidency and vindicated his religious views. Virginia had thousands of Presbyterians who distinguished between Jefferson's religious persuasion and his political system. All over the United States there were Presbyterian Republicans, even among the clergy; but Jefferson was not really disposed to admit it. Nor was he willing to admit equally unwelcome evidence concerning the Unitarians. The relationship between religious and political innovation in New England was remote. Harvard College seemed to entertain no feeling toward Jefferson but antipathy when it appointed a Unitarian professor of theology in 1805.[45]

44. *Autobiography* (Ford, *1*, 55).
45. See Henry Adams, *History of the United States under Thomas Jefferson and James Madison, 4* (New York, 1930), 176.

In Boston Jefferson was denounced as soundly from Unitarian pulpits as from any other.

A second Jeffersonian habit of thought was his conviction that he was a religious nonsectarian. For example, by expressly excluding all questions of supernatural character or endowment from his portrait of Jesus, or by insisting only on morality rather than adherence to a creed as a passport to heaven, he believed he had arrived at an irreducible minimum of religious belief upon which all sects agree and those who held otherwise were dogmatizing venal jugglers.[46] He and Jesus were alike in that vicious frauds had attacked them both for their uprightness and honesty, for their simple, universal, rational morality. Jefferson never realized that his opponents saw the picture very differently. Both he and they had their respective faiths, neither of which was neutral. If the faith of his opponents was repulsive to him, his was as little acceptable to them. His refusal to believe that they could be reasoned with may have made him even more literally sectarian than they.

Related to this is the fact that Jefferson never saw himself as the Unitarian evangelist he really was. Certainly, he never buttonholed anyone and intoned, "Brother, are you saved?" But he devoted his life to the cause of freedom on earth, and essential to this, as he saw it, was the development of moral men in a moral society. To develop them he encouraged the spread of Unitarianism and prophesied its complete victory.[47] Before this could come about, however, education had its role to play in strengthening the general mind and penetrating and dissipating those clouds of darkness, sectarian beliefs.[48]

46. To Francis A. Van der Kemp, March 16, 1817 (Ford, *10*, 77).

47. To John Adams, May 17, 1818 (Ford, *10*, 107); to Benjamin Waterhouse, June 22, 1822 (Ford, *10*, 220) and July 19, 1822 (Ford, *10*, 220–21 n.); to John Davis, Jan. 18, 1824 (Ford, *10*, 287–88).

48. To Francis A. Van der Kemp, 1820 (quoted in Padover, *Jefferson on Democracy*, p. 118).

Jefferson's attempts to relate religion to public education reflected his belief that his own religious persuasion was not only right but neutral, and therefore a constitutionally acceptable basis for developing moral adults and fostering religious freedom. He was particularly sensitive to the potential of education to spread religious belief, and therefore he did his best to hinder the entrance into the field of any group that might pervert it to this purpose. His desire for true religious freedom was genuine. Yet his attitude concerning ministers of the gospel serving as visitors in public schools, and his reaction to criticism aroused by his measures to develop a faculty for the University of Virginia, reveal at many points an unconscious but powerful drive to put his own religious beliefs in a position of unusual strength to receive a hearing from the student. Undoubtedly it never occurred to him in any convincing fashion that his efforts to foster religious freedom in public education might result in discrimination against otherwise qualified people because of their religious beliefs.

CHAPTER 12

Recapitulation

Our Exploration in Brief

We can now review briefly the results of our exploration of Jefferson's thought concerning religion in public education, and relate our findings to the specific questions in the current controversy which originally aroused our curiosity. We started by noticing that no evidence supported the contention that Thomas Jefferson's concept of the proper role of religion in democratic public education was exclusively, or even primarily, determined by his understanding of the principle of separation of church and state. Rather, it was part of a philosophy of education which, along with his understanding of religious freedom, was rooted in his total thought.

An examination of Jefferson's religion provided insight into his concept of the nature of reality and man—a framework in which to place other aspects of his thought—and also into those doctrines which, we later discovered, Jefferson considered essential and legally permissible in any education. We saw that he believed in God as Creator, benevolent Providence, and Supreme Judge. We examined his theism, moralism, and materialism. We noted his conviction that his religious beliefs were scientifically verifiable, and that they agreed with the consensus of religious belief of all people at all times.

We next viewed Jefferson's ambiguous picture of man. According to Jefferson, human beings were created equal in biological needs and natural rights, but endowed unequally with human attributes such as reason, the capacity for imitation, and the moral sense. They were intended for life in society, but behaved repeatedly like social cannibals. They were capable of progress, but obviously subject to corruption. Upon this not completely optimistic concept of man, Jefferson based his understanding of good government. Again the picture was paradoxical. Every man was intended to govern himself, but society required general organization and control. The problem was to develop a government in which every member had his rightful influence and in which the will of the living majority would prevail while the rights of every individual were preserved. Jefferson's solution to this problem was constitutional, representative democracy, a system in which the management of society's affairs was delegated to those members of the Creator's natural elite who were chosen by all the people and given certain specific but limited powers defined in a constitution which could be changed only with the consent of all.

We noted that Jefferson could find no unvarying formula to describe the proper, specific relations between the nation and its members, and that he therefore used the metaphors of the ideal family and the planetary system to communicate his concept of the ideal relationship. Although his basic thought remained consistent, his continuing efforts to guard against whatever specific dangers he perceived caused particular recommendations and practices to vary to the point of apparent inconsistency. He ascribed to government both the negative duty to preserve the natural rights of its citizens and the positive duty to foster their common interests and welfare. When speaking as a "member of the opposition," Jefferson said that the sole function of government is to protect natural rights. When in power, however, he exercised his capacities for positive responsible leadership, anticipating the popular will and making decisions on his own initiative whenever it was not feasible to consult the people first.

We turned from this to consider Thomas Jefferson's thought concerning religious freedom. Although he felt that men's thoughts, like the physical structures of their brains, were unique and beyond their control, he still believed that all people were agreed upon his concept of the fundamentals of religion: a concern for morality and a recognition of God's existence deduced rationally from observation of the natural world. Jefferson held, therefore, that as a demonstration of the existence of God and a support for moral behavior, the testimony of supernatural revelation was superfluous. Furthermore, it could be dangerous, since, like all forms of investigation into the supernatural, it promoted obscurantism, superstition, and immorality. This, to Jefferson, was the problem of Christian Trinitarianism, an irrational, corrupt form of the teachings of Jesus, a demonism which could be promoted only by force and which encouraged fanaticism and persecution. By contrast, Jefferson was convinced that his own belief, Unitarianism, was Jesus' original doctrine: that a benevolent God had created all things and commanded men to be moral. Under conditions of free belief, all men naturally agreed to this and demonism died out.

It was most important, therefore, to restore freedom of opinion. The condition was violated chiefly by government establishment of religion. The alliance of church and state was an unmitigated evil. Whenever the state had enforced belief in doctrine it had always destroyed true religion. Whenever the church looked to the state for support, it inevitably became a parasite on the people. Despite the claims of those who advocated establishment, no improvements in the morals of society had ever been shown to take place. The result was always corruption of government and religion, the death of progress, the stifling of truth.

According to Jefferson, the only condition in which these evils would not occur was absolute freedom of conscience. This included not only the right to "be free to profess, and by argument to maintain . . . opinions in matters of religion," but also the right to refuse to answer any questions concerning religious beliefs and the right not to be questioned at all. Jefferson's writings and actions with respect to religious freedom reveal a paradox similar to his thought on government. In the field of religion, government had both negative and positive duties. It was not to interfere with any man's religious beliefs, but it was to protect all men's freedom of opinion. Here again, as in Jefferson's understanding of the nature of good government, no unvarying formula to describe the proper relationship between the nation and its members could be found. Here again, to communicate his concept of the ideal relationship, he used a particularly graphic metaphor: "a wall of separation between church and state."

Separation of church and state, to Jefferson, was essential in any nation where the citizens were to have freedom of conscience. In this view Jefferson remained utterly consistent. He showed great variety, however, in the specific practices by which he attempted to implement this policy. These were not doctrinaire but flexible, adapted to specific situations; they reflected his own astute resourcefulness. His actions over a period of years often appeared inconsistent with each other because he was constantly trying to guard against whatever specific dangers he perceived. This accounts for his varieties of approach to such matters as governmental proclamation of religious holidays and the right of the clergy to serve in public office.

Separation of church and state was a device intended to develop freedom of religion. Important but not foolproof, the device had to be applied zealously and intelligently by those it was designed to protect. Only a people who had tasted freedom and could maintain it through vigilant, distrustful superintendence of their officials would make this device effective. Jefferson knew that the American people had tasted freedom. He had faith that they would never willingly return to despotism. Yet he also knew that their jealousy and vigilance could never be left to chance. They had to be trained in the art of self-government, to be taught to discern the signs of the times and to act together in intelligent response to their needs. For this task they needed a system of public education designed to develop each man's intellectual power to its fullest.

Jefferson's aim in education was to produce the moral, healthy, industrious individual furnished with all the knowledge necessary to look out for his own interests or those of his associates. He thought in terms of a four-step educational ladder. At the primary level students would learn the "three R's," facts of geography and history, and the "first elements of morality." Secondary school would provide the "tools of learning" for higher education. On the collegiate level the student would receive broad grounding in all the sciences, philosophy, and history. The fourth stage would consist of training for one of the professions or instruction to qualify the wealthy for public or private life. The place of each subject in the curriculum was generally determined by its practical value to the student and by his maturity. Jefferson fought constantly against education which made students ignorant or helpless in the face of practical problems, caused them to become dissipated or morally corrupt, resulted in premature specialization, or led students to metaphysical speculation which could wreck their minds.

For Jefferson a cardinal purpose in education was to inculcate virtuous behavior. He hoped to do this, first, by exhorting the student throughout his schooling to make correct moral decisions until making them became habitual; Jefferson also wanted to include at all levels in the curriculum whatever fiction might help strengthen the moral sense by describing events and situations calculated to evoke right or upright reactions. Second, whenever suitable, Jefferson wanted the student to study Greek, Latin, Hebrew, the writings of the great ancient and contemporary moralists, the rational proofs of the existence of God and their implications for morality, and the utilitarian arguments providing incentive for moral behavior. Jefferson was convinced that the principles of morality and those beliefs upon which he felt all men were agreed—in other words, *his* religion—were essential to sound education. Doctrinal religion, on the other hand, had no place whatever, as he saw it, in the development of healthy, capable, moral individuals. If the study of "sectarian doctrines" could not be avoided, Jefferson suggested approaching them only from the point of view of strict dogmatic rationalism, and only when fully matured reason would give the student maximum invulnerability to sectarian, doctrinal corruption.

There is no conflict between Jefferson's philosophies of education and of democratic public education. Through all of his varied plans and discussions of education in service to democracy, certain themes and purposes remain constant. Properly used, education could train men to do things alone or together. It could safeguard democracy by producing free men. In this way knowledge was power, safety, and happiness. Improperly used, however, education could produce —indeed, was producing—incompetents, fanatics, and tyrants, and through them bring an end to freedom and self-government. These possibilities made a comprehensive system of general instruction the concern of all men intent on governing themselves. The purpose of such instruction, whether received under state or private auspices, was: "to advance its individuals to the happiness of which they were susceptible, by improvements in their minds, their morals, their health, and in those conveniences which contribute to the comfort and embellishment of life." Jefferson planned that every man was to get at least as much education as he desired and could afford. The state's supplying education meant that all men, rather than just the wealthy few, were to be equipped for the business of life. In addition, the common people were to be qualified for the duties of citizenship, and the natural elite to manage the concerns of society. Above all, Jefferson was determined to use public education to bring about student commitment to democratic principles. One of the thorniest problems he faced was doing this without inculcating a blind, dogmatic adherence to his own formulation of the Republican creed.

Jefferson's attempts to relate religion to public education reflected his belief that his own religious persuasion was not only right but neutral, and therefore a constitutionally acceptable basis for developing moral adults and fostering religious freedom. All of Jefferson's proposals for religious instruction in the field of public education were shaped to attain his main goal, the development of moral men who would form the moral society. There is no basic difference between these proposals and the curriculum guidance he gave privately. He felt his "non-sectarian" beliefs to be essential to any education calculated to achieve the moral end. As he saw it, they were also admissible in public education because they did not disturb the equality of the sects. What Jefferson considered to be sectarian doctrines, on the other hand, were, to his mind, educationally deleterious and destructive to the moral purpose. Besides that, in public education they would give some sects advantages over others. Theology had no place in the curriculum, therefore, but if a student did study it, the deleterious effects were to be counteracted by a set of circumstances strongly favoring a general religion of peace, reason, and morality.

Thomas Jefferson was particularly sensitive to the potential of education to spread religious belief, and therefore did his best to hinder the entrance into the field of any group that might pervert it to this purpose. His desire for true religious freedom was genuine. Yet his attitude concerning ministers of the gospel serving as visitors in public schools, and his reaction to criticism of his measures to develop a faculty for the University of Virginia, reveal an unconscious but powerful drive to put his own religious beliefs in a position of unusual strength so as to receive a hearing from the student. That his efforts to foster religious freedom in public education might result in the virtual establishment of his own beliefs or in discrimination against certain people because of their religious opinions undoubtedly never occurred to him in any convincing fashion.

Jefferson and His Current Interpreters

We are now in a position to evaluate the interpretations of Jefferson that were presented so strongly in the discussion following the McCollum decision.[1] Each, as we shall see, is valid up to a point. The first we considered portrayed Jefferson favoring impartial government support of all religions and even of denominational teaching in public schools. J. M. O'Neill, to be specific, maintained that tax support of religion or religious education did not mean establishment to Jefferson, and that Jefferson thought the states could do whatever they thought wise in regard to government provision for religion or religious education,

1. See above, pp. 5–11.

so long as they treated all religions alike and preserved religious freedom. This Jefferson favored "cooperation" between church and state, and advocated the use of public funds for a school of theology for the training of clergymen, partial support for sectarian schools for religious instruction at the University of Virginia, and sectarian use of university facilities for instruction and worship.

Diametrically opposed were those who interpreted Jefferson as a "rigid separatist" against any cooperation between government and religious institutions, against government support of any kind for any one or more churches or for religion in general, and against any form of religion in public education. Three advocates of this interpretation were R. F. Butts, C. Moehlman, and L. Pfeffer. They took issue with O'Neill's picture of Jefferson's understanding of the First Amendment and the Virginia Statute for Religious Freedom, and of Jefferson's intentions concerning religion in elementary schools, in William and Mary College, in the letter to Peter Carr in 1814, and at the University of Virginia.

The third interpretation presented a middle-of-the-road Jefferson who wanted the government to avoid interference in religious matters but nevertheless to support religion as essential to democracy, and who therefore felt that instruction in the fundamentals of Christian theism and Christian worship were both important and proper in public higher education.

None of these interpretations corresponds exactly with Jefferson's position. It is true, as O'Neill says, that Jefferson felt it proper for government to be impartial to all religions, but probably misleading to say he favored "supporting" all religions, even impartially. Jefferson certainly did not favor support of denominational teaching in public schools. Contrary to O'Neill's opinion, tax support of religion or religious education did mean establishment to Jefferson if it included support of the denominations, their particular beliefs, or instruction in tenets not held in common with everyone else. Public education was to include instruction only in those religious beliefs upon which all men agree. This was the extent of the "cooperation" between church and state that Jefferson advocated. It went just far enough to protect every person's freedom of conscience, and no further.

We must weigh carefully O'Neill's statement that Jefferson "never did or said anything at any time to indicate that he thought the states could not do whatever they thought wise in regard to government provision for religion or religious education, so long as they treated all religions alike and preserved religious freedom."[2] O'Neill's point is that to give all denominations similar opportunities for tax support or for access to the public schools is to preserve religious freedom. Jefferson's position was quite different. With respect to those religious beliefs upon which men differ and to the activities connected with them, Jefferson felt strongly that all support must be private and voluntary. No man was to "be compelled to frequent or support any religious worship, place or ministry whatsoever," including any based on his own belief. O'Neill's other comment to the effect that Jefferson might consider the Bill for Religious Freedom to be a good law for Virginia without believing it should be applied to the other states ignores the full implication of the bill's concluding declaration: "that the rights hereby asserted are of the natural rights of mankind, and that if any act shall be hereafter passed to repeal the present or to narrow its operation, such an act will be an infringement of natural right."[3] Natural rights were permanent and universal. They belonged to all people in all states at all times.

Many examples cited by O'Neill to bolster his position that Jefferson favored "cooperation" between church and

2. *Religion and Education*, p. 248.
3. Boyd, *Papers of Jefferson*, 2, 546–47.

state are misleading. For instance, no evidence exists to show that Jefferson advocated the use of public funds to finance the school of "Theology and Ecclesiastical History" mentioned in the letter to Peter Carr of 1814. The "partial support," which Jefferson was supposed to have advocated for sectarian schools to be set up on the confines of the University of Virginia, was limited to allowing students of those schools to have access to regular facilities and lectures at the university. It would seem to be stretching things to call this even partial support. In view of Jefferson's expressed hopes concerning the ultimate results of the arrangement, one wonders whether it was not a subtle attack upon beliefs held in certain denominations. Many other citations reveal O'Neill's tendency to indulge in wishful thinking.

If O'Neill's interpretation of Jefferson can be said not to go far enough, that of the rigid separatists is too extreme. As they say, Jefferson was indeed against government support of any kind for any one or more churches, but unless certain terms are given unusual definitions, it is not true that he was against support of religion in general or against any form of religion in public education. If religion in general means all of the differing religious beliefs, Jefferson was against giving them general public support, whether by aiding them materially or by including their tenets in public education. If religion in general refers instead to those religious beliefs upon which all men agree (and Jefferson believed these did exist), he definitely had a place for it in public education. This must be kept in mind when quoting the provision in his elementary school bill that "no religious reading, instruction or exercise, shall be prescribed or practiced, inconsistent with the tenets of any religious sect or denomination." Jefferson did not mean to exclude religion from public education, but to limit religious instruction to those beliefs upon which he felt all sects agreed.

However, Jefferson's chief reason for including such instruction in public education was not its legality but its educational value. Butts, Moehlman, Pfeffer, and the rest are so concerned with the principle of separation that they miss the importance of educational aims in Jefferson's efforts to develop a sound curriculum for tax-supported schools. Educational standards, rather than separation of church and state, account for religion and theology being "conspicuous by their absence" from the 1817 proposals for a state university after they had been previously included in the 1814 letter to Peter Carr. These subjects were excluded not because what was permissible at a private academy might be illegal in a university supported by public funds, but rather because Jefferson had been reminded of his conviction that theology (like the *theory* of medicine) was a "charlataneric" having no place in *any* sound educational curriculum, whatever its source of support.

The third position, represented by Stokes, that Jefferson wanted the government to avoid interference in religious matters while supporting religion as essential to democracy, is closest to the mark. We must keep in mind, however, that the religion Jefferson felt government should support did not include the various denominational doctrines but only morality and those doctrines he honestly believed to be scientifically verifiable and universally accepted. Stokes is right also in his statement that "even in establishing a quasi-state university on broad lines, the greatest liberal who took part in founding our government felt that instruction in the fundamentals of Christian Theism and Christian worship were both important and proper."[4] But let us not forget that to Jefferson the fundamentals of Christion theism were limited to the principles of morality, the utilitarian arguments for moral behavior, and the rational and philosophic proofs of God's existence. These were not to be confused with denominational beliefs. Similarly,

4. *Church and State, 1,* 338.

Christian worship was to take place only "under such impartial regulations as the Visitors shall prescribe."[5]

In the last analysis Jefferson's concept of religion in public education was guided by two mutually compatible principles. The primary one concerned sound education. Whatever was essential to good education had its place in education in service to democracy. A cardinal purpose of good education was to develop the moral individual. The survival of democracy depended upon moral individuals, and "true religion"—those beliefs upon which Jefferson was convinced that all men agreed—was needed to develop them. His second principle was that democratic government had the duty both to encourage freedom of opinion and not to interfere with the rights of conscience. The inclusion of those religious opinions upon which all men supposedly agreed was, to Jefferson, compatible with government's whole duty respecting freedom of religion. The inclusion in public education of what he held to be the common core of religious belief would, as he saw it, result neither in an establishment of religion nor prevent the free exercise thereof, and, even more important, it would make public education sound.

5. Rockfish Gap Report (Cabell, *Early History*, p. 434).

CHAPTER 13

*R*eflections for Today

Our interest in Thomas Jefferson's thought and practice concerning the proper role of religion in democratic public education is not purely antiquarian. The conflicting values which he attempted to coordinate into a system of general instruction can be seen in the controversy today. The pluralism which was one of the enduring facts of life in Jefferson's time has become even more pronounced. Plurality of faiths and cultures has made it impossible for any one set of religious beliefs and sanctions to be dominant or normative except in particular limited localities or within certain institutions. A system of public education which can produce citizens able to make modern American democracy function will have to deal with these circumstances.

Jefferson's legacy of thought on public education is not a body of doctrine either to be adhered to or rejected *in toto*. He held that each generation has the right and the responsibility to solve its own problems. He also held that subsequent generations would probably be wiser than his own. Certainly this is true in the sense that we, not our forefathers, are in a position to see what conditions now exist, and also in the sense that we can draw upon the experience of our fathers when they could not draw upon ours. One of Jefferson's aims in education was to give us precisely this ability.

As we evaluate Jefferson's understanding of man and government, we will find that many of his beliefs are still uncomfortably valid. Democracy is still the only form of government not eternally at war with the rights of mankind. We have yet to find angels in the form of men to govern us. Government officials still tend constantly to encroach upon the rights of the people. Every government still degenerates when entrusted only to the rulers of the people. Because of this, no safer depository for the power of government yet exists than the hands of the people, who must be educated to exercise that power safely. Today, as always, no people can hope to remain both free and ignorant. More than ever before, education is too powerful a weapon to be left to chance and must become the constant concern of all who wish to remain free.

Other doctrines to which Jefferson subscribed have become dead letters. The evidence has demanded more adequate explanations. As a result, Linnaean biology, Lockean psychology, and the moral sense theory have passed into limbo. In an era when psychological research has shown that people of unquestioned intellectual capacity and mental brilliance—not to mention personal and emotional health—nevertheless have their share of irrationalities and emotional maladjustments, it is difficult to maintain that one irrationality ruins the mind. Nor does contemporary history support the sweeping generalization that supernaturalists become tyrants and materialists become benefactors to all mankind.

Next, it would be well to keep in mind that Jefferson was not doctrinaire. His methods grew out of the specific set of circumstances in which he worked, as well as out of his philosophy. As a result his practice was flexible, adaptable, opportunistic. It was always a means, never an end. For this reason it is futile to ask what specific measures he would have recommended for education in a different age, such as ours. He insisted that education, like all human institutions, had to follow the changes of civilization and the human mind. Given certain principles, their adaptation to specific conditions in time and place was always a matter of compromise. If we construct the best compromise we can between the conflicting forces and principles in democracy today, we will not be false to his legacy.

Even Jefferson's principles must be assessed carefully before we apply them to our problem of determining the proper role of religion in democratic public education. In what manner are we to be guided, if at all, by his enduring beliefs that the object of learning and knowledge, like that of legitimate government, is the freedom and happiness of man,[1] and that public education in a democracy must include instruction in all useful knowledge?

The first principle just enumerated reveals that to the Sage of Monticello education was ineradicably moral. Knowledge was not neutral but involved in the realm of values. Its purpose, the freedom and happiness of man, referred not merely to the individual but to all mankind. By linking the two concepts of freedom and happiness, Jefferson demonstrated that for him freedom had a context of responsibility. Otherwise it would have been anarchy. Though universal ends were not for man to determine, though the efforts of each man to satisfy his own needs could serve the common good only through the guidance of An Invisible Hand, nevertheless the self-interest guiding

1. To Thaddeus Kosciusko, Feb. 26, 1810 (LB, *12*, 369-70).

the individual in making choices had to be enlightened, not selfish. Each man had to learn to respond to the moral sense implanted in him by the benevolent Father of all. Education for freedom had to be moral because the purpose of freedom was to imitate the benevolence of the Creator. Public education had to be moral because democracy itself was a moral enterprise.

This belief reflects Jeffersonian theology, biology, and anthropology, systems of thought which may not command the respect of the reader or may have seen their day. But even if we eliminate them from our thinking, we discover that education is still a moral matter. If we prove to our own satisfaction that science, technology, or a particular academic discipline is neutral, amoral, divorced from the problem of choice, we have only ignored the fact that scientists, technologists, and students are men and can never be amoral. Whether they realize it or not, all people are constantly involved in the business of making decisions, choices, and value judgments on the basis of what they know. They implement these choices through the use of what they know. Knowledge is power. Because their choices inevitably affect others through the flow of events, men are always either moral or immoral. To ignore this is to be no less immoral than it is to deliberately choose evil.

The problem can be bungled but not avoided. Education must always aim to produce responsible men, and especially in a free society or democracy. Conflict over how we achieve this aim must never be allowed to obscure this point. Treat Jefferson's methods in whatever way we will, we cannot ignore the need those methods were intended to satisfy, because the need is inherent in democracy itself. Democracy is still what Jefferson saw it to be, a moral enterprise. The freedom reserved for every man becomes tyranny unless he allows his actions to be governed by moral responsibility—that is, by a recognition of his fellow's inalienable rights.

Let us turn now to a second Jeffersonian principle: public education in a democracy must include instruction in all useful knowledge. This must be handled with care because the word "useful," far from being a simple criterion, can mean all things to all men. Jefferson expressed the desire at one point that the projected state university in Virginia "should comprehend all the sciences useful to us and none others."[2] At first glance this would indicate a narrow curriculum containing only subjects of proved and immediate practicality.

This ignores the fact, however, that Jefferson was attempting to revolutionize the concept of curriculum. He believed that education should make no man useless or parasitic, particularly in a country which needed men of capacity and ability. Where resources were limited, he strove to have merely traditional disciplines replaced by those for which there was more urgent need. He also believed that some truly beneficial disciplines would have to be taught in public institutions because private enterprise had neglected them hitherto and probably never would be able to afford them. But his interpretation of this standard was never narrow. He could find what he considered to be real utility in some surprising subjects. His plans looked forward to an expansion, not a contraction, of curriculum at the University of Virginia. He believed that ornament had as useful a place in education as in architecture. And he never ceased to think of morality as perhaps the most useful of all fields of study. His concept of usefulness was decidedly large-minded.

Yet for us the concept as expressed seems fundamentally too narrow. At Virginia it was probably saved by the needs of a growing nation. The standard of "all the sciences useful to us" will probably serve us best if we express it negatively and interpret it to mean, "No useful field of knowl-

2. To Thomas Cooper, Jan. 16, 1814 (LB, *14*, 60).

edge will be neglected in the total scheme of public education." This should be the minimum standard, never the optimum.

Current usefulness as a standard is realistic but near-sighted. Areas of study that seem trivial may suddenly come to be of central value. The importance of basic research is literally incalculable because it deals with matters of no known use. Yet all knowledge is potentially useful. Further, although every man's education should provide him with a vocation of some sort, no person is merely a vocation. He is a human being—that is, an individual endowed with a rich personality of great potentiality and a member of a society of fellows similarly endowed. His education as a human being is important. As a member of society, particularly in a democracy, he will find himself in common with his fellows facing problems which call for joint action and cooperation. His education must thus make him inquisitive, responsible, communicative, and familiar with the background of problems facing society long before their solution becomes urgent or critical. As an individual his mental and spiritual health will depend upon many other factors besides his ability to fit into the economic scheme. In his education, therefore, he must have opportunity to deal intelligently with basic questions concerning himself and the purpose for which he exists.

Jefferson's proposals for instruction concerning religion in public education were in complete accord with both these principles. They were completely and exclusively moral, and, being so, they included what Jefferson considered to be all that was useful in the area of religion. Nevertheless, his proposals aroused strong opposition. This was due partly to his manner of presenting his proposals. Jefferson's program was to include only those beliefs on which all sects agreed. This presumes a point which ultimately no denomination will accept: that its "gospel" can be divided into parts whose validity can be determined by whether outsiders find them acceptable or not. Every denomination considers its body of belief to be a totality in which tenets most repugnant to nonbelievers may be crucial. Different religious groups in a particular locality *can* get together and agree upon certain tenets held in common to be taught to all children jointly. However, such agreements are stable only when they are entered into voluntarily after deliberation by all concerned. Jefferson instead attempted to impose from the top what he considered to be the common agreement. Not having been consulted, the members of other denominations saw it rather as the entering wedge for the establishment of Unitarianism, a threat to their freedom of belief.

This approach to the teaching of religion in public education depends for its effectiveness upon trust, which in turn requires familiarity and mutual understanding among those parties entering into the agreement. It also presumes limited, fairly stable, mutually recognized and accepted areas of disagreement in the community. The compromise can be expected to endure only as long as no group with a new point of view concerning religion moves into the community, and as long as none of the original subscribers detects within the agreement a threat to its own security.

If approached properly, there is much to be said in favor of dealing with religion in public education as Jefferson hoped to, by emphasizing areas of unified opinion while ignoring troublesome differences. The fact is pointed up that people with widely divergent total points of view can get together on specific issues; this ability is essential if democracy is to exist at all. However, this manner of presenting religion may give the impression that those things on which people agree are more important than those on which they differ. In specific instances the impression may be true, but generally it can be misleading and dangerous.

In Jefferson's day American religious pluralism was limited for the most part to divergencies within Protestant

Christianity. This in turn made the nonsectarian compromise concerning the teaching of religion in public schools a fairly common thing in many communities and states. Since then, the entry into the country of large numbers of Catholics and Jews has made religious pluralism in America more radical and widespread, with the result that localities exist where nonsectarian Protestant compromises have had to be abandoned. "Three-faith" compromises have sometimes been substituted with success. Similar attempts elsewhere have run into difficulties which would serve as good illustrations of the truism that religion can be controversial and is sometimes bitterly divisive.

In localities where no compromise between contending groups has seemed possible, public schools have sometimes resorted to eliminating religion wherever it seemed to be a source of friction. This is the second way to "settle" controversy in a free society: to exclude whatever causes argument from consideration. The result is a truce, which to the ignorant and self-deceiving may give the appearance of unity, tolerance, and good will. The differences have not been settled, however, nor has any mutual understanding between the contending groups been reached; the possibility of renewed conflict is ever present, and educational institutions have done nothing to relieve popular ignorance of the issues. Meanwhile, the "settlement" says essentially, "A plague on both your houses!" Outsiders and students might easily get the impression that these controversial issues are not worth discussing or considering, and perhaps do not even exist.

In specific cases each of these two ways of "settling" controversy may have value. The fact that groups can agree must never be forgotten. Certainly democracy could not continue were its citizens not agreed on several important fundamentals, nor is it wise to impress children with nothing but the contention between groups in society. Nor is the elimination of controversial questions from consideration an unwise measure if it is understood to be a temporary expedient introduced to allow tempers to cool and to let reason, good humor, and understanding become suitably effective. But neither of these ways of "settling" controversy can be called democratic if the matter is allowed to rest with it permanently. Democracy is intended to do one thing more, which public education must take into account.

Jefferson believed that the division of human beings into parties was natural and normal. Difference of opinion could not and should not be suppressed. His concept of democracy was actually a system for making controversy creative. The essence of democracy to him was not suppressing controversy, but getting it out into the open and keeping it there until a decision based on common understanding and willing assent had been reached concerning the issue.

The desire to avoid controversy is understandable. Jefferson shunned it in his private life. Like him, most people find "scenes" distasteful, and prefer peace to war, if the price is not too great. However, many will extend this desire into fields where it does not belong. They may feel that to admit the existence of controversy is to proclaim the failure of a society; in the name of an ideal of community or solidarity, they will do anything to conceal or ignore differences of opinion. Others are Jeffersonians to the extent that they believe basically that controversial matters are unimportant. Whether they have heard the expression or not, they subscribe to the statement, "What all agree in is probably right. What no two agree on most probably wrong!"

Both these excuses for not taking controversy seriously are dangerous. A community which refuses to admit the existence of conflict of opinion within its borders is a fool's paradise. Similarly those who believe that the presence of controversy proves the unimportance of an issue ignore the fact that every great idea has had to fight its way—often bitterly—to achieve acceptance. Even worthless notions that stir up people are important because they stir them up and must be dealt with.

The role of religion in public education is to be determined by the need to make public education as effective a tool as possible in continuing and fostering the functioning of democracy and the development of a free society. The goals of instruction with respect to religion in public schools should grow out of and be properly related to the general purposes of education. If the purpose of democratic public education is to develop adults who can deal creatively and responsibly with the clash of values that inevitably accompanies cultural pluralism, then perhaps the very controversiality of religion may make it a must in education for democratic citizenship. The effect of religion upon the development of human culture cannot be denied. It has had a profound influence upon law, morality, the fine arts, literature, economics, and history. It continues to be a potent political force. We may have become so accustomed to our tradition of religious freedom that we are generally unaware of the importance of religion in shaping or determining the status of specific matters, such as bootlegging in Georgia, high school biology courses in Tennessee, and physician–patient relationships in Connecticut. Nor are we sensitive to the fact that religion may well determine the kind of progress that is possible in India and whether the state of Israel is to be temporarily or permanently among the nations of the world. If religion will influence the outcome of these and many other questions within and outside the United States, an awareness of what it is and does must be included in the training of every American citizen. Certainly, the last impression education for democratic citizenship should give is that conflict due to religious pluralism does not exist or that it has no significance.

Public education is a major common resource for the support and development of the democratic way of life. Democracy is a means of determining courses of action through use of open and admitted conflict of opinion. Its ideal is not the achievement of a homogeneous society, but true cooperation, the working together of different people and groups who have deliberated with each other. The terms in which this ideal is usually put—"majority *rule* and minority *rights,*" "the *will* of the majority with the *consent* of the minority"—throw a tremendous responsibility upon all the participants in the decisions of government. Minority rights cannot be safeguarded unless the minorities are known and unless what they have to say is heard out. Provision must always be made for the unhindered expression of unpopular points of view. Since one of the most important ways by which human beings are divided and grouped is through religion, a school which trains students for democratic citizenship should help the student appreciate all religious traditions, his own and those of others. A basic requirement of democratic citizenship is to recognize that the existence of conflicting positions on all issues is normal in a democracy.

To eliminate from public education the consideration of religion because it is controversial is to make that education defective as a training ground for democratic citizens. To limit consideration to those matters on which all members of local denominations agree is good in earlier stages of student development, but is ultimately insufficient because democracy requires that people stay in communication at points over which they differ. A truly adequate curriculum of public education in a democracy will contain opportunities for the student to become intelligently aware of the effect of religion upon human culture, and of the basic beliefs of all American religious groups, including free thinkers, atheists, agnostics, and others considered by many to be antireligious. The American citizen today must also become acquainted with major world faiths and the effects they have in international affairs and events. The development of methods of joint action and cooperation between nations realistically aware of their differences is as urgent as it is for the many popular groupings in the United States.

The last provision we should rivet upon all public education is a doctrinaire adherence to Jefferson's words: "no religious reading, instruction, or exercise shall be prescribed inconsistent with the tenets of any religious sect or denomination." Indoctrination obviously has no place in the public school, but instruction concerning religion need not be indoctrination. Christian theological seminaries offer courses in comparative religion, giving fair presentation of non-Christian faiths such as Islam, Hinduism, and Buddhism, without seriously risking defections from among their students. "Understanding of" and "belief in" are not synonymous. If the interpretation of Jefferson's clause is that religion and its effects cannot be discussed in public education, the meaning is unrealistic and therefore unwise. It flies in the face of his own standard that public education should provide instruction in "all useful sciences."

Acquainting the student with religious pluralism is part of democratic public education's duty to introduce future citizens to pluralism of all types: economic, political, ethnic, racial, and others. Schooling should enable the student to face the actualities of free society. If instead it gives him only silly, sentimental notions concerning the unity of all Americans he will be an incompetent citizen. Later disillusionment will usually either confirm his ineffectiveness or make him positively antidemocratic. In this sense there is wisdom in Jefferson's belief that man's morality is jeopardized unless he learns to apply his mind to facts, not systems. Facing realities may be tougher than hearing sentimental platitudes, but maturity includes knowing lessons which do not have to be unlearned.

Nor can the recognition of human differences stop with their mere acknowledgment. They must be studied. Whoever says, concerning others, "I respect their conclusions, however different from my own," and means, "I pay no attention to those points at which we differ," is shirking his democratic responsibility. Democracy requires a man to maintain a respect for his opponents and their rights in the midst of clash and conflict of opinion. This respect is no more granted by whoever withdraws from discussion with others concerning matters over which they disagree, than it is by those who ride roughshod over the opinions of their opponents.

Here we have returned once more to the point that democracy is a moral enterprise, that freedom must be exercised within the context of responsibility. Schooling for future citizenship must take into account the fact that democracy basically depends for its survival upon its citizens sharing a common attitude with two facets. Each citizen must have, first, a sense of commitment, a sense of loyalty or final responsibility to a supreme value, principle, or source of law, to an ideal transcending himself, his nation, and any other particular local or temporal interest bidding for his support. This should be the motivation behind all his actions. It would be well to note that this was a characteristic of Jefferson and the Founding Fathers. Their god was God and not a human institution. Second, each individual must recognize that every man is finite and fallible, especially himself. No matter how completely and constantly motivated to action he may be by a transcendent and supreme ideal, his understanding of that ideal, his expression of it, and his plans to embody it in time and place must necessarily be faulty and to some extent corrupted by particularity, self-interest, and limitation of view. Thus he has reason to listen to others and to seriously consider their views on any common problem.

These two facets are the essence of a morality which must be characteristic of the citizens of any democracy that is to survive. Religions deal consciously with both facets. They do not all agree on the details of the ideal moral structure, nor can it be said that subscription to a particular creed makes a man moral. But they do take the problem of morality seriously, and for reasons which are urgent, even though they are often sentimentalized. It makes no sense to ignore the seriousness with which they treat the problem of morality or the insights into it which they can bestow. If morality is of importance to the continuation of democracy, an understanding of religions and religion is essential to public education.

No, our interest in Thomas Jefferson is not purely antiquarian. Many of his insights into the problems facing free peoples and democratic governments are permanently valid and valuable. Yet we must use caution when invoking his words and actions as guides. We must endeavor constantly to understand the thought behind his expression. We must also make the effort to judge both thought and expression with intelligence and discrimination. His drive to establish a system of democratic public education grew out of a desire to enable us, in the last analysis, to do those two things: to know history and to use our heads. We do no honor to the memory of the author of the Declaration of Independence by slavish imitation of his words or actions. To accept or reject them after making earnest efforts to determine their actual, current merit is the only way to keep faith with this patriot and educator. He meant it when he said that subsequent generations would be wiser than his own; only we can understand the problems that face us, and determine whether his ideas and measures can be fruitfully applied to them. He meant it when he said that the land belongs to the living, and that the will of the living majority must be the law of the nation. We will benefit greatly from close study of his thought, but ultimately, as far as Jefferson is concerned, we have not only the right but also the responsibility to make our own decisions.

Jefferson's Use of History

In his concept of history Jefferson shared many attitudes common to other *philosophes*. First, history to him was a valuable form of knowledge in the Lockean sense. It consisted of reflection upon experience. It could be depended upon to have all reasonable and necessary certainty for the guidance of man in solving his problems.[1] As Bolingbroke had said, it was "philosophy teaching by examples."[2]

Second, history's meaning to Jefferson, as to many other members of the Enlightenment, was essentially a secularized form of the traditional Christian story of man. Man had had a golden age or Garden of Eden period, from which he fell into his present deplorable state, and from which he was to rise again in the future into a state of happiness or bliss.[3] To Jefferson man's golden age was the Anglo-Saxon period of English history or the state of those tribes of American Indians who had yet to come into contact with

1. See R. G. Collingwood, *The Idea of History* (Oxford, 1946), pp. 72–73.
2. H. T. Colbourn, "Thomas Jefferson's Use of the Past," *William and Mary Quarterly*, 3rd ser. *15* (1958), 56–57.
3. See Becker, *Heavenly City*, pp. 119–30.

civilization. (Gibbon's golden age was the period of the Antonines; Hume's, that of the Tudors; Rousseau's, man's original state in nature before he discovered how to possess property, etc.)

Jefferson assigned man's "fall" in English history to the period subsequent to the Norman invasion of England, when feudal customs were forced upon the people and Christianity was fraudulently engrafted onto the common law. (To Gibbon man's "fall" was the fall of Rome, the triumph of barbarism and religion which led to the Dark Ages; to Rousseau it occurred when the first man fenced off a piece of property and said to his neighbors, "This is mine!") Jefferson's view of history also had its eschatology. Like Condorcet and Turgot, he looked forward to the day on this earth when man would live in a state of religious respect for personal liberty and labor, inviolability of the right of property, equal justice for everyone, multiplication of the means of subsistence, and augmentation of enjoyments, enlightenment, and all means to happiness.[4] To Jefferson that day was already dawning in North America.

The roots of this understanding of history are easy to find. History books made up the majority of the titles that recurred in all three of Jefferson's libraries. An overwhelming number of his English histories were written by Whigs such as Henry Spelman, John Dalrymple, Francis Sullivan, Roger Acherly, Lord Kames, Edward Coke, and Catharine Macauley. Rapin's *History of England,* which Thomas Jefferson recommended to a student in 1825, was in Peter Jefferson's library.[5]

The interpretation of English history known as the "Saxon myth" was common to all these historians. According to this view the Anglo-Saxons were the ancient Germans described by Tacitus, whose government was a form of primitive democracy which respected all natural rights.

4. See Löwith, *Meaning in History,* p. 101.
5. To ———, Oct. 25, 1825 (LB, *16,* 124–28).

When the Anglo-Saxons moved to England, they brought with them their democratic institutions, including elective monarchy and parliamentary procedure. This democracy was overturned in 1066 by Norman treachery. Feudalism was an alien element, which, according to this view, had not been in England previously but was imposed by William the Conqueror upon the people.

In the succeeding centuries, according to the Whigs, the people struggled to release themselves from slavery and regain their birthright, liberties, and privileges. At times they were victorious. According to the "Saxon myth," for instance, the Magna Carta was a reaffirmation of Saxon common law and ancient customs. On the other hand, there were also frequent monarchical encroachments. The people asserted themselves finally by expelling the Stuarts in 1688. That revolution should have solved the problem but, according to the Whigs, it stopped where it should have begun, converting England into a fixed, standing aristocracy. The Whigs felt that currently the English had insufficient regard for their glorious Saxon heritage and had sadly forgotten the liberties to which they were entitled.[6]

This interpretation of history was made to order for the justification of revolution. As Jefferson saw it, history was in the process of repeating itself on the North American continent. Like their Saxon forebears, the English in North America had left their homes and carved out new settlements for themselves in a foreign land. They were not a conquered people, but the British monarchy was attempting to reduce them to a new form of feudal slavery. Revolution was justified to prevent George III from becoming a second William the Norman. This, essentially, was the message of *The Summary View of the Rights of British America*.[7]

History was thus a valuable extension of political experi-

6. See Colbourn, pp. 59–65, 68.
7. See Chinard, *Jefferson*, pp. 31–32, 48–53; Malone, *Jefferson*, *1*, 184–90.

ence, supplying Jefferson with an understanding of his political and economic problems. It was etiology in that it described the golden age and how that age had been lost. By the same token, however, it was also eschatology, for in the description of the golden age it presented a model for the future state, and by showing the errors which had caused the downfall of their ancestors it would enable men to avoid similar mistakes in the future.[8] This was Bolingbroke's "philosophy teaching by example," the past illustrating both the dangers to be avoided and the democratic delights to be recaptured. Thus, although Jefferson believed history was repeating itself, he subscribed to no cyclic theory of history. Man was perfectable and could control the future if he knew the past.

Jefferson was a strangely reactionary revolutionary. He wanted change but not innovation. He wished to advance to the idealized political perfection of an earlier age. He wanted to restore Saxon principles of polity. In America this involved sweeping away all vestiges of feudalism, primogeniture, entails, quitrents, and even the established church.[9] His constant aim was to avoid the political pitfalls into which he believed England had fallen, and to establish a democracy which would not be prey to petty ambition and political corruption. He accepted the possibility of decline as normal, but was imbued with enough eighteenth-century optimism to believe that an awakened historical consciousness would serve his fellow citizens as it had served him, giving them adequate warning of encroachments of tyranny in all its predictable forms.[10] The preservation of democracy depended upon the inclusion of instruction in history in public education.

8. See Colbourn, pp. 56–57. See also Becker, *Heavenly City,* pp. 95–111, to compare Jefferson's position with that of other *philosophes.*

9. E.g. letter to Edmund Pendleton, Aug. 13, 1776 (Boyd, *Papers of Jefferson, I,* 492).

10. See Colbourn, pp. 68–69.

Bibliography

WRITINGS OF JEFFERSON AND HIS CONTEMPORARIES

Boyd, Julian P., et al., eds., *Papers of Thomas Jefferson,* 15 vols. to date, Princeton, Princeton University Press, 1950–.

Cabell, Nathaniel F., ed., *Early History of the University of Virginia as Contained in the Letters of Thomas Jefferson and Joseph C. Cabell,* Richmond, 1865.

Chinard, Gilbert, ed., *The Commonplace Book of Thomas Jefferson: A Repertory of His Ideas on Government,* Johns Hopkins Studies in Romance Literatures and Languages, extra Vol. II, Baltimore, Johns Hopkins Press, 1926.

—— ed., *The Correspondence of Jefferson and Dupont de Nemours,* Baltimore, Johns Hopkins Press, 1931.

—— ed., *Jefferson et les idéologues,* Johns Hopkins Studies in Romance Literatures and Languages, extra Vol. I, Baltimore, Johns Hopkins Press, 1925.

—— ed., *The Literary Bible of Thomas Jefferson: His Commonplace Book of Philosophers and Poets,* Baltimore, Johns Hopkins Press, 1928.

Cousins, Norman, ed., *In God We Trust: The Religious Beliefs and Ideas of the American Founding Fathers,* New York, Harper, 1958.

Ford, Paul L., ed., *Writings of Thomas Jefferson,* 10 vols. New York, 1892–99.

Hunt, Gaillard, ed., *Writings of James Madison,* 9 vols. New York, G. P. Putnam, 1900–10.

Knox, Samuel, *A Vindication of the Religion of Mr. Jefferson, and a Statement of His Services in the Cause of Religious Liberty,* Baltimore, 1800.

Koch, Adrienne, and Peden, William, eds., *Life and Selected Writings of Thomas Jefferson,* New York, Modern Library, 1944.

Lipscomb, Andrew A., and Bergh, Albert E., eds., *Writings of Thomas Jefferson,* 20 vols. Washington, D.C., 1903.

Padover, Saul K., ed., *The Complete Jefferson,* New York, Duel, Sloane and Pearce, 1950.

—— ed., *Thomas Jefferson on Democracy,* New York, New American Library, 1946.

Price, Richard, *A Review of the Principal Questions in Morals,* ed. D. Daiches Raphael, Oxford, Oxford University Press, 1948.

Priestley, Joseph, *A History of the Corruptions of Christianity,* London, 1871.

WORKS INTERPRETING JEFFERSON
AND HIS CONTEMPORARIES

Arrowood, Charles Flinn, *Thomas Jefferson and Education in a Republic,* New York, McGraw-Hill, 1930.

Bowers, Claude G., *Jefferson and Hamilton: The Struggle for Democracy in America,* Boston, Houghton Mifflin, 1926.

—— *Jefferson in Power: The Death Struggle of the Federalists,* Boston, Houghton Mifflin, 1936.

—— *The Young Jefferson, 1743–1789,* Boston, Houghton Mifflin, 1945.

Chinard, Gilbert, *Thomas Jefferson: The Apostle of Americanism,* 2d rev. ed. Ann Arbor, University of Michigan Press, 1957.

Colbourn, H. Trevor, "Thomas Jefferson's Use of the Past," *William and Mary Quarterly,* 3rd ser. *15* (1958), 56–70.

Dodd, William E., *Statesmen of the Old South,* New York, Book League of America, 1929.

Fabian, Bernhard, "Jefferson's *Notes on Virginia:* The Genesis of Query xvii. *The different religions received into that State?*" *William and Mary Quarterly,* 3d ser. *12* (1955), 124–39.

Foote, Henry Wilder, *Thomas Jefferson: Champion of Religious Freedom, Advocate of Christian Morals,* Boston, Beacon Press, 1947.

Freeman, Douglas Southall, *Young Washington,* Vol. I of *George Washington, a Biography,* New York, Scribner, 1948.

Hall, J. Lesslie, "The Religious Opinions of Thomas Jefferson," *Sewanee Review, 21* (1913), 164–76.

Henderson, John C., *Thomas Jefferson's Views on Public Education,* New York, 1890.

Himes, Charles F., *Life and Times of Judge Thomas Cooper,* Carlisle, Pa., Dickinson School of Law, 1918.

Hirst, Francis W., *Life and Letters of Thomas Jefferson,* New York, Macmillan, 1926.

Honeywell, Roy J., *The Educational Work of Thomas Jefferson,* Cambridge, Harvard University Press, 1931.

Johnson, Allen, *Jefferson and His Colleagues, a Chronicle of the Virginia Dynasty,* Chronicles of America, 15, New Haven, Yale University Press, 1918–21.

Kelley, Maurice, *Additional Chapters on Thomas Cooper,* University of Maine Studies, 2d ser. 15, Orono, Me., University Press, 1930.

Kimball, Marie, *Jefferson: The Road to Glory, 1743–1776,* New York, Coward-McCann, 1943.

—— *Jefferson: The Scene in Europe, 1784 to 1789,* New York, Coward-McCann, 1950.

—— *Jefferson: War and Peace, 1776 to 1784,* New York, Coward-McCann, 1947.

Knoles, George Harmon, "The Religious Ideas of Thomas Jefferson," *Mississippi Valley Historical Review, 30* (1943), 187–204.

Koch, Adrienne, *Jefferson and Madison, the Great Collaboration,* New York, Alfred A. Knopf, 1950.

—— *The Philosophy of Thomas Jefferson,* New York, Columbia University Press, 1943.

Lehmann, Karl, *Thomas Jefferson, American Humanist,* New York, Macmillan, 1947.

Lerche, Charles O., Jr., "Jefferson and the Election of 1800: A Case Study in the Political Smear," *William and Mary Quarterly*, 3rd ser. 5 (1948), 467–91.

Malone, Dumas, *Jefferson and His Time*, Boston, Little, Brown, 1948–; Vol. 1, *Jefferson the Virginian;* Vol. 2, *Jefferson and the Rights of Man.*

—— *The Public Life of Thomas Cooper*, New Haven, Yale University Press, 1926.

Martin, Edward T., *Thomas Jefferson: Scientist*, New York, Henry Schuman, 1952.

Mead, Sidney, "Thomas Jefferson's Fair Experiment," *Religion in Life, 23* (1954), 566–79.

Monk, Samuel H., "Samuel Stanhope Smith 1751–1819, Friend of Rational Liberty" in *The Lives of Eighteen from Princeton,* ed. Willard Thorp, Princeton, Princeton University Press, 1946.

Morison, Samuel Eliot, *The Young Man Washington*, Cambridge, Harvard University Press, 1932.

Nock, Albert Jay, *Jefferson*, New York, Harcourt, Brace, 1926.

Padover, Saul K., *Jefferson*, New York, New American Library, 1955.

Randall, Henry S., *The Life of Thomas Jefferson*, 3 vols. New York, 1858.

Rossiter, Clinton, "Which Jefferson Do You Quote?" *The Reporter, 13* (1955), 33–36.

Schachner, Nathan, *Thomas Jefferson: A Biography*, 2 vols. New York, Appleton–Century–Crofts, 1951.

Schlesinger, Arthur M., Jr., "Comments on Dr. Govan's Article on Jefferson and Hamilton," *Christian Scholar, 40* (1957), 19.

Sensabaugh, George F., "Jefferson's Use of Milton in the Ecclesiastical Controversies of 1776," *American Literature, 26* (1955), 552–59.

Wiltse, Charles M., "Thomas Jefferson on the Law of Nations," *American Journal of International Law, 29* (1935), 66–81.

WORKS INTERPRETING JEFFERSON'S ERA

Adams, Henry, *History of the United States under Thomas Jefferson and James Madison*, 4 vols. New York, Albert and Charles Boni, 1930.

Adams, Herbert B., *Thomas Jefferson and the University of Virginia*, Washington, D.C., U.S. Bureau of Education Circular of Information No. 1, 1888.

Baillie, John, *The Belief in Progress*, London, Oxford University Press, 1950.

Bainton, Roland H., *The Travail of Religious Liberty: Nine Biographical Sketches*, Philadelphia, Westminster Press, 1951.

Becker, Carl L., *The Declaration of Independence: A Study in the History of Political Ideas*, New York, Harcourt, Brace, 1922.

—————— *The Heavenly City of the Eighteenth-Century Philosophers*, New Haven, Yale University Press, 1932.

Berlin, Isaiah, *The Age of Enlightenment*, New York, New American Library, 1956.

Boorstin, Daniel J., *The Lost World of Thomas Jefferson*, New York, Henry Holt, 1948.

Brinton, Crane, *The Shaping of the Modern Mind*, New York, New American Library, 1956.

Bruce, Philip Alexander, *The History of the University of Virginia, 1819–1919*. 5 vols. New York, Macmillan, 1920.

Bryson, Gladys, *Man and Society: The Scottish Inquiry of the Eighteenth Century*, Princeton, Princeton University Press, 1945.

Bury, J. B., *The Idea of Progress: An Inquiry into its Origin and Growth*, London, Macmillan, 1928.

Cassirer, Ernst, *The Philosophy of the Enlightenment*, trans. F. C. A. Koelln and J. P. Pettegrove, Boston, Beacon Press, 1955.

Channing, Edward, *The Jeffersonian System: 1801–1811*, The American Nation: A History, 12, New York, Harper, 1904–18.

Charles, Joseph, "Adams and Jefferson: The Origins of the American Party System," *William and Mary Quarterly*, 3rd ser. *12* (1955), 217–67.

Collingwood, R. G., *The Idea of History*, Oxford, Clarendon Press, 1946.

Cragg, G. R., *From Puritanism to the Age of Reason: A Study of Changes in Religious Thought within the Church of England, 1660–1700*, Cambridge, Cambridge University Press, 1950.

Ekirch, Arthur Alphonse, Jr., *The Idea of Progress in America, 1815–1860,* New York, Columbia University Press, 1944.

Gaustad, Edwin Scott, *The Great Awakening in New England,* New York, Harper, 1957.

Gouhier, Henri, *Sous la signe de la liberté,* Vol. I of *La Jeunesse d'Auguste Comte et la formation du positivisme,* Paris, Librairie Philosophique J. Vrin, 1933.

Greene, M. Louis, *The Development of Religious Liberty in Connecticut,* Boston, 1905.

Halévy, Elie, *The Growth of Philosophic Radicalism,* trans. Mary Morris, Boston, Beacon Press, 1955.

Jones, Howard Mumford, *The Pursuit of Happiness,* Cambridge, Harvard University Press, 1953.

Löwith, Karl, *Meaning in History,* Chicago, University of Chicago Press, 1957.

Miller, John C., *Crisis in Freedom: The Alien and Sedition Acts,* Boston, Little, Brown, 1951.

Morison, Samuel Eliot, and Henry Steele Commager, *The Growth of the American Republic,* rev. ed. Vol. I, New York, Oxford University Press, 1940.

Nelson, Lowry, *American Farm Life,* Cambridge, Harvard University Press, 1954.

Pattison, Mark, "Tendencies in Religious Thought in England, 1688–1750," *Essays and Reviews,* 12th ed. (London, 1865), pp. 306–98.

Perry, Ralph Barton, *Puritanism and Democracy,* New York, Vanguard Press, 1944.

Peterson, Merrill D., *The Jeffersonian Image in the American Mind,* New York, Oxford University Press, 1960.

Randall, John Herman, *The Making of the Modern Mind: A Survey of the Intellectual Background of the Present Age,* Cambridge, Mass., Riverside Press, 1926.

Robinson, William A., *Jeffersonian Democracy in New England,* New Haven, Yale University Press, 1916.

Rossiter, Clinton, *The American Presidency,* New York, New American Library, 1956.

Schneider, Herbert W., *A History of American Philosophy,* Columbia Studies in American Culture No. 18, New York, Columbia University Press, 1946.

Shinn, Roger Lincoln, *Christianity and the Problem of History*, New York, Scribner, 1953.

Stephen, Leslie, *The English Utilitarians*, 3 vols. London, 1900.

—— *History of English Thought in the Eighteenth Century*, 2 vols. New York, 1876.

White, Leonard D., *The Jeffersonians: A Study in Administrative History, 1801–1829*, New York, Macmillan, 1951.

Willey, Basil, *The Eighteenth Century Background*, London, Chatto and Windus, 1940.

Wiltse, Charles Maurice, *The Jeffersonian Tradition in American Democracy*, Chapel Hill, University of North Carolina Press, 1935.

WORKS ON CHURCH, STATE, AND EDUCATION

Blanshard, Paul, *American Freedom and Catholic Power*, Boston, Beacon Press, 1949.

—— *Communism, Democracy, and Catholic Power*, Boston, Beacon Press, 1951.

Brubacher, John S., *Modern Philosophies of Education*, rev. ed. New York, McGraw-Hill, 1950.

Butts, R. Freeman, *The American Tradition in Religion and Education*, Boston, Beacon Press, 1950.

Everson vs. Board of Education, 330 U.S. 1, 1947.

Hallowell, John H., *The Moral Foundation of Democracy*, Chicago, University of Chicago Press, 1954.

Johnson, Frederick Ernest, ed., *American Education and Religion: The Problem of Religion in the Public Schools*, New York, Harper, 1952.

Mattox, Fount William, *The Teaching of Religion in the Public Schools*, George Peabody College for Teachers Contribution to Education No. 386, Nashville, George Peabody College for Teachers, 1948.

McCollum, Vashti Cromwell, *One Woman's Fight*, Boston, Beacon Press, 1952.

Modern Philosophies and Education, see National Society for the Study of Education.

Moehlman, Conrad Henry, *School and Church: The American Way*, New York, Harper, 1944.

———— *The Wall of Separation between Church and State,* Boston, Beacon Press, 1951.

National Society for the Study of Education Yearbook 54, ed. Nelson B. Henry, Pt. I, *Modern Philosophies and Education,* Chicago, University of Chicago Press, 1955.

———— Yearbook 41, ed. Nelson B. Henry, Pt. I, *Philosophies of Education,* Chicago, University of Chicago Press, 1942.

O'Neill, J. M., *Religion and Education under the Constitution,* New York, Harper, 1949.

People of the State of Illinois, ex. rel. *Vashti McCollum* v. *Board of Education of School District No. 71, Champaign County, Illinois,* et. al., 333 U.S. 203, 1948.

Pfeffer, Leo, *Church, State, and Freedom,* Boston, Beacon Press, 1953.

Philosophies of Education, see National Society for the Study of Education.

Politella, Joseph, *Religion in Education: An Annotated Bibliography,* Oneonta, N.Y., American Association of Colleges for Teacher Education, 1956.

Shields, Currin V., *Democracy and Catholicism in America,* New York, McGraw-Hill, 1958.

Stokes, Anson Phelps, *Church and State in the United States,* 3 vols. New York, Harper, 1950.

Tewksbury, Donald G., *The Founding of American Colleges and Universities,* New York, Teachers College, Columbia, 1932.

Index